Being Prepared

Disasters are even more upsetting when you don't ha[ve] documents that will help you deal with agencies—pu[blic] that could help you recover. Here's what you should have:

- ➤ Birth certificates for each family member
- ➤ Passports of all family members who have them
- ➤ Driver's licenses
- ➤ Automobile registrations and insurance documentation
- ➤ Health insurance membership cards
- ➤ Inoculation records for each family member
- ➤ Continuing prescriptions for each family member
- ➤ Extra copies of eyeglasses and contact lens prescriptions
- ➤ Any medical care instructions that would be needed if the patient was not treated in the usual place
- ➤ Insurance policies for houses, cars, and livestock
- ➤ Copies of mortgages or leases
- ➤ Records for pet and livestock healthcare, and licenses if required in the area
- ➤ Documents pertaining to any businesses owned, including articles of incorporation, business insurance, and leases
- ➤ Bills of sale for any recently transferred objects
- ➤ Tax returns for the past three years
- ➤ Contracts
- ➤ Living wills for any family members who have them
- ➤ Trusts and deeds
- ➤ Powers of attorney for any family members who have them
- ➤ Last wills and testaments for any family members who have them

Keep copies of all documents in a single, portable strongbox in a location that will allow you to pick it up easily if you need to evacuate. This box also should have a chance of withstanding damage to your house.

alpha
books

Knowledge Is Power

In a natural disaster or its aftermath, he who knows the ropes probably has less chance of being strung up or strung out by them. Here's the least you should be in touch with if disasters are expected or if you're recovering from one:

➤ **NOAA Weather Radio**—The National Oceanic and Atmospheric Administration provides continuous broadcasts of the latest weather information from local National Weather Service offices. Weather messages are repeated every 4 to 6 minutes and are routinely updated every 1 to 3 hours, or more frequently in rapidly changing local weather or if a nearby hazardous environmental condition exists. Most stations operate 24 hours daily.

➤ **The Federal Emergency Management Agency Web site**— On this site (www.fema.gov), you can get information about how to find insurance and how to apply for federal assistance.

➤ **The University of Illinois Cooperative Extension Service (UIUC)**—This service (www.extension.uiuc.edu) hosts a disaster home page that contains news releases and information on current disasters, plus information on preparing for disasters, getting disaster assistance, and helping disaster victims.

➤ **Quake Safe**—Provided by Stanford University, this is a program and Web site (www.stanford.edu/dept/EHS) that tells you what to do during an earthquake. It offers tips on how to prepare your home, office, and community for earthquakes; there's also a section on how to make a three-day survival kit.

➤ **Putting Down Roots in Earthquake Country, Southern California Earthquake Center at the University of California**—This Web site (www.scecdc.scec.org/eqcountry.html) provides tons of earthquake preparation information, including how to prepare your house. It also explores and explodes some earthquake myths.

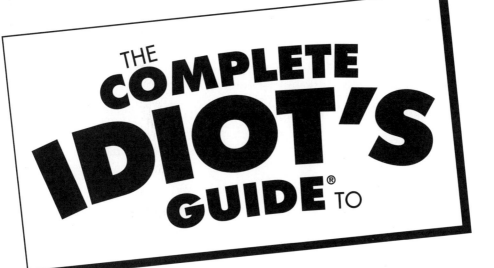

THE COMPLETE **IDIOT'S** GUIDE® TO

Natural Disasters

by Laura Harrison McBride

alpha
books

Macmillan USA, Inc.
201 West 103rd Street
Indianapolis, IN 46290
A Pearson Education Company

Publisher
Marie Butler-Knight

Product Manager
Phil Kitchel

Managing Editor
Cari Luna

Acquisitions Editor
Randy Ladenheim-Gil

Development Editor
Michael Thomas

Production Editor
Billy Fields

Copy Editor
Krista Hansing

Illustrator
Jody P. Schaeffer

Cover Designers
Mike Freeland
Kevin Spear

Book Designers
Scott Cook and Amy Adams of DesignLab

Indexer
Tonya Heard

Layout/Proofreading
Darin Crone
John Etchison

Contents at a Glance

Contents

Foreword

The first disaster survivor may well have been Noah, who was smart enough to build an ark when he was warned about a great flood. Some scientists believe there really was a catastrophic deluge on the Black Sea 7,500 years ago that might have been Noah's disaster.

Whether Earth's ongoing spate of disasters began with Noah or not, humankind remains fascinated with catastrophic events. More than 300 world cultures have a story about a universal flood. But we're also preoccupied with earthquakes, volcanic eruptions, tidal waves, mudslides, sinkholes, waterspouts, drought, lightning, fires, hurricanes, floods, blizzards, avalanches, insect plagues, disease epidemics, and hunger too! And that's not because we're pessimistic.

It's because disasters affect us all. No country is completely safe from disaster.

As you will find in the following pages, the disaster business has its own vocabulary. Did you know, for instance, that a fumarole chimney is an opening in a volcanic area from which smoke and gases escape? And that there are three kinds of sinkholes—subsidence, solution, and collapse?

Knowing some basic information about disasters could save your life—or at the very least make you the life of a party. Did you know, for instance, that escape from New York City might not be possible if a really big hurricane blew in? That even six inches of fast-moving water can knock you off your feet—and two feet can float your car? That the U.S. experiences about 1,000 tornadoes a year, averaging 70 deaths? That it's impossible to outrun a lava flow (don't even try it)? As you sit there reading this, do you really know your chances of getting struck by lightning? (Don't worry, the majority of people who get struck by lightning live through it.)

If you haven't been in the heart of a disaster, these pages will help you see what it's like. Eyewitness accounts from disaster survivors are included throughout *The Complete Idiot's Guide to Natural Disasters*.

You'll also learn a bit about the science of disasters—how hurricanes are formed, how El Niño triggers global weather events, how fishermen and farmers are affected by disasters.

The study of disasters also involves the study of our own society and how we treat our neighbors. Why do more people in underdeveloped countries die from disasters? Why do we put increasing numbers of people in vulnerable locations? Are we treating our environment in ways that promote disaster?

Whether you're in New York City, rural Montana, Mongolia, or the Lesser Antilles, there will always be a "next disaster." This book gives you the basics about what to do after a disaster, what to keep on hand, and will even remind you to take care of your pets.

This book also suggests some disaster benefits. Precious gems and metals are created by volcanic flow. Disaster beauty is in the eye of a beholder—just ask any storm chaser who's about to shoot up-close footage of a tornado. And get this: In the year before the London fire, 75,000 Londoners had died of the Great Plague. In the aftermath of the London fire, which broke out in 1666, the plague declined, the rats whose fleas transmit it having been killed or displaced in large numbers. So, although the flames took 16 lives or so, they may have saved many thousands.

And saving lives and property is a big reason for all this hoopla about disasters. Whenever we write about disasters, we call the people who have lived through disasters "survivors"—not victims. And whatever disaster comes next, with a little information and a little preparation, chances are you'll join the ranks of disaster survivors worldwide. Now, sit back and enjoy the book. But first—go turn your weather radio on.

—The Disaster News Network

The Disaster News Network (http://www.disasternews.net) is an online news service that reports disaster occurrence and suggests appropriate ways to respond.

Introduction

Why this, why now?

For one thing, the climate is changing. Had you noticed? The summer of 1999 was vicious in many parts of the United States. The mid-Atlantic states suffered drought, to the point that the steamy estuary of the Chesapeake threatened to resemble the bottom of a crab boil that had been on the fire too long. It was scorched, with just a few dead, smelly things on the bottom. Water was rationed. People from inner-city Washington, D.C., took shelter in air-conditioned light rail stations overnight. Even as this is being written, things are not totally back to normal there.

Nature runs over all of us sooner or later, in some big or small way. The Earth can do it, with earthquakes and volcanoes. The sea can do it, with tidal waves and storm surges. The skies can do it, with tornadoes, hail storms, and blizzards. Squirrels can do it; they carry hanta viruses, which cause plague-like diseases (but I still feel bad if I squash one as it stupidly darts under the wheels of my car). And, of course, microbes can do it, with Ebola, dengue fever and two "boutique" diseases that hold lots of promise for misery: Mad Cow Disease and flesh-eating strep.

If you live on Earth, you are a potential victim. Period. No place is completely safe from everything. There's either weather, the Earth's antics, or disease, or all of the above to contend with.

That being the case, it is helpful to know what's up and where. Unless your desire to live on the edge is overwhelming, there are a few places you might not want to move. Coastal California would be one. (If you already live there, never fear; there are more dangerous places, for a variety of reasons. The Sudan suggests itself as well; civil war added to drought and disease are much more likely to affect you than an earthquake, mudslide, or tsunami.)

Some places might be much safer, if you can give up the life you've built wherever you live now. Try Kuching. Where? No, it's not in China. But it is exotic.

How This Book Is Organized

In talking about the incredible things that can happen on Earth, it's best to begin at the beginning, as this book does, with the Earth itself.

Part 1: Solid Ground, or Not? Earthquakes. Mostly, it's not. A thin crust floats above a roiling, boiling mass of Earth soup. Here, you'll read about the worst the Earth can do, and how it happened in San Francisco, Turkey, and Pompeii. And there are some mighty odd ways people are trying to predict the next big shake up. Some of them actually work. Hint: The Amazing Randy might want to debunk them.

Part 2: Earthly Wrath: Ground-Breaking Events. What's a volcano? It's a big hole in the ground that spits hunks of granite. It also oozes rivers of glowing chemicals that become earth when they cool down. It puffs out tons of pollutants that crash airplanes and grow coffee beans. It has some cousins, hot springs and such that spew boiling water into the air. And it has a relatively calm relative, the sinkhole, also an earth engineer, that changes the look of the landscape awfully suddenly sometimes. Look into this stuff—but don't stand too close to the edge.

Part 3: Wind. Right, this the second part of the phrase "Earth, wind, and fire." And, as volcanoes are to Earth, so tornadoes are to the atmosphere. They're big, bad, ugly, and so exciting that some people pay other people to help them find one—to watch from afar, that is. Then there are tornadic winds, up-close and sometimes personal. There's also El Niño and lower-level winds that turn windmills in quaint Dutch landscapes, send Frenchmen screaming through the streets of Marseilles, set California forests on fire, fling airplanes to the ground, trash climbers in the Alps, and, of course, move mountains.

Part 4: Fire. Here we talk of lightning, cows, and trash-burning. No matter how it starts, fire has the potential for enormous harm. It destroyed London more than once. It also destroyed Chicago; you think a cow was responsible? That's a natural sort of thing, but it's probably not true. Burning rags put a New York factory on the list of worst fires of all time as well. (Sometimes good comes of tragedy: Fire laws and procedures were changed nationwide after that one.) Baltimore also burned. And, of course, Beverly Hills lights up regularly—and not just with stars' palatial homes.

Part 5: Water. Douse it. Water's good for that. It's also good for creating storm surges, floods, hurricanes, blizzards, and other atmospheric events that make life miserable. But the survivors' stories are exciting. And then there's the flip side: draining, deadly, disease-bearing drought.

Part 6: Bugs, Bugs, and More. There are bugs and then there are BUGS. Bugs are spiders; BUGS are fleas infected with bubonic plague, mosquitoes carrying dengue fever, and flies carrying sleeping sickness. There are other BUGS as well: teeny little bugs called microbes by another name. Cows go mad, and flesh rots as doctors whack away at the limbs above the point of infection, blocking its spread by removing its pathway. Worse than leprosy? Perhaps—and brand new.

Part 7: Where and How to Live. In some places on earth you can experience just about any sort of natural disaster you'd like to see. And in other places you'll be lucky to find any disaster in an average lifetime.

Extras

Throughout *The Complete Idiot's Guide to Natural Disasters,* you'll find four types of boxes that contain special information about natural disasters.

Sound the Alarm

The sections called "Sound the Alarm" are warnings, things to look out for or be aware of in times of disaster.

To Ensure Preservation

"To Ensure Preservation" sections offer tips and insights into disasters or human nature.

Research Findings

"Research Findings" boxes provide interesting, bet-you-didn't-know tidbits. (Hey, sometimes you've just gotta have some brain food for its own sake!)

Earthy Language

"Earthy Language" sidebars define words, concepts, and cultures of people involved in natural disasters now and in times past.

Acknowledgments

My first husband, geologist Dr. Paul B. Basan, got me up-close and personal with a lot of the Earth's antics. I wasn't sure I liked it at the time, but serendipity is a wonderful thing—even if it takes 25 years to resolve itself.

Thanks also to my dog, Murphy Brown. I didn't name her; a friend did, after my favorite TV sitcom character, to whose show I referred as the training tapes. My dog acts just like her namesake and keeps me on target, one way or another.

And, in no particular order, thanks also to those who put up with me through this manuscript: the Rev. Dwight Smith; the Rev. Jeffrey Proctor; Don Gillson; Larry and Donna Box, and Caitlin; Dede and Peter Bierbrauer; Kaye McCally; Noelene Downing; Bertha De Souza; Tory Tolia; Natalie McIntyre; and Dick Piet.

Thanks to Claire Trent, geologist, for pointers. Thanks also to "Dr. Steve" for insights bestowed as we groomed our horses to ride. More thanks to my editor, Randy Ladenheim-Gil, for professionalism, but also for sharing.

And thanks to my agent, Karl Weber, for service above and beyond the call of duty.

Trademarks

All terms mentioned in this book that are known to be or are suspected of being trademarks or service marks have been appropriately capitalized. Alpha Books and Macmillan USA, Inc., cannot attest to the accuracy of this information. Use of a term in this book should not be regarded as affecting the validity of any trademark or service mark.

Part 1

Solid Ground, or Not? Earthquakes

One thing is for sure—if you've been through even a small earthquake, you have no need for another to convince you of the Earth's awesome power.

Worse yet, no place on Earth assures your escape from the possibility of earthquake, except one of the poles. (And you wouldn't want to live there.)

So, forget it, and accept that somewhere, somehow, no matter how cautious a life you live, you might well experience an earthquake. Even in Manhattan. Even in Missouri. And almost assuredly in Mission Viejo.

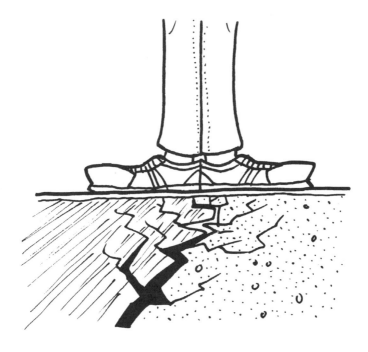

Chapter 1

Global Upheaval: Earthquake 101

In This Chapter

➤ A subject for discussion from earliest times

➤ What causes the shaking and quaking

➤ The New Madrid Seismic Zone

➤ Why California has always rocked and rolled

➤ Is the Big One at hand?

It's amazing how often the ancient Greeks, who had no computers—not even the abacus of the ancient Chinese—got scientific facts substantially right, even facts about natural forces deep within the Earth.

Consider this possible tableau from, say, 559 B.C.E.: Several men are sitting around, discussing reports of recent earth movements they heard from sailors stopping on their way from Italy to Alexandria. Says Thales, a scientist from Miletos, a town in what is now Turkey, "There has been, no doubt, an agitation of the great sea on which Greece and our trading partners float."

The other men, five or six of them, disagree. An argument ensues, and before long, one tosses the retsina (a wine preserved and flavored with resins of evergreen trees) they've been sharing all over Thales.

Thales' view—that a great sea underlay the lands of the Earth—was in opposition to the view generally held in the sixth century B.C.E. about the causes of earthquakes. His dinner companions believed that air moving wildly through subterranean chambers caused the earth to move. But Thales was closer to being right than they were.

What an Earthquake Is

The fact is that the land we live on *does* float on a great sea. It's not the water that Thales thought it was, but it's molten material that moves deep within the Earth.

To Ensure Preservation

The Greek word for earthquake was *seismos*. Today, anything to do with earthquakes is likely to include the descriptive term *seismic*. So watch out for Greek words bearing rifts.

Earthy Language

Tectonic means "of or having to do with construction." So, although humans think of earthquakes as being destructive—of our towns, roads, and buildings—they actually are constructive as far as Mother Earth is concerned because they create more land mass.

All this molten stuff jostling around under the relatively rigid surface of the Earth creates tension. The Earth's crust is cooler than the molten material, which gets increasingly hotter under the pressure created by the Earth's crust itself and starts looking for a way out. The molten rock pushes up where it can, moving the solid stuff around as it looks for new nooks and crannies to fill.

Usually, in response to *tectonic* forces, the earth bends a little. But just as too much wind will snap even a flexible tree, too much force building up within the Earth will break the crust, snapping it into a new position. As the roiling, boiling "earth batter" rumbles around, it causes vibrations known as seismic waves. These waves travel both under the crust and within the layer of crust itself. They ultimately cause the sudden, jolting break in the crust that we call an earthquake.

Three Ways to Cut It: Types of Quakes

Earthquakes are destructive, but they are also one way in which the Earth adds to its existing land mass. Geologists categorize the physical action of earthquakes in creating land three ways:

➤ **The Continental Crush**—When two land masses meet, neither one gives. Result? They sort of climb each other, making mountain ranges like the Himalayas (which are still growing), the Alps, and even the ancient, eroded Appalachians, which once were craggy peaks.

➤ **The Continental Slide**—When a land mass meets ocean floor, the ocean floor takes the low road, sliding its heavier, denser mass (which has been compacted by all that heavy water) under the continent, making a trench. The Marianas Trench is an example. It reaches a depth of at least 38,500 feet near Guam, making it part of the Pacific Ring of Fire.

➤ **The Continental Transformation**—Sometimes two continents pass against each other like ice dancers doing the *paso doble*. The San Andreas Fault is the most famous of the "transform" faults. In 16 million years, the North American continent will have moved so far south in relation to the Pacific Ocean that Los Angeles will be north of San Francisco. (It's also called a strike-slip fault.)

Research Findings

The Mid-Atlantic Ridge is a 47,000-mile mountain range that runs from the North Pole to the South Pole under the Atlantic Ocean. Along the ridge, the earth is spreading apart through "sea floor spreading," the oozing up of the Earth's interior through huge cracks. The Mid-Atlantic Ridge mountains rise above sea level in Iceland and comprise the only exposed active spreading zone in the world.

The Earth Is Not Without Its Faults

Theoretically, an earthquake can happen anywhere on Earth. But in fact, they most often occur along existing weaknesses in the crust, or *faults*—places where two blocks of the Earth's crust have been slipping or moving against each other for a long, long time.

Often, it's pretty obvious where these faults are: Mountain ranges are the telltale signs. When they occur in the middle of a tectonic plate, it's not so obvious. There is a fault under the Mississippi River, for example; most people don't know that the nineteenth century was marked by a lot of movement there, in the New Madrid earthquakes.

Earthy Language

A **fault** is a place where two blocks of the Earth's crust have been slipping or moving against each other for a long, long time.

New Madrid: A History of Quakes

Despite their size, the New Madrid quake and two really big rumbles in Iran before the year 1000 C.E.—and doubtless unremarked shakings of the New World before it was found by Old Worlders like Christopher Columbus—have not played a major role in our thinking about earthquakes. Why? Because they happened in the middle of a plate and even now are not fully understood. However, they have been fully described. The Center for Earthquake Research and Information (CERI), at the University of Memphis, has done a pretty good job of describing the New Madrid quake. In the winter of 1811–1812, CERI scientists write, these events occurred:

> The region was struck by three of the most powerful earthquakes in United States history. These magnitude 8 quakes, centered near the town of New Madrid (Missouri), devastated the surrounding region and rang church bells 1,000 miles away in Boston. The scars that those great earthquakes made on the landscape remain—the quakes locally changed the course of the Mississippi River and created Reelfoot Lake, which covers an area of more than 10 square miles in northwestern Tennessee.

The USGS has this to say of the nineteenth-century midplate quakes:

> Survivors reported that the earthquakes caused cracks to open in the earth's surface, the ground to roll in visible waves, and large areas of land to sink or rise. The crew of the New Orleans (the first steamboat on the Mississippi, which was on her maiden voyage) reported mooring to an island only to awake in the morning and find that the island had disappeared below the waters of the Mississippi River. Damage was reported as far away as Charleston, South Carolina, and Washington, D.C.

That's fairly amazing stuff, and no minicams to record it!

The area is still subject to earthquakes. Few people are aware of it, however, so it's possible that residents of the area could still get as rude an awakening as their ancestors did. At the time of the New Madrid quakes, the area was sparsely populated. Today, though, the region is very well populated, with large cities such as St. Louis and Memphis in the quake zone. Therefore, it is important to the USGS to warn the population that this is an active seismic zone and to urge residents to begin building structures accordingly.

Getting the Word Out

The topography of the Mississippi Valley makes belief tough, though, because the faults and other geological structures related to earthquakes there have been deeply buried over hundreds of millions of years by thick layers of sediment. The central Mississippi Valley is nearly level, and nothing about the surface geology gives a clue to earthquake activity in the region—at least to a layman's eye.

Sound the Alarm

The central Mississippi Valley has more earthquakes than any other part of the United States east of the Rocky Mountains, says the United States Geological Survey (USGS). The geological structures related to the causes of these quakes lie deeply buried by sedimentary deposits. Ongoing geophysical studies are revealing these hidden features, enabling residents of the region to better prepare for future earthquakes.

So alternative methods are being tried, most notably mapping variations in the Earth's magnetic field. One such map made by USGS geophysicists clearly shows a buried feature known as the Reelfoot Rift, a northeast-trending structure around which most central U.S. earthquakes occur.

A rift (see Chapter 2, "Plates and Rifts") happens when tectonics pull the crust apart. If this happens long enough, the crust separation forms an ocean basin, such as the one under the Atlantic Ocean. At the Reelfoot Rift, the crust didn't separate enough to create a new ocean basin—yet. But there is a mighty large lake. And, as Yogi Berra said, it ain't over 'til it's over.

The locations of earthquakes within the New Madrid Seismic Zone appear to be strongly influenced by large bodies of igneous rock, which were formed by the cooling and solidification of molten rock beneath the Earth's surface. These igneous rock bodies show up as areas of high magnetic intensity on the magnetic map of the region. Since 1974, pinpointing dozens of minor earthquakes and dotting them onto an area map gives a good outline of the rift itself.

The New Madrid faults break the surface of the earth near the town of Commerce, Missouri. If you dig a trench, you'll find sedimentary deposits as young as 12,000 years old that have already been broken by movement along the fault. Could this feature, which also displays magnetic field anomalies, pose a seismic threat today? Yup, says the USGS.

Sound the Alarm

Scientists estimate that there is a 9-in-10 chance of a magnitude 6 to 7 quake occurring in the New Madrid Seismic Zone (NMSZ) before the middle of this century. (See Chapter 3, "Weird Science? Quake Prediction," for a discussion of magnitude.)

But since everything is so flat, a quake would at least be less destructive than one that occurred in the canyons of California. Right?

Wrong, says the USGS:

> Because of differences in the geology east and west of the Rocky Mountains, the effects of a magnitude 7 quake in the midcontinental United States could be far worse than those of the 1989 magnitude 7 Loma Prieta, California, earthquake. That quake, which struck the San Francisco Bay region during the World Series, killed 63 people and caused $6 billion of property damage.

Historic California Quakes—Worse Than the Movies

We think that modern quakes are especially bad partly because electronic media cover them in such excruciating detail. But quakes don't tailor their destructiveness to the times.

This table, culled from a USGS list of more than 200 California quakes with a magnitude of 5 or higher, are quakes that certainly would have garnered 24/7 coverage if minicams had been around:

Year	Month and Day	Magnitude	Area
1769	July 28	6.0	Los Angeles Basin
1800	November 20	6.5	San Diego Region
1808	July 24	6.0	San Francisco Region
1812	August 15	7.0	Wrightwood
1812	December 21	7.0	Santa Barbara Channel
1836	June 10	6.75	Hayward Valley
1838	June ?	7.0	San Francisco Peninsula
1857	January 9	8.25	Great Fort Tejon Earthquake
1857	September 3	6.25	West Nevada or East Sierra Nevada
1858	November 26	6.25	San Jose Region
1868	October 21	7.0	Hayward Fault
1871	March 2	6.0	Cape Mendocino
1872	April 11	6.75	Owens Valley
1873	November 23	6.75	Crescent City
1875	November 15	6.25	Imperial Valley to Colorado River Delta

Year	Month and Day	Magnitude	Area
1885	April 12	6.25	South Diablo Range
1889	May 19	6.25	Antioch
1892	February 24	7.0	Laguna Salada, B.C.
1892	May 28	6.5	San Jacinto or Elsinore Fault Region
1899	April 16	7.0	West of Eureka
1906	April 18	8.25	Great 1906 Earthquake
1906	April 23	6.4	Arcata
1910	August 5	6.6	West of Crescent City
1911	July 1	6.5	Calaveras Fault
1915	October 3	7.3	Pleasant Valley, Nevada
1915	November 21	7.1	Volcano Lake, B.C.
1915	December 31	6.5	West of Eureka
1922	January 31	7.3	West of Eureka
1923	January 21	7.2	Cape Mendocino
1927	November 4	7.3	Southwest of Lompoc
1932	December 21	7.2	Cedar Mountain, Nevada
1934	December 21	7.0	Colorado River Delta
1941	October 3	6.4	West of Cape Mendocino
1942	October 24	6.5	Fish Creek Mountains
1946	March 15	6.3	Walker Pass
1947	April 10	6.4	Manix
1952	July 21	7.7	Kern County Earthquake
1954	July 6	6.6	Rainbow Mountain, Nevada
1954	August 24	6.8	Stillwater, Nevada
1954	December 16	7.1	Fairview Peak, Nevada
1954	December 16	6.8	Dixie Valley, Nevada
1970	February 9	6.5	San Fernando
1980	November 8	7.2	West of Eureka

The first significant quake of the minicam era, arguably, was this one:

1989	October 18	7.1	Loma Prieta

And its sisters:

1991	August 17	7.1	West of Crescent City
1992	April 25	7.2	Cape Mendocino
1992	June 28	7.3	Landers

The Great 1906 San Francisco Earthquake

This is the quake most people think of when the subject of recent earthquakes comes up.

Although the planet lacked minicams, it did possess legions of big old tripod cameras. Between those and the plethora of good writers—both professional and amateur—around at the time, we have lots of images.

Research Findings

The U.S. Army relief unit that helped after the San Francisco earthquake estimated 700–800 dead. More recent research, reports the USGS, puts the toll at about 3,000. The population of San Francisco at the time of the quake was about 400,000; 225,000 were left homeless. About 28,000 buildings were lost, and the cost in 1906 dollars was $400 million, most of that caused by the fires. Only $80 million was directly caused by the earthquake.

It was early morning, 5:12 A.M., when the first *foreshock* was felt. Within 20 to 25 seconds, the great earthquake, with its *epicenter* near San Francisco, broke loose. Shocks were felt from southern Oregon to south of Los Angeles and into central Nevada.

A contemporary account, reported by the Exploratorium Web site, is chillingly descriptive:

Earthy Language

A **foreshock** is a minor shock preceding the main shock of an earthquake. An **epicenter** is the part of the Earth's surface directly above the locus of an earthquake.

John Farish, a mining engineer who was staying at the St. Francis, one of the city's finest hotels, wrote that he was awakened by a noise, "which might be compared to the mixed sounds of a strong wind rushing through a forest and the breaking of waves against a cliff. In less time than it takes to tell, a concussion, similar to that caused by the nearby explosion of a huge blast, shook the building to its foundations, and it began a series of the most lively motions imaginable. Accompanied by a creaking, grinding, rasping sound, it was followed by tremendous crashes as the cornices of adjoining buildings and chimneys tottered to the ground."

Farish's terror lasted more than 40 seconds, an eternity. The size of the quake was later estimated by seismologists to be 8.3 on the Richter scale (see Chapter 3). Its wake of destruction, as the world's two largest tectonic plates (the North American and the Pacific) slid past each other, was 290 miles long, stretching from Mendocino to Monterey.

Local reports said it seemed like doomsday; all the church bells were set clanging.

Those citizens whose doors were not jammed or blocked ran into the streets in their nightclothes. In an area south of Market Street, on land that had been created from part of the Mission Bay swamp, dozens were killed instantly, and hundreds of others were trapped in flimsy, substandard rooming houses.

Collapsing brick chimneys killed dozens more, including fire chief Dennis Sullivan. Sullivan would have been needed: Ruptured gas mains, wood stoves, and toppled lanterns all conspired to set off conflagrations that only intensified the "end of the world" panic started by the church bells. As it turned out, firemen were helpless; all but one water main had been broken by the quake, with 80 million gallons leaking uselessly onto the ground. The whereabouts of two dozen antiquated cisterns were known only to the dying fire chief.

The stockyards were damaged, and steers ran amok in the streets; most were killed when a building fell on them. A few escaped the buildings and police pistols and ran through Chinatown.

Research Findings

In 1906, the Richter scale hadn't been invented. Seismologists used the Rossi-Forel scale, which ranked earthquakes from 1 to 10. The San Francisco quake got a 9, meaning that it fell just short of opening huge chasms and destroying all life. (See Chapter 3 for a discussion of earthquakes and scale measurements.)

Thousands of San Franciscans packed picnics and went up to Nob Hill to watch the spectacle. Some went to Market Street to see if any of the new "skyscrapers" might fall down. The tallest, as it happened, lost only a few decorative elements, but the buildings surrounding it were consumed by fire. Novelist Jack London described the "rose color that pulsed and fluttered with lavender shades. There was no sun. So dawned the second day on strickened San Francisco."

A refugee camp in San Francisco after the 1906 earthquake.

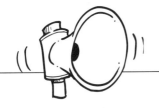

The fires destroyed 2,831 acres, or more than 490 city blocks. They burned 30 schools, 80 churches, and 250,000 homes.

Mom, Did You See Candlestick Park?

The 1989 Loma Prieta quake, the first major rupture since the 1906 quake, struck as 62,000-plus fans filled Candlestick Park for the third game of the World Series. It lasted 20 seconds and was centered 60 miles south of San Francisco on a 30-mile segment of the San Andreas Fault. It was felt as far away as San Diego and western Nevada.

The collapse of the Cypress Street section of I-880 in Oakland caused most of the 63 deaths. A section of the San Francisco–Oakland Bay Bridge also collapsed. Areas including Santa Cruz, Watsonville, Hollister, and Los Gatos suffered heavy damage. A disaster area was declared for the seven hardest-hit counties, from Monterey in the south to Solano in the north. More than 12,000 people lost their homes. More than 18,000 homes were damaged, and 963 were destroyed. More than 2,500 other buildings were damaged, and 147 were destroyed.

An automobile lies crushed under the third story of this apartment building in the Marina District. The ground levels are no longer visible because of structural failure and sinking due to liquefaction. (Courtesy J.K. Nakata, U.S. Geological Survey)

For a California quake, it was deep—11 miles, as opposed to the usual 4 to 6 miles. There was a 5.2 aftershock (a minor shock following the main shock of an earthquake) 2.5 minutes after the main shock; in the week following, a total of 300 more aftershocks of 2.5 or greater, and 20 greater than 4.0 were felt.

Runways at Oakland airport, bridges along the Pajaro and Salinas rivers, and the San Jose State Marine Station in Moss Landing were all damaged by *liquefaction*. The I-280 skyway suffered severe damage.

Thousands of landslides occurred as far north as the area below San Francisco. Large fissures opened throughout the Bay area. Thirty-four fires broke out, with a major fire in the Marina district.

Earthy Language

Liquefaction occurs when seismic waves cause sediments below the water table to temporarily lose strength and act as a liquid rather than a solid. Most often, clay-free deposits of sand and silt will liquefy.

And Then There's Palmdale ...

On June 28, 1992, sleeping residents of Yucca Valley and Big Bear Lake were shaken awake—and not by Mom with a cup of cocoa. In fact, they were awakened by an unusual geological event, especially for the San Andreas Fault region. The largest quakes in 40 years in the continental United States were caused by four separate, lesser-known fault lines in the Mojave Desert, near Palmdale, California. The quake registered 7.3 and was called the Landers earthquake, after the hardest-hit town.

Research Findings

The USGS was formed by the U.S. Department of the Interior in 1879 to discover and map the geological features of the nation. Today, in addition to mapping topography, its mission includes "providing reliable scientific information to: describe and understand the Earth; minimize loss of life and property from natural disasters; manage water, biological, energy, and mineral resources; and enhance and protect our quality of life."

Three hours later, a 6.5 quake struck 30 miles away. The worry was that the four fighting faults would set off the somnolent San Andreas Fault, which might have broken where Interstate 15 cuts through the San Bernardino Mountains. That would have produced the 8.0 quake experts have been expecting. It didn't happen, proving, for good or ill, that geologic forces do not conform to human expectations, even those of USGS scientists.

The Earth didn't do what the experts thought it would then. But scientists theorize that the Landers quake activity has linked the Gulf of California with slip systems east of Mount Whitney, the site of an 1872 quake that is one of California's three known 8.0 magnitude quakes.

Stay tuned for further developments.

The Least You Need to Know

➤ Earthquakes are caused by the molten interior of the Earth, forcing itself upward through tremendous pressure and expansion against the cooler exterior of the Earth.

➤ Earthquakes can theoretically happen anywhere, but they typically occur along faults.

➤ Scientists predict that the New Madrid Seismic Zone, which has experienced quakes since 1811, will experience a major quake in the next 50 years.

➤ The 1906 San Francisco earthquake and the 1989 Loma Prieta earthquake were two of the major earthquakes of this century.

➤ Central and coastal California may yet experience the 8.0 earthquake scientists have been expecting.

Chapter 2

Plates and Rifts

In This Chapter

➤ Incredible beauty from imponderable disruption

➤ The Pacific Rim and the Anatolian Plate

➤ Rifts and trenches

➤ Precariously perched Puerto Rico

The Earth's surface is divided like a jigsaw puzzle into giant pieces called tectonic or crustal plates. Moving slowly over the partially melted rock just below—the mantle—they slide past each other, bang into each other, repel each other, or slip below or climb over each other. The plates are a mile thick and weigh more than a small planet. The interaction of these plates causes 95 percent of the world's earthquakes.

Rings of Fire, Dances of Doom

These subterranean rock movements can be terrifying, but in combination with other forces of nature such as glacier activity and wind and stream erosion, they also create great beauty. Much of that beauty is found in the humid mountains of the romantic Pacific islands, or in the craggy, desolate ice castles of the Arctic. It may be found in the weathered igneous rocks of the Cappadocian area of Turkey, where people have carved whole cities and monasteries into the crumbling leftovers of lava or *uplift* or *subsidence*. It may be found in the whispering, tree-covered slopes of the Great Smoky Mountains, or thundering in with the Bay of Fundy's spectacular tides.

Map of tectonic plates.

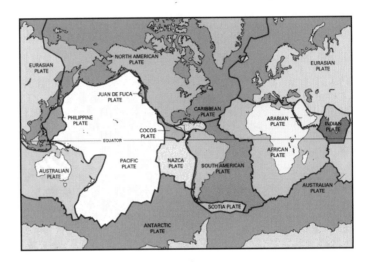

Never forget, though, that the beauty was born in terror, if not for people recently, then for prehistoric animal life and even for the rudimentary intelligences of primordial microorganisms.

The Pacific Rim

You might almost think that writers of rock songs knew a lot about earthquakes: "Shake, rattle and roll," "Whole lot of shakin' goin' on."

The truth is, for all the mountains so high caused by seismic action, there are also valleys so low. The San Andreas fault in California has created a lovely valley where the city of San Francisco stores its drinking water in the Crystal Springs Reservoir.

Seismic activity could deprive San Franciscans of their baths in a couple ways. Seismic creep—slow, steady movement along the fault line—could drain off some of the water by shifting the slope of the land and creating drainage, or at least make the shoreline of the reservoir look different. If you had time-lapse eyes, of course, set for a couple thousand years between blinks, you could see this movement.

Or, San Franciscans could lose their water supply as if it were a jar of stewed tomatoes that was packed wrong and popped its cork under pressure.

Earthy Language

The Earth maintains a balance. So, if one huge chunk of the Earth's crust is raised above the surrounding material (**uplift**) by earthquakes, another area—somewhere—will have to sink below the level it formerly held (**subsidence**) to maintain the balance.

Research Findings

A river runs through it! Commonly, a strike–slip fault produces a nice valley with a river running through it, or a picturesque lake. Why? This sort of fault will push up, over eons of time, easily erodable rocks along the zone. By contrast, the land below the material that was pushed up will seem to be a depression and, in fact, may have lost rock material to the heights. Rivers flowing in that general direction may be channeled toward the hollow land left by the rising rocks.

Creeping segments of the fault produce many small to moderate quakes that cause minor damage or none at all. But when it comes to stuck or locked places, watch out! Think about opening that jar of tomatoes. It won't budge, not at all. With a tremendous input of wrist-twist energy, the top finally pops off. You were expecting maybe a little spillage onto your clean counter. Ha! Little did you know that the tomatoes weren't cooked properly and that gases had been building up and expanding in there for weeks. If you hadn't opened the jar, you might have come home one day to find that the tomatoes had "quaked"—found a weak spot in the glass, popped through and pushed the other plates of glass all over your refrigerator as they released the pent-up energy.

In the Earth's crust, locked segments of faults store tremendous amounts of energy that can build up for centuries. The Great San Francisco Earthquake of 1906 ruptured a previously locked 430-kilometer segment extending from Cape Mendocino to San Juan Bautista.

That's the way it goes in California. And that's the way it goes for the seismic region that California is part of, the Pacific Rim, also called the Ring of Fire. The Ring of Fire is an arc stretching from New Zealand, along the eastern edge of Asia, north across the Aleutian Islands of Alaska, and south along the coast of North and South America. It contains more than 75 percent of the world's active volcanoes. At its edges, called *subduction zones*, it is seismically as well as volcanically active.

Earthy Language

A **subduction zone** is an elongated area of the Earth's crust along which one plate or even a smaller block that is part of a plate descends in relationship to another block or plate.

To Ensure Preservation

Nope, California won't slip into the ocean. The San Andreas Fault is only about 15 kilometers deep, a quarter of the thickness of the crust at that point. Because California is pretty much all crust (and not much North American Plate), it has low-density rocks and rides high on the ocean of Earth.

When the Ring of Fire is quiet, and when no volcanoes are spewing and oozing and flinging their superheated nuggets skyward, earthward, and seaward, the plates might be causing a much less photogenic Reign of Terror: a series of earthquakes.

In the United States, the best-known expression of the Ring of Fire's power is, of course, the San Andreas Fault, responsible for the Great San Francisco Earthquake of 1906 and the Northridge quake in 1994 that killed 60 people. Less well known is the Calaveras Fault, located near the city of Hollister in central California. Why is it not so well known? Because it creeps at a steady pace, about 5 to 6 millimeters a year, without tossing people out of their beds or cars off the interstate.

Top moving-and-shaking billing always goes to the big cities on the coast. But a smaller city, Parkfield, California, might get top billing in the future—certainly, it has been a sterling "bit part" player for more than a century. Since 1881, Parkfield has experienced earthquakes of 6.0 magnitude every 22 years. This would tell local residents when to take a sabbatical and get out of town for a while.

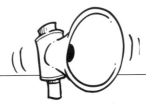

Sound the Alarm

A powerful earthquake (7.7 on the Richter scale) killed as many as 800,000 people in China's Hebei province in 1976. Another powerful quake struck in January 1998, killing only 47 but injuring more than 10,000. Of course, the more recent quake is nothing compared to the 1976 disaster. But imagine, in a nation that has always been populous, how many people have been killed or injured in Chinese quakes. Your best chance of surviving one there might be by living in a yurt in Mongolia.

Indeed, it tells the United States Geological Survey when to come into town. The USGS and various state agencies have parked seismographs, creep meters, stress test meters, and other ground-motion measurement devices all around Parkfield so that they can begin to get a handle on what happens before a quake. Then, perhaps, they can begin to use science to predict them, rather than the historical record or behavior of farm animals and other folksy methods.

To Ensure Preservation

Human beings are notorious for thinking "it can't happen to me" or "it can't happen here." Forget it. There are earthquakes everywhere, at the edges of plates and in the middle, on flat land and in the mountains. Be especially careful of complacency if you live beside a long, thin, quiet, peaceful lake .... Lake Champlain, for example. It may be between two states (New York and Vermont), but it is also between two subplates, and the area does jiggle from time to time.

But the Earth Gods seem to be listening and don't want to reveal their secrets. Based on the Parkfield research, not to mention earlier quakes (1934 and 1966), scientists claimed that there was a 95 percent chance of a 6.0 quake shaking Parkfield before 1993. It didn't happen. The only thing that got shaken was the scientific belief that one could get a handle on earthquakes based on various physical and chemical predictive parameters. However, never say die. The USGS continues the experiments.

Neither the USGS nor any other group is likely to be embarrassed by similar claims on the East Coast. There is no Atlantic Ring of Fire; rather, two oceanic plates meet mid-ocean, where movement happens via magma bursting through rather than plates slipping under or past each other. Still, quakes on the East Coast are possible. In 1985, New York City experienced a quake measuring 4.0 magnitude; two quakes, measuring 4.0 and 4.5, shook Reading, Pennsylvania, and caused minor damage.

The Anatolian Plate

The ancient Greeks—and the current ones—live atop the Anatolian Plate. The 1999 Turkish and Greek earthquakes were caused by movement of the Anatolian Plate.

Most of Turkey and its surrounding areas, including the Aegean Sea and Cyprus, are all atop the Anatolian Plate and, in fact, were once known as Anatolia. This area is bounded on the north by the North Anatolian Fault, and on the south by the Hellenic Arc. Turkey, from the Aegean region in the west to the Caucasus in the east, contains many seismically active regions. The Aegean region, the Caucasus, and the North and East Anatolian Fault zones are the best known and have been responsible for countless damaging quakes throughout recorded time and before.

Research Findings

The prevalent theory of the Earth's formation is the Pangea Theory, which holds that all of today's continents were once one supercontinent called Pangea, a Greek word meaning "all lands." What evidence suggests that this is true? First, it is known that hot stuff expands while cold stuff contracts, meaning that the Earth's top, cold crust more or less has to crack when the hot interior wants more room. Here are four more reasons to believe in Pangea:

➤ The coastlines of the continents appear to fit together.

➤ Distinctive rock strata found on one continent are found in what would be adjacent places on the sister continent.

➤ Ditto for fossil distribution.

➤ Ditto for coal distribution. (Simplistically, coal is made from dead stuff being heated up, say, from volcanic activity or pressure.)

But Anatolia does not stand alone. In a sort of "knee-bone-connected-to-the-thigh-bone" way, it is part of the Alpine-Himalayan *orogenic* system, which reaches from Italy to Burma.

Earthy Language

Orogenic comes from *orogeny*, which means "the formation of mountains, especially through a disturbance in the Earth's crust."

One researcher claims the system is identified with high mountain ranges and shallow seismicity, which nonetheless constitutes one of the most seismically active continental regions in the world, and one with the greatest documented history of quakes. Indeed, that same researcher identified 37 earthquake source zones. That's not a good location for your house if you're a light sleeper. On the other hand, he also identified zones where no sizable quakes have happened for centuries.

What about the Anatolian Plate and the 1999 Turkish earthquake disaster? The Anatolian Fault Zone is a huge strike-slip fault running from the Aegean Sea east of Istanbul to the border shared by Turkey, Iran, and the Republic of Georgia. The earthquake originated at a shallow depth where the Arabian Plate is colliding with the Eurasian Plate. As a result, the Anatolian Plate was squeezed just a bit more toward the Mediterranean Ocean. Thousands died.

Historically, seismologists have contended that one quake does not set off another. And yet, after the 1999 Turkey quake, the revered USGS indicated that a magnitude 7.1 quake in southern California might have been related to it in some way. They didn't say so right out. They simply grouped it in a single Web site with other geological events that happened surrounding the Izmit quake, including the eruption of a volcano in Alaska.

Here's what they said about the Hector Mine quake in the Mojave Desert:

> This earthquake was almost as strong as the recent ones that caused major damage and many casualties in Taiwan and Izmit. So how come only minor damage and few injuries occurred in California?

> The Hector Mine earthquake caused minimal damage because the epicenter was in a sparsely populated region in the Mojave Desert. But even then, it cut a 40-kilometer gash through the Mojave Desert and derailed a passenger train. It also cracked highways and rocked buildings in nearby cities.

Amos Nur, a Stanford University researcher, studied recent Mediterranean area quakes to determine that early civilizations probably met unfortunate ends because of a "swarm" of quakes. He certainly believes one quake might set off another, which sets off another, and so on. It seems other scientists, even the USGS, are beginning to lend credence to the possibility that when the Earth shifts in one place, necessarily, it must shift in another until all possible shifts have been completed. Until next round. Until the tension and pressure build up within the Earth again, and then .... Earthquakes!

Causing a Rift

If you pull at the edges of a couple continents, or pieces of continents, you get a rift. A *rift* is an elongated valley formed by the depression of a block of the planet's crust between two faults or groups of faults of approximately parallel strike. The presence of rifts is a good way to tell whether there were some earthquakes in the vicinity in prehistoric times.

Here are some examples of well-known rifts. Keep in mind that the magnitude of the rift as it appears today might give you some clue as to the magnitude of the disaster that would have occurred if people had been around to see this stuff when it happened.

Earthy Language

A **rift** is an elongated valley formed by the depression of a block of the planet's crust between two faults or groups of faults of approximately parallel strike.

Death Valley

Death Valley is the –est in a lot of ways. It is the hottest place in North America. It is the deepest valley, at 282 feet below sea level. Some would say it has the greatest display of wildflowers and the greatest views of snow-covered peaks.

In the 1870s, geologist G.K. Gilbert found rock layers there that, with modern study, reveal a nearly complete record of the Earth's past. So, Death Valley is also the revealing-est place on Earth.

It was relatively recently, during Mesozoic time (225 to 65 million years ago), says the USGS, that "A chain of volcanoes rose along the present Sierra Nevada, the sea withdrew while the Death Valley region became a highland, and all the older rocks were broken and deformed." At the same time, "A sea-floor trench (on the later site of California's Mother Lode) became a zone of under-thrusting when the east-moving Pacific plate plunged beneath the continent's edge." In short, the midcontinental plate and the Pacific plate bumped into each other as the Pacific plate moved eastward. Deep folds and high ridges—a rift—were the result.

To Ensure Preservation

If you go to Death Valley, you may think you're losing your mind. Rocks strewn across the sandy valley floor often appear to move by themselves during the night in an area known as The Devil's Racetrack. How? Your guess is as good as anyone else's.

Africa's Rift Valley

Africa's Rift Valley is 4,000 miles long, stretching from Lebanon to the Mozambique Channel. It is the greatest single rupture on Earth's land surface, and it can be clearly seen from the moon. It contains the lowest point on land, lower than Death Valley, at 510 feet below sea level. It is surrounded by some of the world's greatest peaks, including Kilimanjaro.

Mankind may have originated there. Hominid (man-like ape, or ape-like man, as you please) fossils found by Louis and Mary Leakey in Olduvai Gorge in Tanzania—part of the rift—opened up research into man's prehistoric past.

A trip through the gorge reveals lush rain forests that give homes to mountain gorillas, lakes thronged with flamingoes, and great plains (the Serengeti and Masai Mara) that support a variety of animals unique on Earth. Incredible varieties of fish inhabit both the chains of lakes within the rift and the coral reefs at its terminal sea.

The Great Rift Valley was formed by the repeated contact of four major plates moving across the Earth, and one subplate. The Arabian Plate, north of the Red Sea, bumped into the African Plate, over which the Nile River flows. The Madagascar Plate (logically, under Madagascar, as well as the rest of the Indian Ocean) bumped the African Plate from the west, with the added attraction of the East African Subplate, which just complicated their contact. And then, there's the wedge, to the east and south of the Arabian Plate, of the Indo-Australian Plate, a mighty hunk of Earth carrying two major continents. No wonder the Rift Valley is deep, wide, and still active.

Sequatchie Valley, Tennessee

This 125-mile long rift occurred when a plateau literally split apart in an earthquake before recorded time. That was a long, long time ago. These days, there are green farmlands, forests of hardwoods, towns, and even quaint old bridges to see in the valley. It's a nice day trip from Chattanooga: a cheaper jaunt than hiking to Africa!

The Bay of Fundy

A drive, preferably in warm weather, into eastern Canada will show you a rift valley unlike all the others—a rift valley that is a bay.

In 1841–1842, Sir Charles Lyell, considered the father of modern geology, found the Bay of Fundy. He was surrounded by steep red sandstone cliffs and basaltic lava remains from 200 million years before, when Nova Scotia was wedged near the equator between North America and Africa in the middle of Pangea.

As the continental plates pulled apart, rift valleys formed; this one is part of the Newark Supergroup, extending from Nova Scotia to South Carolina. The Bay of Fundy occupies one of that slew of rift valleys and hosts the world's highest tides, rising and falling 40 to 50 feet a day.

Deep Sea Fissuring

What is a rift on land is a trench in the ocean. The United States owns the biggest one, near the U.S. territory of Guam.

Marianas Trench

The Marianas Trench is the deepest spot on Earth, 35,840 feet under the ocean surface in the western Pacific Ocean, near Guam. It is a prime example of sea-floor spreading, the rifting that happens as tectonic plates recede from each other. Of course, they aren't pulling away quickly; even this deep trench is spreading the earth apart at only about plus or minus 2 centimeters a year. And it's doing it at one side—the volcanic side—more than the other. The volcanic side includes Guam, an island of volcanic origin with active volcanoes on the not-too-distant islands of Pagan and Agrihan. In fact, notable volcanic activity in the Marianas Trench has occurred as recently as October 1995. Gerard Fryer, at the Hawaii Institute of Geophysics and Planetology, described it in this way:

A *seamount* 25 miles northwest of Saipan is currently erupting. Two weeks ago fishermen saw discolored water. Personnel of the CNMI (Commonwealth of the Northern Mariana Islands) Wildlife and Emergency Management Office (EMO) surveyed the site and measured a bottom depth of 200 meters. More recently, fishermen reported "explosions" (though nothing broke surface). EMO went back on October 25, confirmed the submarine explosions, and measured a bottom depth of 60 meters. It isn't clear what navigation equipment was used, so we cannot really conclude yet that the seamount grew 150 meters.

Activity continues. CNMI has issued a tsunami alert, not because a major catastrophic eruption is expected, but because near surface activity could build a very unstable structure that might collapse, generating waves that would threaten the nearby islands of Saipan, Rota, and Tinian. Residents have been advised to be ready to evacuate low-lying areas on short notice or immediately on feeling any ground tremors (the tsunami travel time would be about 15 minutes).

Earthy Language

A **seamount** is not a horse you ride in the water. It is a noun, entered into Webster's Dictionary as late as 1941, meaning "a submarine mountain rising above the deep-sea floor."

Think Puerto Rico, Think Rift

Just because nothing has happened lately, don't think that the Commonwealth of Puerto Rico, so close to U.S. shores and a major vacation destination, couldn't shake things up again. After all, it is very close to some of the deepest parts of the Atlantic Ocean. The Puerto Rico Trench rings it at the deepest point in that ocean, at 28,374 feet.

Puerto Rico is rife with the sorts of seismically challenged land types that made the Loma Prieta (1989), Guam (1993), and Kobe, Japan (1995), earthquakes so dangerous. The land is made up of shallow layers of low-density, saturated, granular sediments or low-strength clay, both of which tend to liquefy from intense shaking.

Worse yet, greater San Juan is perched on both of these materials. And Puerto Rico is seismically active, sited at the convergence of the North American and Caribbean plates. Development of the area near San Juan has led to artificial filling over soft clay and loose sand—and now buildings are on top of that. Result: Danger, danger, danger.

Large earthquakes in 1787, 1867, and 1918 indicated that widespread liquefaction is indeed a likely result of a good-sized quake.

The October 11, 1918, earthquake measured 7.5. It was accompanied by a tsunami and killed about 116 people. It also did about $4 million in damage.

On November 18, 1867, Puerto Rico caught a double whammy, with a 7.5 earthquake just 20 days after Hurricane San Narciso. This earthquake's tsunami ran 490 feet inland and did lots of damage to buildings.

On May 2, 1787, a huge earthquake, estimated at 8.0, hit the island. Its epicenter may have been the Puerto Rico Trench. The quake demolished the Arecibo church and the El Rosario and La Concepcion monasteries, and damaged churches at Bayamon, Toa Baha, and Mayaguez. It also did a lot of damage to the castles of San Felipe del Morro and San Cristobal.

If you're planning to move to Puerto Rico, avoid the margins of Bahia de San Juan and Laguna San Jose, and the beach; instead, look to the mountains for safety. Heading for the hills seems a good idea during any Puerto Rican earthquake.

The Least You Need to Know

➤ California is part of the Pacific Rim, also known as the Ring of Fire, an arc that contains more than 75 percent of the world's active volcanoes and a good deal of seismic activity.

➤ The cradle of civilization, often viewed as Anatolia, is still very seismically active.

➤ The probable birthplace of mankind is located in the biggest tectonically produced feature on Earth, Africa's Rift Valley.

➤ Rift valleys on land are trenches at sea. The deepest trench in the world is the Marianas Trench.

Chapter 3

Weird Science? Quake Prediction

> **In This Chapter**
>
> ➤ The Richter and Mercalli scales
>
> ➤ Ancient Chinese prediction methods
>
> ➤ Modern methods of prediction, from the scientific to the screwball
>
> ➤ Historical upheavals and how they've been explained

The Earth moves about every 30 seconds, on average. Through measurement devices more cunning than anything the seafaring ancients even dreamed of, we know that there are earthquakes happening all the time. More than a million a year occur, in fact, including a number too small to be felt by mere mortals—but not too small to be measured by the sacred seismographs of modern science.

Sacred Seismographs See Slippage

Measuring earthquakes requires a language all its own. Two main scales are used to measure earthquake intensity. The Mercalli Intensity scale utilizes a range of Roman numerals from I to XII. The Richter scale is the measuring stick most of us are familiar with. The Richter scale describes the size of an earthquake through single digits with decimal points, 0 to 9.

The Mercalli Intensity scale can be more descriptive to the layman in terms of the damage we might expect. For example, Mercalli I means that earth vibrations are recorded by instruments. Mercalli II means that people resting on the second floor of houses notice shaking. Mercalli III means that anyone indoors will feel shaking and that hanging objects will swing back and forth.

On the Richter scale, 0 to 4.3 covers these three degrees. To the layman, Mercalli I, II, or III describes the earthquake pretty accurately. To the scientist, 3.7 tells the story. The Mercalli Intensity scale is more descriptive, telling us what that force is capable of doing. The Richter scale is completely quantitative, telling scientists the precise amount of force that an earthquake generated.

Modified Mercalli Intensity Scale

  I. People do not feel any earth movement.

 II. A few people might notice movement if they are at rest and/or on the upper floors of tall buildings.

III. Many people indoors feel movement. Hanging objects swing back and forth. People outdoors might not realize that an earthquake is occurring.

 IV. Most people indoors feel movement. Hanging objects swing. Dishes, windows, and doors rattle. The earthquake feels like a heavy truck hitting the walls. A few people outdoors may feel movement. Parked cars rock.

  V. Almost everyone feels movement. Sleeping people are awakened. Doors swing open or close. Dishes are broken. Pictures on the wall move. Small objects move or are turned over. Trees might shake. Liquids might spill out of open containers.

 VI. Everyone feels movement. People have trouble walking. Objects fall from shelves. Pictures fall off walls. Furniture moves. Plaster in walls might crack. Trees and bushes shake. Damage is slight in poorly built buildings. No structural damage occurs.

VII. People have difficulty standing. Drivers feel their cars shaking. Some furniture breaks. Loose bricks fall from buildings. Damage is slight to moderate in well-built buildings, and considerable in poorly built buildings.

VIII. Drivers have trouble steering. Houses that are not bolted down might shift on their foundations. Tall structures such as towers and chimneys might twist and fall. Well-built buildings suffer slight damage. Poorly built structures suffer severe damage. Tree branches break. Hillsides might crack if the ground is wet. Water levels in wells might change.

 IX. Well-built buildings suffer considerable damage. Houses that are not bolted down move off their foundations. Some underground pipes are broken. The ground cracks. Reservoirs suffer serious damage.

X. Most buildings and their foundations are destroyed. Some bridges are destroyed. Dams are seriously damaged. Large landslides occur. Water is thrown on the banks of canals, rivers, and lakes. The ground cracks in large areas. Railroad tracks are bent slightly.

XI. Most buildings collapse. Some bridges are destroyed. Large cracks appear in the ground. Underground pipelines are destroyed. Railroad tracks are badly bent.

XII. Almost everything is destroyed. Objects are thrown into the air. The ground moves in waves or ripples. Large amounts of rock may move.

To Ensure Preservation

Some regard the lesser known Mercalli Intensity scale, devised by Italian geologist Giuseppe Mercalli, as easier to follow than the better known Richter scale, invented in 1935.

From the U.S. Federal Emergency Management Agency (FEMA)

Every earthquake has a unique magnitude (measured by the Richter scale, these days), although its effects vary according to distance from the epicenter, ground conditions, local construction standards, and so on (estimated by the Mercalli Intensity scale).

Richter Scale

What Richter Numbers Really Signify	Richter TNT for Seismic Example	Magnitude Energy Yield (approximate)
1.5	6 ounces	Breaking a rock on a lab table
1.0	30 pounds	Large blast at a construction site
1.5	320 pounds	
2.0	1 ton	Large quarry or mine blast
2.5	4.6 tons	
3.0	29 tons	
3.5	73 tons	
4.0	1,000 tons	Small nuclear weapon
4.5	5,100 tons	Average tornado (total energy)
5.0	32,000 tons	
5.5	80,000 tons	Little Skull Mountain, Nevada, quake, 1992
6.0	1 million tons	Double Spring Flat, Nevada, quake, 1994
6.5	5 million tons	Northridge, California, quake, 1994

continues

Richter Scale   (continued)

What Richter Numbers Really Signify	Richter TNT for Seismic Example	Magnitude Energy Yield (approximate)
7.0	32 million tons	Hyogo-Ken Nanbu, Japan, quake, 1995; Largest thermo-nuclear weapon
7.5	160 million tons	Landers, California, quake, 1992
8.0	1 billion tons	San Francisco, California, quake, 1906
8.5	5 billion tons	Anchorage, Alaska, quake, 1964
9.0	32 billion tons	Chilean quake, 1960
10.0	1 trillion tons	(San Andreas-type fault circling Earth)
12.0	160 trillion tons	(Fault cutting Earth in half through center)

Research Findings

Charles Francis Richter (1894–1979) invented the first standard measurement tool for earthquakes. *Richter* means "judge" in German; how fitting that he should be the judge of how big an earthquake is.

Charles Francis Richter, of Richter scale fame, wasn't just a scale maker. He demonstrated a correlation between the intrinsic energy of the earthquake and the amplitude—the destructive effects—of the ground motion at any given distance.

Earthquakes and Waves

Would you like a body wave or a surface wave? Those are the two types of waves the Richter scale measures to determine an earthquake's magnitude.

Surface waves travel along the Earth's surface, and body waves are vibrations that travel through the Earth. Both originate at the focus, or internal origin, of the earthquake; the epicenter is the area on the surface of the earth above the focus. Surface waves are stronger and cause the most damage, making the ground literally roll.

Body waves come in two varieties—compression waves, which roll through anything and carry the earthquake far and wide, and shear waves (also called transverse waves), which stop when they encounter liquid.

Richter used measurements of shear waves (or transverse waves) to calibrate his scale of magnitudes. The measurements had to be obtained using a Wood-Anderson seismograph, which is particularly sensitive to shear waves and can measure their amplitudes at one-second periods. Although Richter's work was originally calibrated only for these specific seismometers, and only for earthquakes in southern California, seismologists have since adapted his magnitude scale to all types of seismometers, all over the world.

Compression waves are, excuse the pun, the movers and shakers of earthquakes. They reach the surface first, and so are often called primary waves—p-waves, for short. Although their velocity decreases as they near the surface, they are still the fastest of all earthquake waves. They cause less damage, though, than the short, lethargic shear or surface waves, also called s-waves. Whereas p-waves displace material directly ahead of and behind them in a sort of domino effect, s-waves displace the material that is at right angles to them, like a billiard ball striking other billiard balls at angles.

To Ensure Preservation

Want to find oil? Use an earthquake. Using earthquake p-waves or manufactured sound waves, scientists map the ocean floor. The ways the waves are reflected to the surface of the ocean tells what sedimentary structures are below. Some types of these structures—faults, folds, and domes—are known to often trap oil. Give me a good earthquake, and I'll give you a good idea where to drill for oil below the ocean floor.

These multi-monikered waves are useful as well as destructive. By recording exactly when each type of wave reaches seismic stations globally, we can determine when and where an earthquake happened, almost exactly.

If your house is a pile of rubble, however, these analytical niceties might not mean much to you. A good, accurate prediction would have meant a great deal more. It wouldn't have saved your house, but at least you'd be returning to the rubble instead of digging out from under it.

Taking the Quaking out of Shaking

If we can pinpoint the precise place to set humans down on the moon's surface, why can't we tell what our own planet is doing under our feet? That's an imponderable question. Still, earthquake prediction has been an art and a science for most of recorded history.

Many ancient Oriental manuscripts mention earthquake-detection devices. In 132 C.E., Chinese philosopher Zhang Heng used a pendulum, a jar, and a few balls in carved dragon heads to rig up a temblor detector. The jar was 6.5 feet in diameter, and a pendulum hung inside it. Connected to that were the dragon heads on the outside, each with a ball in its hinged mouth. The jar sat on a stand. On the stand was a bronze toad with its head up and mouth open. The theory was that when the earth shook, the dragon's mouths would open and drop the balls, one of which would roll into the toad's mouth. The direction of the quake would be known by which dragon dropped a ball.

Sounds screwy, but it worked. It perceived a shaking too small to be felt, more than 600 miles away. Verbal news of it reached Zhang a few weeks later, confirming his instrument's accuracy.

Of course, Zhang's instrument merely detected a quake. It didn't predict it. Predictions and forecasts would have to depend on something other than recognizing ground that was already shaking. There's also a difference between a prediction and a forecast, with forecasting being far easier.

A prediction assigns a specific date, place, and magnitude to an earthquake. A forecast simply assigns the probability of an earthquake, along with probable years and magnitudes, to a region. It's about as precise as, one often thinks, weather forecasting. And that may be as good as it gets: Can you imagine your TV weather-gal *predicting* the weather: "It will rain exactly .5 inches from 4:14 P.M. to 6:07 P.M. on Thursday, March 5, 2001, in a radius of 20 miles around Dover-Foxcroft, Maine." Right. Sure. Any day now.

Predictions may fail, but forecasts have often been on target. The earthquake that occurred in northern California on October 17, 1989, was not predicted, but it was forecast by the United States Geological Survey. It fell within the magnitude range, time span, and approximate region that the USGS had said would probably experience a seismic event. Doubtless, the USGS used all the tools at its disposal, not the least of which its extensive data on past quakes and its huge network of seismographs that plotted every little shiver in the Earth's mantle.

Here are the current "best methods" for attempting to forecast earthquakes.

Magnetic Readings

The Earth's magnetic field might be useful in predicting earthquakes, if we learn to read accurately the meaning of the Meissner effect as it occurs naturally.

The Meissner effect is simply any change in the Earth's magnetic field that causes magnets to repel things that they normally attract. A *superconductor* repels a magnet and might be a useful tool for recognizing upheavals in the Earth's magnetic field caused by the kind of subterranean chaos that precipitates earthquakes. The effect was named for German physicists W. Meissner and R. Ochsenfeld, who discovered it in 1933. What makes it so difficult to use is that different elements that make up the Earth demonstrate various degrees of magnetic weakness at various temperatures.

Anecdotal evidence for using magnetic changes to predict earthquakes comes from Japan, at the time of an 1855 earthquake. A shopkeeper in Tokyo had a large horseshoe magnet on display, with several iron objects placed on it to demonstrate its strength. One day they clattered to the ground as the magnet failed. A few days later, a big earthquake struck. When it was over, the objects once again were attracted to the magnet.

A Rising Issue: Gas

Another possible avenue for predicting earthquakes is through measurements of escaping gases. A major proponent of this method is geologist Thomas Gold.

The generally accepted belief about earthquakes is that they are caused by forces inside the Earth that build up strains in the crust to the breaking point. The moment of fracture is the moment of earthquake. But why, asks Gold, would there often be multiple large quakes in the same area over a few days or weeks? Why wouldn't the crust break in all the locations where it is already stressed at the moment of violent shaking?

"Why would the ground shake sometimes for periods longer than a minute? Why would quakes cause tsunamis, the massive ocean waves? A brief tremor, however fierce, would not have such an effect," Gold proposes.

Earthy Language

A **superconductor** is a substance in which there is the complete absence of electrical resistance, especially at very low temperatures. Such substances are perfect conductors of electricity, offering no other force to impede the electric current.

To Ensure Preservation

This is an experiment you could try at home with little risk. Get a big magnet. Hang it on the wall. Place doodads on it. (Bonus: This doubles as a work of art.) If your "artwork" disintegrates, you'll know that an earthquake might be coming.

He believes that gases are the answer. Gases are subject to rapid large changes of volume and could, in fact, correlate to the "subterranean air movements" posited by the ancient Greeks (except Thales).

When predictions (not forecasts) are based on gas-related phenomena, Gold says, lives are saved. "One city has been successfully evacuated two hours before a massive earthquake, and thereby probably many thousands of lives were saved. This was the city of Haicheng in China, in February of 1975. That prediction was based almost entirely on gas-related phenomena."

Gold chronicles a number of eyewitness earthquake accounts that suggest to him that gases are involved. He quotes from a contemporary report of the series of New Madrid quakes 1811–1812, referred to in Chapter 1:

> On this day [December 16, 1811] twenty-eight distinct shocks were counted, all coming from the southwest and passing to the northeast, while the fissures would run in an opposite direction, or from the northwest to the southeast.

> One family, in their efforts to reach the highlands by a road they all were well acquainted with, unexpectedly came to the borders of an extensive lake; the land had sunk, and water had flowed over it or gushed up out of the earth and formed a new lake. The opposite shore they felt confident could not be far distant, and they traveled on in tepid water, from twelve to forty inches in depth, of a temperature of 100 degrees, or over blood heat, at times of a warmth to be uncomfortable, for the distance of four or five miles, and reached the highlands in safety.

> On the 8th of February, 1812, the day on which the severest shocks took place, the shocks seemed to go in waves, like the waves of the sea, throwing down brick chimneys level with the ground and two brick dwellings in New Madrid, and yet, with all its desolating effects, but one person was thought to have been lost in these commotions.

> About four miles above Paducah, on the Ohio River, on the Illinois side, on a post-oak flat, a large circular basin was formed, more than one hundred feet in diameter, by the sinking of the earth, how deep no one can tell, as the tall stately post-oaks sank below the tops of the tallest trees. The sink filled with water, and continues so to this time. The general appearance of the country where the most violent shocks took place was fearfully changed, and many farms were ruined.

Gold cannot fathom why no one thought of gases at that time or since. "I know of no way in which an area of land could suddenly sink by tens of feet, except by the release of large amounts of gases whose pressure had previously held open a large total volume of pore-spaces in the underlying rocks," he says.

Gold also believes the gas theory explains other places that are not on a fault line but that are still "earthquake spots." One of these is in northern Norway, where, for a long time, you could be guaranteed an earthquake that you could feel (at least a small one) once in every 24 hours. In the United States, there's a similar area on the western tip of Flathead Lake in Montana, and still another near the town of Enola, Montana.

Deep earthquakes also argue for gas, says Gold. "Earthquakes are known at depths down to 700 kilometers, and the pressure there is so great that sudden fracture cannot occur. So, it would have to be some force other than fracture that caused the ground to move."

Gas is explosive, and even at minor depths, could move, excuse the pun, mountains. Add to that the thoughts of Amos Nur, that quakes sometimes occur in 50-year swarms: it could be, one might suppose, that the gases that had built up had all been released by that approximate number of shifts of ground, allowing the gas to escape through the fissures and the loosely packed, jiggling earth. And, too, the ancients often had things right—recall Thales and friends—without really knowing why.

At the very least, it is suggestive.

Celestial Augury

Others believe in syzygy. No, it isn't the last name of some tin-pot central European dictator. It's pronounced "si," as in *sister*; "zi," as in *zither*; and "gee," as in "Oh, golly gee." What this weird word means is an alignment of the sun, moon, and Earth; it happens twice each month, at the new moon and the full moon. And it's another big concept, like Gold's, this one from geologist Dr. James Berkland.

The in-line spinning of the celestial bodies increases the gravitational forces, pulling ocean tides to their max—and, says Berkland, no doubt "Earth tides" as well. Recall that the Earth isn't as solid as it looks. And there was that cagey Greek, Thales, who thought that the subterranean ocean was what caused quakes anyway.

The Earth and the moon are closest (that is, in perigee) once a month; the Earth and the sun are closest (in perihelion) once a year, in January. So, the greatest gravitational stress on the Earth's innards occurs then. Does it make a difference?

Berkland says it does. "The optimum such example in 600 years was on January 4, 1912, when syzygy and perigee were only 6 minutes apart. On that day, the strongest quake (5.5 magnitude) in California/Nevada in two years occurred near Bishop, California."

Berkland cites some more unhappy celestial coincidences and quakes. Within 24 hours of syzygy, there were these temblors:

➤ Long Beach, California (1933)

➤ Tehachapi, California (1952)

➤ Olympia, Washington (1949)

➤ Hebgen Lake, Missouri (1959)

➤ Anchorage, Alaska (1964)

➤ San Fernando, California (1971)

➤ Tangshan, China (1976)

➤ Eureka, California (1980)

➤ Landers, California (1992)

➤ Kobe, Japan (1995)

*Road scene after 1964
Alaska earthquake.*

But best of all was the Loma Prieta "World Series Earthquake," which was publicly predicted when the maximum tidal force in two years occurred on October 14, 1989, less than four days before the very serious 7.1 magnitude quake.

The Seattle quake of January 28, 1995, was predicted on Seattle television and radio less than six days before the strongest Seattle shaker in 30 years struck. January 28 was the day after perigee and two days before the new moon.

Earthy Language

Piezoelectricity is electricity or electric polarity due to pressure, especially in a crystalline substance (such as quartz).

Weird Science

Charlotte King hears earthquakes. Not voices in her head, not Martians landing in the yard—earthquakes. And there is some scientific evidence to back her up.

Investigation over more than a decade proposes that Charlotte King's sensitivity to earthquake "noises" before they happened is an ability to pick up signals from *perovskites,* which generate waves as a result of tectonically generated *piezoelectricity.* Perovskites, although infinitely more superconducting, are similar to the substances used in speakers and the microphones of telephones.

In about 1973, Jerry Gallimore invented a device that measured the same signals King heard and could be used to predict earthquakes. His device, like King's ears, used the vibrations of perovskites to make predictions.

Gallimore's work was followed up by a French scientific team. They apparently didn't understand fully why it worked, but they did manage to get some of the magnetic interference out of the vibration-detection process.

Two other U.S. researchers, Elizabeth Rauscher, Ph.D., and William L. Van Bise, an electrical engineer, called the Library of Congress Earthquake Prediction Registry on January 8, 1994, to report impending events within 30 days in the Los Angeles area. Their report was based on unusual surges of signals from 3.8 to 4.0 Hz—the same sort of frequencies King hears. The Northridge quake struck on January 17.

Rauscher and Van Bise don't discount Charlotte King. In fact, in predicting the Landers quake on June 28, 1992, near Lake Arrowhead, California, the researchers had used antennae near Reno, Nevada, to pick up signals at 3.8 cycles per second. They consulted with King about the area, timing, and strength of the quake.

Warnings, Warnings Everywhere

At the moment, accurate earthquake predictions are more the exception than the rule. So you can't bet the farm on getting out of Dodge to dodge the flying bricks. What can you do?

Remember that there will be aftershocks—usually smaller temblors—for hours, days, and even weeks or months to come. So you'll have plenty of incentive to mull over what has happened as you rebuild your chimney, or your house.

Earthy Language

Perovskite refers to a yellow, brown, or grayish black mineral sometimes containing rare Earth elements. The word was coined in 1840 from the surname of Russian statesman Count L.A. Perovskii, who died in 1856.

Research Findings

Seismic activity is not all that Charlotte King feels. As she reported on television's "That's Incredible" in 1981, she feels abdominal pain whenever a volcanic eruption begins anywhere in the world. With Mount Saint Helens, she was doubled over. When it blew, she had a minor stroke.

You might also monitor the USGS Web site; it won't give you predictions any more than your wisdom teeth will (although there are people who say theirs act up when there are changes in the earth's magnetic field). But it will keep you abreast of what—post Gallimore—science is working on to get a handle on earthquake forecasting and prediction.

The Least You Need to Know

➤ The Richter scale is the more well-known scale for measuring quakes, but it means more to scientists than to laymen.

➤ The Mercalli Intensity scale puts quakes' damage in terms the layman can understand.

➤ Earthquake predictions are rarely 100 percent accurate; earthquake forecasts are about the best way to alert an area to a probable earthquake.

➤ Current methods of earthquake prediction range from interpreting disturbances in the magnetic field, to measuring escaping gases, to syzygy, to readings based on vibrations of perovskites.

Chapter 4

Earth's Greatest Recent "Rock and Roll" Hits

In This Chapter

➤ Demographics of earthquake casualties

➤ Verbal snapshots of earthquake survival

➤ What a small quake feels like, up close and personal

➤ Tips to help you survive one

The world powerhouse in earthquake research is, arguably, the United States Geological Survey National Earthquake Information Center. So it is prudent to believe them when they say that in 1998, earthquake deaths (8,928) were three times higher than in the year before (2,900). Of course, 1999 beat both totals combined, with 1997's 419 casualties thrown in.

What's going on? Is the Earth getting rowdier, more rapacious? Actually, it is just getting back to normal. Believe it or not, the average annual death toll from earthquakes in the twentieth century was in excess of 10,000.

Yikes! No wonder earthquakes are studied so intensely—they kill in five figures. But that just returns us to the question of why the death toll is getting back to normal.

The answer: Although builders have gotten more earthquake-conscious and are building safer buildings—which have accounted for the decreasing tolls—populations continue to grow and to move into more earthquake-prone locations. And exactly why is *that*?

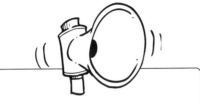

Sound the Alarm

Don't be fooled just because rock looks stationary and seems to erode only through geological ages. When an earthquake unleashes huge amounts of energy, rock can transmit waves—that is, it can move—at up to 5,000 miles per hour. Try not to get in its way.

Two reasons. First, typically, the only land poor people can afford to buy or build—or squat—on is unstable land on which they erect even less-stable shelters. Second, wealthier people flock to areas of natural beauty—that is, mountains—which are now reachable easily with four-wheel drive sport utility vehicles.

Take a chilling example of scenario no. 1: The Afghan earthquake on May 30, 1998, killed more than 4,000; most of the victims were living in huts or worse, with little infrastructure to rescue them after it happened.

Scenario no. 2 has not produced a horrific death toll yet. But most experts think it's just a matter of time. After all, if the largest earthquake of 1998—a magnitude 8.3—had happened in Missouri rather than under the ocean between Australia and Antarctica, there's no telling how horrific it would have been.

Selected News Accounts About Recent Earthquakes

A quick read of news accounts of earthquakes the past few years should be enough to convince the most die-hard Pollyanna that major quakes are nothing to laugh about.

A Mexican Quake: October 1999

Selected sections from a *San Francisco Examiner* October 1, 1999, report are enough to make anyone living in an earthquake zone build a bunker or move:

> OAXACA, Mexico—Dozens of the sick and injured shivered in the drizzle Friday under tents outside Oaxaca's public hospital, which was evacuated after a magnitude 7.5 earthquake. The death toll rose Friday to 20 ....

> The quake forced authorities to evacuate 62 patients to the hospital plaza, where they spent the night under a 55-degree drizzle beneath two large plastic canopies.

> In the plaza, 16-year-old Serafina Perez huddled under a blanket with her 1-year-old son Alfonso, who was being treated for a cold and fever ....

> Teresa de Jesus Garcia, 18, died when she ran out from the stationery store where she worked and was hit by falling bricks. Since her 300-peso ($32.00) weekly pay was her family's main income, friends appealed for help for the girl's mother and grandmother ....

Aureliano Salmoron, a 76-year-old farm worker, expressed thanks that he and his family escaped physical harm but bemoaned the loss of his adobe home.

"I'm going to continue fighting. What else can I do?" he said, his voice breaking. "But at this age, how much more can I fight?"

If you think it is just impoverished Mexican citizens affected by the quake, think again, and think Puerto Vallarta, an extremely popular resort destination for North Americans, which was rocked by a quake in 1995 (no dead were reported).

To Ensure Preservation

"Must be jelly, 'cause jam don't shake like that," said the old song. Mexico City is essentially resting on jelly and is highly vulnerable to earthquakes, say geologists. What's the "jelly"? An old, soft lakebed—which, with enough shaking, could easily liquefy. Don't build a house—much less a city—on that sort of land, especially if it's in an active fault zone. If you can't tell, ask a geologist: The United States Geological Survey and most universities have plenty.

August 1999: Turkey

Whether due to the staggering death tolls or the exotic locale, the devastating earthquake in Turkey in the summer of 1999 generated hundreds of grisly reports, both print and broadcast. Following are parts of a pithy offering from NBC News.

Sound the Alarm

Just because the ground stops shaking doesn't mean that the earthquake is over. Turkey experienced at least 210 aftershocks of the 1999 earthquake, said Ahmet Mete Isikara, head of Istanbul's Kandilli Observatory.

Voices of Trapped People Still Heard; Death Toll Tops 10,000; Police Detain Three Contractors

U.N. officials were quoted as saying as many as 35,000 were still buried beneath rubble, but Turkish officials refused to confirm that figure. There were, no doubt, thousands still buried.

Research Findings

The worst earthquake in Turkish history killed an estimated 40,000 people in the eastern province of Erzincan in 1939.

Authorities took their first steps today against contractors whose shoddily made apartment buildings have been blamed for many of the deaths ....

Although Turkish government officials admitted building codes had not always been followed in the quake area, they also insisted that a quake that strong—7.4—would have destroyed many buildings even if all had been constructed according to code.

The governor of the nation's central bank estimated the cost of the quake could rise to $5 to $7 billion.

When those statements were made, the count had risen to 10,009 dead and 34,000 injured; the government had ordered 10,000 additional body bags. Burials in mass graves had begun, and helpers—from those burying the dead to clerics—didn't know where to turn.

"Who should I pray for?" asked Rustu Korkmazer, Imam of the stricken Turkish town of Adapazari. "Which of the thousand dead should I rush to?"

Taiwan's Unusual 1999: Big Quake, Few Dead

Scientists said Taiwan's quake of 1999 was unrelated to the quake in Turkey. But the earth is round, after all. How can what happens in one section inside that ball not affect another?

Still, that pronouncement isn't what's unusual about this quake (seismologists typically say that). What was unusual—and frightening—is that while Taiwan's rocking and rolling has usually begun far out to sea, this quake began inland, close to the city of Taichung. Like the Turkey quake, it was not deep in the earth, but relatively near the surface.

Research Findings

"The building codes are better in Taiwan than in Turkey," said USGS seismologist Walter Mooney at the time of the Taiwan quake, explaining the vast difference in death tolls between the two similar-size quakes.

"It looks as if this one was peculiar in some way," Dr. Chris Browitt of the British Geological Survey in Edinburgh told the BBC. "It looks like it was much shallower than usual and in a different area."

For a more clinical look at the big quake with the light casualties, here's the report from the BBC:

The island's last tremor on this scale was on 14 November 1986 but occurred under the ocean, and the resulting death toll was restricted to just 15.

The last time that Taiwan experienced an earthquake of this magnitude on land was in 1935, resulting in more than 3,000 deaths.

"A magnitude 7.5 earthquake will occur maybe four times a year somewhere in the world," said Dr Browitt. "It's just that this one happened to hit at a place where a lot of people and buildings are exposed."

Where the Philippine plate is grinding against the enormous Eurasian plate, there's a very active region, seismologically, with plate movement measured at as much as 7 centimeters a year. The movement pushes the mountains up by as much as five millimeters a year. That's where Taiwan perches.

Combine that with an intensely tropical climate—lots of rainfall—and you get major landslides, rockfalls, and other naturally hazardous landscapes all over the island. Material eroded from those constantly rising mountains forms the land on which cities are built; it's notoriously unstable, and has an odd effect on earthquake waves. Indeed, in this sort of *topography,* aftershocks are sometimes as bad as the earthquake itself. In 1935, there was a magnitude 7.1 earthquake, which killed more than 3,000 in the western part of the nation. Three months later, an aftershock killed only a handful fewer.

Earthy Language

Topography is, literally, an accurate, detailed description of surface features of the earth—hills, valleys, rivers, lakes. Topographic maps also include buildings and roads, generally.

Quaking at the Numbers

Here's a list of the most damaging earthquakes of the current generation by year, place, death toll, and magnitude—before the disasters of 1998 and 1999:

➤ 1971, Southern California: 65 deaths, 6.5 magnitude

➤ 1972, Managua, Nicaragua: 5,000 deaths, 6.2 magnitude

➤ 1976, Guatemala: 22,000 deaths, 7.9 magnitude

➤ 1977, Tangshan, China: 250,000+ deaths, 7.6 magnitude

➤ 1980, Romania: 2,000 deaths, 7.2 magnitude

➤ 1980, Algeria: 35,000 deaths, 7.7 magnitude

➤ 1981, Southern Italy: 3,000 deaths, 7.2 magnitude

➤ 1982, Southern Iran: 3,000 deaths, 6.9 magnitude

➤ 1983, Yemen: 28,000 deaths, 6.0 magnitude

➤ 1985, Turkey: 1,342 deaths, 6.0 magnitude

➤ 1989, Mexico: 10,000 deaths, 7.0 magnitude

➤ 1989, Armenia: 25,000 deaths, 6.9 magnitude

➤ 1989, Northern California: 67 deaths, 7.1 magnitude

➤ 1990, Iran: 40,000 deaths, 7.7 magnitude

And Then, the Real People

What are your chances of experiencing an earthquake? Pretty good. The Center for Earthquake Research and Information has this to say:

> There is a 100 percent chance of an earthquake today. Though millions of persons may never experience an earthquake, they are very common occurrences on this planet. So today, somewhere, an earthquake will occur. It may be so light that only sensitive instruments will perceive its motion; it may shake houses, rattle windows, and displace small objects; or it may be sufficiently strong to cause property damage, death, and injury.

> It is estimated that about 700 shocks each year have this capability when centered in a populated area. Fortunately, most of these potentially destructive earthquakes occur in relatively unpopulated areas.

Research Findings

The greatest number of people killed in one earthquake was 830,000 in a 1556 earthquake in China.

Living to Tell About It

What's it like to experience an earthquake—say, something under 5.0 on the Richter scale?

My husband and I were staying in the end room of a motel built out over Lake Luzerne in upstate New York. The room had a great view of the lake and was the only room completely perched above it on pilings. It was the middle of the night, or at least, my body thought so, for it was deeply asleep. I was having a dream. I was a sausage, and I was in a big pan with other sausages being shaken around.

About that time, my husband leaped out of bed. I sat up. The dogs we were sleeping with, Daisy and Cagney, bounded off the bed and began to twirl (well, Cagney did—Daisy was too old to bound).

"Quick! Shoes, coats, leashes," I yelled, jumping into my own shoes, snapping the leash onto Cagney's collar, and throwing my coat over my arm. My husband was doing pretty much the same thing and reached the door first. We ran up the boardwalk from our room in the motel to solid—somewhat solid—ground.

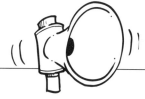

Sound the Alarm

Better to sound the alarm a bunch of times for little things than once for something catastrophic. Although Greece is tectonically challenged, it benefits from having small frequent quakes. Records show that very few occur that are bigger than magnitude 6.5 on the Richter scale. So, if you want to experience an earthquake and probably not get hurt, Greece is probably the place to court the experience.

Standing 100 feet from the lake shore, in as open a space as we could find, it was apparent what was going on. It had been obvious to me the minute my consciousness returned; we were having an earthquake.

The *temblor* was just about over by the time we got out where we could see the tall pines swaying. No one else was out; almost no one else was staying at the lake in October. We went back in and got back into bed with our dogs.

My first husband had been a geologist, a "soft rocker" (one who studies sediments, both those being currently deposited in oceans and rivers, and ancient remains of oceans and rivers) rather than a "hard rocker" (one who studies volcanic rocks). When one hangs out with "rockers" of any sort, one learns a bit about how the Earth works (if only to keep from coming unglued at otherwise boring graduate student dinner parties).

Earthy Language

Temblor means, simply, earthquake, but it's an interesting word. One might ask why it lacks an "r" right after the "T". Why isn't it like the English word tremble, which means to shake? Because the word is derived from the Spanish word temblar, "to tremble." And *they* left out the r.

So, although I was long divorced from the geologist, I knew about aftershocks. And it occurred to me now to tell my husband that we would probably feel more shaking in about 20 minutes. Oh, goody.

We did. It turned out that the epicenter of that quake was actually quite far away, near Cortland, New York, where my mother lived alone. She felt it all right, and was scared to pieces.

Saving Yourself

Even a small earthquake can bring down the chimney and Aunt Maybelle's frightful china (at last!) down out of the vitrine to its doom. (Every cloud has a silver lining.) So, you should think about getting your wits about you before the earth moves under your feet. Here's how:

1. Have a well-thought-out family plan about what to do if you are not together when the earthquake strikes—where each member will go, how you will contact each other.

2. Use a flashlight or other battery-operated lighting source—no matches—until you are sure that there are no gas leaks.

3. Have shoes handy that will protect you from cuts as you walk over debris.

4. Assess everyone's physical condition; if necessary, treat injuries until help arrives.

5. Avoid eating or drinking anything that could be contaminated by broken glass or leaking chemicals.

6. Have enough properly stored food and water on hand to feed your family for three days. Food should not need refrigeration before or after opening. Water should be stored in a cool place and should have been changed every six months. (If the lines are broken, remember that you have between 30 and 50 gallons of fresh water in your water heater.)

7. Have on hand emergency medical kits sufficient for injuries to your entire family, plus all medications for a week. These would include such regular medications as heart or blood pressure medications and insulin.

8. Have a portable radio and extra fresh batteries. (If your radio fails, you can use the radio in your car, providing that your car's gas tank has not been ruptured, making the spilled gasoline dangerous.)

9. Have a chart of where your gas, water, and power main switches and valves are located, and know how to turn them off.

10. Keep ready preselected changes of clothing, including warm outerwear, for each family member.

11. Obtain emergency pet supplies, and figure out a way to confine the pets when the shaking starts so that they will not become injured unnecessarily or run away in fright.

Here's a list of recommended survival supplies:

➤ At least 2 quarts to 1 gallon of boiled water per person, per day.

➤ Ample and freshly stocked first-aid kit.

➤ First-aid manual with instructions on how to use the kit.

➤ Canned or individually packaged food—precooked, requiring minimum heat and water. Consider infants, pets, and others with special dietary requirements.

➤ Can opener.

➤ Blankets.

➤ Portable, battery–operated radio, with spare batteries.

➤ Critical medication and eyeglasses, contact cases, and supplies.

➤ Fire extinguisher (dry chemical, type ABC).

➤ Flashlight, with spare batteries and bulbs.

➤ Battery-operated or spring-wound watch or clock.

➤ Barbecue (use outdoors only), charcoal and a lighter, or a portable stove with self-contained fuel source.

➤ Various sizes of sealable plastic bags.

➤ At least two pots.

➤ Paper plates, plastic utensils, and paper towels.

➤ Large plastic trash bags for trash, waste, and water protection.

➤ Ground cloth.

➤ Large trash cans.

➤ Hand soap, liquid detergent, and shampoo.

➤ Toothpaste, toothbrushes, and dental floss.

➤ Premoistened towelettes.

➤ Deodorant.

➤ Feminine supplies.

➤ Infant supplies.

➤ Toilet paper.

➤ Powdered chlorinated lime to add to sewage, to disinfect, and to keep away insects.

➤ Newspapers to wrap waste and garbage; may also be used for warmth.

➤ Heavy shoes and gloves for every family member for cleaning debris.

➤ Candles.

To Ensure Preservation

During an earthquake, keep calm. Inside, stand in a doorway, or crouch under a desk or table away from windows, and glass doors and dividers. Outside, keep away from buildings, trees, and telephone and electrical lines. On the road, drive away from underpasses and overpasses, stop in a safe area, and stay in the vehicle.

➤ Matches, dipped in wax and kept in a waterproof container.

➤ Garden hose for siphoning and firefighting.

➤ Complete change of clothes, kept dry.

➤ Ax.

➤ Shovel.

➤ Broom.

➤ Rope or bailing wire.

➤ Plastic tape.

➤ Pen and paper.

➤ Flares.

➤ Tools—screwdriver, pliers, wire, knife, hammer, crescent wrench (for turning off gas main).

Unless you're a geologist, you probably won't go seeking an earthquake. Nonetheless, no matter how quietly you like to live, one may find you. So there's no harm in being prepared. No matter where you choose to live, think about making sure that any building you move into meets earthquake-resistance standards for that locale. Think about putting together a "disaster kit." And hope that local officials where you live have done the same.

The Least You Need to Know

➤ An average year will see 10,000 earthquake casualties.

➤ People are building more structures in earthquake-prone zones, not fewer.

➤ Whether on a poor Mexican farm or in a Taiwan luxury hotel, quakes are terrifying.

➤ An area with frequent small quakes might be safer for living than an area with few big ones.

➤ You have an excellent chance of being in an earthquake.

➤ Somewhere, each day, there is an earthquake.

Chapter 5

The Earthquake's Twin: The Tsunami

In This Chapter

➤ A tidal wave by any other name is just as deadly

➤ Dangerous shores: places to avoid to escape the wave

➤ Is death inevitable? Tips from FEMA to fool the flood

➤ New information: meteors and subaqua slides

➤ The worst tsunamis in history

You've heard of *tsunamis* (pronounced "soo-nahm'ee"). They are also called tidal waves. You figure they're just science fiction, or maybe a good image for those old Japanese woodblock artists to play around with. Big curvy wave, with lots of blue paint and black lines, maybe a view of a shoreline in the background through the curl of the wave. But real? Come on. You might as well believe in the Eggplant That Ate Chicago.

You couldn't be more mistaken. According to the Federal Emergency Management Agency (FEMA), until the 1999 earthquakes in Turkey, tsunamis had killed more people since 1945 than earthquakes.

Surf's Up

Although some hot-doggers would have you believe otherwise, a tsunami is not a surfer's wildest dream. Rather, it is the worst nightmare for people living in coastal

Earthy Language

The word **tsunami** comes from *tsu*, which is Japanese for harbor, and *nami*, Japanese for wave. Today, we use this word to mean any destructive wave caused by an earthquake under or near the ocean, or sometimes, a volcanic eruption undersea.

Sound the Alarm

People who are near the seashore during a strong earthquake should listen to a radio for a tsunami warning and should be ready to evacuate at once to higher ground.

areas of the world. Where there's ocean, there's potential for tsunamis, although areas at greatest risk are less than 50 feet above sea level and within 1 mile of the shoreline.

While tsunamis are often caused by earthquakes, they can also be caused by landslides, volcanic eruptions, or even meteorites (as scientists believe happened a time or two in the eons before recorded history). From the point of origin, waves travel outward in all directions, much like the ripples caused by throwing a rock into a pond. The time between wave crests may be from 5 to 90 minutes, and the wave speed in the open ocean will average 450 to 600 miles per hour.

What You Can't See Can *Hurt* You

In the open ocean, tsunamis are invisible. Ships at sea cannot detect a passing tsunami, nor can the waves be seen from the air. Weather planes and satellites are useless.

While still in the deep ocean, a tsunami is merely a series of waves that are only a few feet high and a hundred miles or more apart, but they are typically traveling at 600 miles per hour. When these ungentle giants reach shallow water and begin to compact, they slow down (the troughs are compressed) but grow in height (the crests are magnified). Same wave force, different format. A series of waves may reach the coast at intervals of 5 to 40 minutes at speeds of up to 30 miles per hour.

Where Not to Be

In the United States, the main place not to be to avoid tsunamis is Hawaii, followed by Alaska and then the Pacific Coast of the continental United States.

Hawaii

Hawaiian tsunamis can be locally generated, in which case there will be little warning; after all, Hawaii is an active volcanic zone. Tsunamis strike almost immediately after an earthquake occurs. Tsunamis may also come from two main tectonically active areas, Chile or the Aleutian Islands. Chilean tsunamis are better for Hawaiians; they take about 15 hours to reach Hawaii, affording lots of time to evacuate the low-lying areas. Aleutian Islands tsunamis reach Hawaii in about 4½ to 5½ hours. That's still time to evacuate, but barely.

Of the 50 or so tsunamis reported in Hawaii since the early 1800s, seven caused major damage and loss of lives. Two of those—the tsunamis of 1868 and 1975—were of local origin, generated by earthquakes beneath the southern coast of the island. The 1868 waves destroyed several coastal villages in the Ka'u and Puna districts, most of which were never rebuilt. The 1975 tsunami claimed two lives and caused widespread damage along the Kalapana coast. Although there were obviously better warning systems then than in 1868, it would have been tough to beat that tsunami. The wave reached Hilo in just 20 minutes from the time of the earthquake.

To Ensure Preservation

If you live near a shore and suspect that you may be in line for a 100-foot soaking but don't have a radio, observe the shoreline. Rapid changes in the water level indicate an approaching tsunami.

If you live in a coastal area, remember: Any earthquake strong enough to cause difficulty in standing or walking should be regarded as strong enough to cause a tsunami. Head for higher ground immediately—crawl along the shaking earth, if you have to.

Research Findings

Consider this frighteningly visual description of a tsunami, from a *Seattle Times* article about Washington state's new tsunami-safety warning signs:

"Like a grasping hand, the first wave penetrates up to a mile onshore, hauling back cars, trucks, and anything else it can snag as it returns to sea. That debris gets mixed up with the second wave and is spat, like a shotgun blast, at the battered coastline, making the second waves often the most damaging ones."

Philippines

The Philippines is another place not to be if you want to avoid tsunamis. The 1994 Mindoro earthquake, magnitude 7.1, caused a tsunami that struck about 40 kilometers of the shoreline of Mindoro Island, as well as Verde Island and the Baco Islands north of the Mindoro mainland.

The Baco Islands lost near-shore houses completely, as well as 41 people, mainly children and the elderly, who drowned in the dark of night. One child was carried away during the rundown of the wave at its highest spot and was never found.

Most people reported that there was less than a 5-minute interval between the ground shaking and the ocean rising. Still, many were able to rush landward for 50 or 60 meters before the wave hit. Most of them also saw the shoreline recede for a great distance—about 50 to 100 kilometers—right after the main earthquake was felt. The approaching wave was accompanied immediately with a very loud, jet-like gushing sound.

Despite the short lead time, there were many survivors because the wave struck at the lowest tide and because the topography near the populated areas was flat, diminishing the effect of the waves.

Research Findings

Although most deaths during a tsunami are caused by drowning, other loss of life can be attributed to flooding, polluted water supplies, and damaged gas lines that explode in the hours after the waves recede.

Most eyewitnesses of the tsunami that hit the Philippines said that there were three waves, with the first one the strongest. Luckily, it was low tide, but the tide oscillated for an hour after the three waves. The area it hit, near Batangas Pier, is shallow coast with large tidal flats, causing friction that probably helped the waves dissipate more than they would have coming up a steep beach. Because of the flatness, though, the wave did reach quite far inland, as much as 250 meters; its greatest height was 8.5 meters.

Aside from the 41 deaths—really remarkable, considering the time (night) and rapid arrival of the tsunami—several fishing boats were destroyed, 1,530 houses were destroyed or washed away, another 6,036 houses were partially destroyed or partially washed away, and 7,566 were damaged.

New Guinea

New Guinea is another place to avoid if you don't want to see a tsunami. According to the United States Geological Survey, the tsunami that struck Papua New Guinea on July 17, 1998, and claimed 2,200 lives may have been the most devastating tsunami in the twentieth century.

The tsunami followed a magnitude 7.1 earthquake, similar in size to the Mindoro quake. But in New Guinea, the wave reached 15 meters, almost twice the size of the Mindoro wave.

Scientists examined this event closely in an attempt to explain the exceptionally high waves. *Science News Online* reported in September 1999 that the investigation into the cause of the deaths of those 2,200 residents of Papua New Guinea had thrown a bucket of water on prevailing popular theories of how tsunamis are caused. Tsunamis typically were attributed to undersea earthquakes, reporter R. Monastersky wrote, but evidence collected off the New Guinea coast indicated an underwater landslide, caused by a quake.

Also from Monasterky's report comes this:

> "This really is one of those big paradigm shifts in science," says team member Philip Watts of Applied Fluids Engineering in Long Beach, Calif., who uses computer models to simulate tsunamis. "We suspect that a lot of the bigger, known tsunamis involved some landsliding."

The scientists reached their conclusion after mapping the seabed and drilling for sediment samples. A robotic submarine photographed a 4-kilometer trench in the ocean floor, marking the place where the Pacific Ocean floor had crashed into New Guinea before diving beneath it into the Earth.

Researchers discovered a fresh, amphitheater-shaped scar, created when a giant chunk of sediment had slumped downhill. When, they wondered, did it break loose?

The fact that there was a delay between the earthquake and the wave—unlike at Mindoro—could point to a *seafloor slump* as the cause rather than the earthquake itself. If the quake had caused the wave, it would have struck in about 5 minutes, as in Mindoro. But it didn't arrive for 20 minutes, about the time that it would take for the slump to start and finish after the earthquake caused it.

Earthy Language

A **seafloor slump** is much like a landslide. The difference is that the water slows the slippage of the material which has either been shaken loose by an earthquake or extruded by volcanic activity. A slide that would take only seconds on land, where air offers little resistance, may take many minutes underwater.

A computer model supports the theory. But, of course, there is dissension. One researcher says there was evidence of small, quake-caused slides, or slumps, but not one big enough to have caused the big wave.

The bright side of the New Guinea tsunami is that it has cast doubt on accepted theories and has engendered more research, which might eventually save more lives. On the other hand, it also makes it possible that modest quakes, like those that visit

California as often as frequent fliers fasten their seatbelts, could trigger giant waves by setting off even modest subocean slides.

Tsunami Warnings

It was the 1946 Hilo tsunami that fostered the creation of the Pacific Tsunami Warning System, headquartered in Honolulu and administered by the National Weather Service and National Oceanic and Atmospheric Administration (NOAA).

A "tsunami watch" goes up when seismometers and tide-gauge stations around the Pacific report ominous readings. Once the presence of a wave is confirmed, the Honolulu center issues an estimated time of arrival for the first wave, and civil authorities evacuate low-lying coastal areas.

The speed of a tsunami depends on the depth of the water, so the arrival point from anywhere on the Pacific Rim is predictable. (At least, it was until the New Guinea tsunami.)

No matter what the cause, though, the size of the wave is tougher to calculate because it depends on the configuration of the sea bottom and initial landfall of the tsunami. The destructiveness, then, is determined by local underwater and land-based topography. Because the precise path across the ocean, the precise journey across underwater features close to shore, and the current tide level (high or low, spring or *neap*) will be different for each tsunami, it would be unwise to think that just because the last one delivered only a few feet of water, the next will do the same.

Biggest Tidal Waves in History

Tsunami waves have killed more than 4,200 people since 1992; until the New Guinea wave, the total was only 2,000. Needless to say, one Big Kahuna of a wave can create a truly horrible human disaster.

Following is a list of the biggest waves on record:

➤ **April 1, 1946**—A cruel April Fool's joke, this Pacific-wide tsunami followed a magnitude 7.8 quake in Alaska's Aleutian Islands. More than 165 died, including children at school on Hawaii's Laupahoehoe Point. Damage? In 1946 dollars, $26 million.

Research Findings

In the 1946 tsunami, the newly built (1940) Scotch Cap Lighthouse on Unimak Island was swept away, along with the five men running the light. The lighthouse was 40 feet above the sea and five stories high. That's a big wave, for certain.

➤ **May 22, 1960**—This Pacific-wide tsunami was spawned by a magnitude 8.6 quake off the coast of central Chile. An estimated 2,300 died. Damage? More than $500 million.

➤ **March 28, 1964**—This Pacific-wide tsunami caused damage on Washington's coastline. It was triggered by a magnitude 8.4 quake in Alaska's Prince William Sound. More than 120 died; damage was more than $106 million.

➤ **November 4, 1952**—A Pacific-wide wave was triggered by an 8.2 earthquake off the coast off the Kamchatka Peninsula, in Russia. It affected not only Hawaii, but also Midway Island and its U.S. Naval installation. It also affected the Kamchatka Peninsula. Damage estimates in Hawaii (in 1952 dollars) ranged from $800,000 to $1 million. No humans died, but six cows were lost.

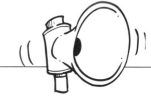

Sound the Alarm

Just because tsunami waves are not a problem for big ships in deep ocean, don't think that small boats near shore will save you if a wave is predicted. Inhabitants of Chile who feared the earthquake in the 1960 tsunami took to the sea in small boats to escape the shaking. In a thunderous breaker, all the boats were lost.

➤ **March 9, 1957**—An 8.3 magnitude quake shook the Andreanof Islands in the Aleutian Islands off Alaska. Although no lives were lost, the Hawaiian Islands suffered damages amounting to about $5 million in 1957 dollars.

➤ **May 22, 1960**—An 8.6 magnitude earthquake occurred off the coast of South Central Chile. The range of casualty estimates is great, between 490 and 2,290. Damage cost estimates were over half a billion dollars.

➤ **June 3, 1994**—A magnitude 7.8 earthquake occurred off the southeastern coast of Java near the east end of the Java Trench in the Indian Ocean. More than 200 East Java coastal residents died.

➤ **November 15, 1994**—At 3:15 P.M. (local time), an earthquake occurred near Verde Island, Philippines. The magnitude 7.1 earthquake spawned the 1994 Mindoro tsunami, which destroyed 1,520 houses and killed 41 people.

Can Anyone Survive?

If you want to survive a tsunami, the best way is not to be in one. The Federal Emergency Management Agency (FEMA) suggests that you line up your ducks in advance.

If you plan to move to (or are already living in) an area susceptible to tsunamis, you should heed these tips:

1. Find out whether your home is in a danger area.

2. Know the height of your street above sea level and the distance of your street from the coast. Evacuation orders may be based on these numbers.

3. Be familiar with the tsunami warning signs:

   ➤ An earthquake or sizable ground rumbling

   ➤ A noticeably rapid rise or fall in coastal waters

   ➤ Broadcast warnings from the NOAA or local channels

To Ensure Preservation

Most tsunami bulletins have warned of tsunamis that didn't materialize. In 1948, Honolulu was evacuated, as was Hilo after a 1994 magnitude 8.1 quake in Japan's Kuril Islands. Both bulletins were busts. Millions of dollars were lost in effort and lost work time. But better safe, and a little poorer, than to be swept away. Heed all tsunami bulletins.

Warnings won't help unless all family members know how to respond to them, so make evacuation plans in advance. Choose an elevated inland location to run to, separately or together. Also, choose more than one route to get there, as disasters tend to clog roads, either with debris or people in cars trying to get away. Teach family members how and when to turn off water, electricity, and particularly gas. Teach children how and when to call 911 and the police or fire department, and which radio station to listen to for official information.

FEMA also recommends having these disaster supplies on hand:

➤ Flashlight and extra batteries.

➤ Portable, battery-operated radio with extra batteries.

➤ First-aid kit and manual.

➤ Emergency food and water. Some portable things, such as granola bars to grab in a flash, might be a nice touch.

➤ Nonelectric can opener (just in case, when it's over, your house is intact and food supplies are untouched, but the power is out).

➤ Essential medicines. Again, really essential medicines should be with you, in a purse or gym bag that you can grab easily.

➤ Cash and credit cards; keep these items with you.

➤ Sturdy shoes.

Develop an emergency communication plan. In case family members are separated from one another during a tsunami (a real possibility during the day, when adults are at work and children are at school), have a plan for getting back together.

FEMA recommends making an out-of-state relative or friend the family contact. After a disaster, often it's easier to call long distance. Make sure everyone knows the name, address, and phone number of the contact person.

All this assumes that you have been listening to a radio or television for the latest emergency information, including evacuation orders.

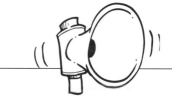

Sound the Alarm

At all costs, stay away from the beach. Never go down to the beach to watch a tsunami come in. If you can see the wave, you are too close to escape it.

In the aftermath of a tsunami, continue to monitor the situation from your battery-operated radio. Help the trapped and injured as much as you can, as long as it is safe for you to do so.

Re-enter your own home with caution, and only after authorities say it is safe to return. Don't turn anything on until specialists—electricians and gas company employees—have checked out your appliances and systems (remember the exploding gas lines).

If your house was drenched, open windows and doors to help with drying. Shovel mud while it is still moist; it's heavy, but it will help the building dry, and you won't have to breathe in nasty particles.

Don't drink the water until you hear that it is safe; drink bottled water as long as the seals are intact.

Checklist for Utility/Appliance Damage

Once you've said, "Oook, mud, slime, geesh, wah, darn it!" several hundred times upon seeing your home, now perched porchless in Tsunami Shores subdivision, you need to do a few other things before life can begin to return to normal. (These same procedures should follow any disaster through which your house is still left standing—hurricanes, ice storms, floods, narrow escape from forest fire, tornado, and so on.)

➤ Check for gas leaks. If you smell gas or hear a blowing or hissing noise, open a window and quickly leave the building. Turn off the gas at the outside main valve if you can, and call the gas company from a neighbor's home. If you turn off the gas for any reason, it must be turned back on by a professional.

➤ Look for electrical system damage. If you see sparks or broken or frayed wires, or if you smell hot insulation, turn off the electricity at the main fuse box or circuit breaker. If you have to step in water to get to the fuse box or circuit breaker, call an electrician first for advice.

➤ Check for sewage and water line damage. If you suspect that sewage lines are damaged, avoid using toilets and call a plumber. If water pipes are damaged, contact the water company and avoid the water from the tap. You can obtain safe water by melting ice cubes.

The Least You Need to Know

➤ Tsunamis are caused by earthquakes and earthquake-triggered underwater landslides.

➤ Any shoreline in the world is susceptible to tsunamis, but particularly the Pacific Rim nations.

➤ Tsunamis kill in other ways besides drowning; floods, polluted water supplies, and damaged gas lines that explode hours after the waves recede can also claim many lives.

➤ You can run, but you can't hide: Escaping an earthquake by putting out to sea is a bad idea.

➤ If you live in a coastal area, make sure that you know the tsunami warning signs and have an evacuation plan for your family in advance.

Part 2
Earthly Wrath: Ground-Breaking Events

Volcanoes are the bad boys of the Earth's formation: They're exciting, but not too nice. Their friends are pretty foul, too: landslides, rockfalls, that sort of thing.

Volcanoes make big holes in the Earth (craters and fissures), as do sinkholes, a feature of the landscape unrelated to volcanoes, but equally terrifying to those whose houses slide out from under them quietly and with no warning.

"What goes up must come down" is a pretty good aphorism for this section.

Blowing Its Stack: Volcanoes

Most people have a favorite volcano image. For some, it is derived from a movie—*Joe vs. the Volcano*, or *One Million Years B.C.* (either the 1940 movie with Victor Mature or the hubba-hubba version more than 30 years later with Raquel Welch). *Dante's Peak*, with Pierce Brosnan, and *Volcano*, with Tommy Lee Jones are two other recent disaster movies that provide plenty of graphics of volcanic eruptions.

The directors of those films could have gotten their images from any number of documentary films of modern eruptions. Or, they could have based them on reading assignments they might have had in college—for instance, two letters from Pliny the Younger to Roman historian Tacitus, giving details of the death of his uncle Pliny (the Elder) and his deadly mission to return to Stabiae, Pompeii's harbor, to try to save some of the populace from the 79 C.E. eruption.

One thing is certain about volcanoes: Modern ones and ancient ones are stunningly similar, and efforts to escape them are often futile.

Sound the Alarm

Scientists have estimated that at least 200,000 persons have lost their lives as a result of volcanic eruptions during the last 500 years. Between 1980 and 1990, volcanic activity killed at least 26,000 people and forced nearly 450,000 to flee from their homes.

Not Quite One Million B.C.

The eruption of Mount Vesuvius in 79 C.E. is probably the most famous eruption of all time. It claimed the lives of common men, women, children, and pets as well as Roman soldier/philosophers such as Pliny. Following are two passages about Pliny the Elder, translated by Professor Cynthia Damon of Amherst College.

[Pliny] was at Misenum in his capacity as commander of the fleet on the 24th of August [in 79 A.D.], when between 2 and 3 in the afternoon my mother drew his attention to a cloud of unusual size and appearance …. He called for his shoes and climbed up to where he could get the best view of the phenomenon. The cloud was rising from a mountain—at such a distance we couldn't tell which, but afterwards learned that it was Vesuvius. I can best describe its shape by likening it to a pine tree. It rose into the sky on a very long "trunk" from which spread some "branches." I imagine it had been raised by a sudden blast, which then weakened, leaving the cloud unsupported so that its own weight caused it to spread sideways. Some of the cloud was white, in other parts there were dark patches of dirt and ash. The sight of it made the scientist in my uncle determined to see it from closer at hand ….

Research Findings

There were dozens of erotic murals on walls in ancient Pompeii, but these were hidden from public view—and even public knowledge—until very recently.

He launched the quadriremes and embarked himself, a source of aid for more people than just Rectina, for that delightful one. He hurried to a place from which others were fleeing, and held his course directly into danger. Was he afraid? It seems not, as he kept up a continuous observation of the various movements and shapes of that evil cloud, dictating what he saw.

Ash was falling onto the ships now, darker and denser the closer they went. Now it was bits of pumice, and rocks that were blackened and burned and shattered by the fire. Now the sea is shoal; debris from the mountain blocks the shore. He paused for a moment wondering whether to turn back as the helmsman urged him. "Fortune helps the brave," he said, "Head for Pomponianus …."

An onshore wind forced Pliny's ship into the harbor. He and his crew disembarked, and he asked to be taken to the baths. He ate and went to bed. Ash piled up to three or four feet outside his door before he awoke. He joined the others.

They discussed what to do, whether to remain under cover or to try the open air. The buildings were being rocked by a series of strong tremors, and appeared to have come loose from their foundations and to be sliding this way and that. Outside, however, there was danger from the rocks that were coming down, light and fire-consumed as these bits of pumice were. Weighing the relative dangers they chose the outdoors; in my uncle's case it was a rational decision, others just chose the alternative that frightened them the least.

They tied pillows on top of their heads as protection against the shower of rock. It was daylight now elsewhere in the world, but there the darkness was darker and thicker than any night. But they had torches and other lights. They decided to go down to the shore, to see from close up if anything was possible by sea. But it remained as rough and uncooperative as before. Resting in the shade of a sail he drank once or twice from the cold water he had asked for. Then came a smell of sulfur, announcing the flames, and the flames themselves, sending others into flight but reviving him. Supported by two small slaves he stood up, and immediately collapsed.

To Ensure Preservation

If you want a glimpse of how people lived in Pompeii before 79 C.E., when Mount Vesuvius erupted and destroyed the city, visit the Metropolitan Museum of Art in New York City. You can see a restored Pompeian bedroom, murals intact, and a spine-cracking bed floating on the mosaic floor of the tiny room.

Research Findings

During the first eight hours of the eruption of Vesuvius, dust, ashes, cinders, and rocks fell on Pompeii to depths of 2 to 4 meters (8 to 10 feet). The heaps of small rocks that landed on the houses caused many roofs to collapse.

And died, suffocated by the ash and noxious fumes.

The next day, his nephew and sister were forced out of Misenum by ash crossing the bay, but they were able to return and resume their lives.

Mount Vesuvius erupting,
Italy, 1944.

The residents resumed their lives—at least, the well-to-do residents—in houses they had left. It is unlikely that modern homes, which were not supported by columns of marble, would remain inhabitable after an assault by volcanic ash.

How Volcanoes Happen

Some ancient peoples thought fire-breathing dragons caused volcanoes. Others thought it was the wrath of the gods. The scientific explanation is a little more complex.

Inside Inner Earth

The Earth is hot inside, some places so hot that what we know as rock up here is liquid down there, called magma. (Once the hot stuff breaks the Earth's surface, and before it is cooled to rock, it is called lava.) Hot liquid is less dense than cold solids (rock, earth), so it rises toward the surface, like a hot air balloon rising. (Same principle, different substances!)

The magma doesn't always escape. Sometimes it forces its way up under the cone of a volcanic mountain, causing the mountain to rise (like a cake), but never breaking through (like a potato bursting its skin in the microwave). Which process occurs depends on the relative density and the pressure and heat (and lack thereof) in the magma and the rock layers above it. Magma (and heat, pressure, steam, and gases) can escape through volcanoes of various types, or through extrusions—vents, *fumaroles,* and so on.

Earthy Language

A **volcano** is a mountain but is not formed by folding and crumpling, uplift, or erosion. Rather, volcanoes are built by their own eruptive products—lava "bombs," ash, and dust—falling back to earth and creating a cone-shaped mound that grows with each eruption, or alternatively, by seepage of lava down the sides. Volcanoes also grow by being pushed up from within by magma that doesn't break through the surface.

Naming Volcanoes

The people who built Pompeii and Herculaneum thought the volcano—Mount Vesuvius—was extinct. Or, at least, they regarded any activity—in the age before science as we know it—as just something the gods were up to that wouldn't really affect the people, unless the people crossed the gods somehow.

Nonetheless, the extravagantly pyrotechnic explosion of Mount Vesuvius—with its mushroom cloud of ash and gases, falling ash and exploding debris, flows of lava and rocks, burning trees, and pulverized houses, cows, and people—gave a name to the most visually compelling type of volcano: plinian, after Pliny the Elder.

Earthy Language

A **fumarole** (from the Latin *fumarium*, for "chimney") is an opening in a volcanic area from which smoke and gases escape.

At the other end of the scale, very mild eruptions may merely discharge steam and other gases, or they may be slightly more violent and extrude large quantities of lava. For quick mental indexing, scientists commonly use the name of a spectacular eruption to describe others of the same general type. Some may be uniformly of one type; others may display a sequence of types.

Phreatic (also called steam-blast) eruptions are relatively mild and occur when explosive, expanding underground steam contacts cold earth, or when colder surface water comes into contact with hot rock or magma. No new molten rock is exploded or extruded; rather, fragments of existing solid rock in the volcanic conduit are ejected.

Earthy Language

The term **phreatic** derives from the Armenian word *albiwr*—goodness knows how—for "spring" and the Old High German *brunno*, for "burn." It means relating to or being an explosion caused by steam derived from groundwater.

Sound the Alarm

Don't think that you can ignore warnings to evacuate and plan to outrun a volcano's flows. Scientists and historians have figured that it took only about four minutes for boiling mud to flow from Vesuvius to Herculaneum, a distance of about four miles.

Strombolian eruptions (named after the volcano Stromboli, one of the Aeolian Islands north of Sicily) cause huge clots of molten lava to burst from a summit crater, forming luminous arcs through the sky; lava clots (balls of molten material flung out of the volcano rather than extruded) combine to stream down the slopes in fiery rivulets.

Vulcanian eruptions are typified by the 1947 eruption of the Paricutin Volcano in Mexico. A dense cloud of ash-laden gas explodes from the crater and rises high in the sky, with steaming ash forming a cloud near the top of the cone.

Vesuvian eruptions cause ash-laden gas to be violently flung above the crater into a cauliflower-shaped cloud, also known as the plinian phase of multitype eruptions. Other phases might include phreatic events, in which only superheated water and water-vapor arises, or there might even be extrusions from vents and fumaroles for a time, rather than continuous explosive events.

Pelean volcanoes (typified by the Mayon Volcano in the Philippines in 1968) fling large quantities of gas, dust, ash, and incandescent lava boulders out of a central crater. These then fall back and form glowing avalanches moving downslope at as great a speed as 100 miles per hour. The Mayon eruption is a recent example; the name comes from Mount Pelee on Martinique, Lesser Antilles, which erupted in 1902.

"Hawaiian" eruptions may occur along fissures or fractures that serve as linear *vents* (as happened in the eruption of the Mauna Loa Volcano in Hawaii in 1950). Or, they may occur at a central vent, as they did during the 1959 eruption in Kilauea Iki Crater of Kilauea Volcano, Hawaii. In Hawaiian eruptions, molten, incandescent lava spurts from a fissure in the volcano's *rift zone* and feeds lava streams that flow downslope. In *central-vent eruptions,* a fountain of fiery lava spurts to a height of several hundred feet or more. "Such lava may collect in old *pit craters* to form lava lakes, or form cones, or feed radiating flows," says the USGS.

Earthy Language

A **vent** is simply a crack in the earth through which molten material or steam can escape. A **rift zone** is an area marked by cracks, faults and vents, and overlies a dike, a sheetlike body of igneous rock that has intruded the rock around it. A **central-vent eruption** is one occurring at a cylindrical, or pipe-like, opening in the Earth's surface. A **pit crater** is one formed by a sinking in of the surface because of shifting material below, and it is not primarily a vent for lava.

Mexican Volcanoes: The Fires Next Door

The Pacific Ring of Fire is regarded by many as the hotbed of all real volcanic activity. Mexico, as a long, sweeping arc in that ring, has more than its fair share of active volcanoes.

Popo

Popocatepetl ("smoking mountain" in the Aztec tongue) rises to 17,883 feet. Despite Mexico's warm climate and the heat of the volcanic core, it remains snow-capped year-round. It is almost perfectly conical up to 16,400 feet, where a peak called Pico del Fraile (the remains of the older volcano) gives it an irregular appearance. "Popo's" crater is oval and deep, and the walls are nearly vertical. The cone is covered with yellow sulfur spots; gases escape from numerous vents in its wall as well as from walls in the main crater.

Research Findings

In Polynesia, the people attributed eruptive activity to the beautiful but wrathful Pele, goddess of volcanoes, whenever she was angry or spiteful.

Most recently, Popo erupted from 1995 through 1997, capping the 36th known eruption; good historical records date back to the Spanish conquistadors.

NASA has been studying Popo and has concluded that there were several major events in the past 5,000 years, not unlike the Vesuvius eruption; one occurred in 822 C.E., and another happened sometime during the long period between 400 and 800 B.C.E. Around 3100 B.C.E., Popo had a huge blowout that produced pyroclastic flows all around the volcano to distances of 10 kilometers. Thick ash deposits were dispersed by west-southwest winds toward the Puebla Valley, and years of destructive

Earthy Language

A **lahar** is a type of mudflow, a torrential flow of water-saturated volcanic debris down the slope of a volcano in response to gravity.

mudflows (*lahars*) filled the Puebla valley. An even larger eruption occurred about 23,000 B.C.E., when the entire southern flank of Popo collapsed and/or exploded, accompanied by a major plinian eruption—or so the geological record suggests.

Says Michael Abrams, a volcanologist with the NASA/Jet Propulsion Laboratory, in Pasadena, California: "Clearly the people living in the valley were massively affected." That's an understatement of cosmic proportions, perhaps.

Why would NASA study volcanoes? The simple answer is "because they can." With the advent of good photos from space of everything that goes on on Earth, it was natural for NASA to not only provide photos to other scientific agencies, but to develop its own staff in many specialties so that they would know what was important to photograph, and how, if nothing else.

Archaeological evidence suggests that the city of Cholula was abandoned. The difference between it and Vesuvius? No Pliny around to comment. At least, none that eurocentric researchers have found and made public.

Popo is not fully asleep, though. NASA has reported this:

Sound the Alarm

If Popocatepetl erupted today as it has in the distant past, pyroclastic flows would endanger everyone within 10 kilometers of the volcano. If it happened in the summer or fall, ash would blow over Mexico City to the west, choking or suffocating men, women, children, dogs, parakeets, and other small animals. (In the other seasons, the less populous Puebla Valley 45 kilometers away would be ravaged.) But the greatest impact might be the many years of mudflows that would happen every rainy season. They would have great economic impact, if anyone still lived there.

After midnight on December 21, 1994, a series of earthquakes signaled that eruptions had started. That morning a gray ash cloud was visible over the top of the volcano, and ash fell on Puebla.

During the afternoon, the eruptions increased. Because most of the ash was blowing to the east, civil defense authorities decided to evacuate 19 villages (31,000 people) east of Popo. Moderate eruptions have continued, and according to newspapers the total number of evacuees was about 75,000 people by December 26.

The USGS sent a team of volcano experts to Mexico to help Mexican scientists evaluate what the volcano might do in the near future. This is one of the most active volcanoes in Mexico, having had 15 eruptions since the arrival of the Spanish in 1519 C.E. Volcanologists have studied Popo because most volcanoes tend to have future eruptions that are like their earlier ones.

Colima

Colima, Mexico, 280 miles west of Mexico City, has what is considered that nation's most dangerous and active volcano. In 1991, the 13,448-foot mountain produced a *dome* that rose 100 feet above the crater rim. The dome collapsed, covering the upper slopes with lava flows. *Bombs* were also shot, causing brush fires.

And then there's more recent history:

➤ October 29, 1999—Colima Volcano released two small ash events. The ash rose to approximately 19,000 feet above sea level. On November 4, there was another ash eruption to 18,000 feet above sea level.

➤ October 28, 1999—Colima Volcano released smoke and ash 2,950 feet into the sky. Colima continued to accumulate energy, and volcanologists feared an even more powerful eruption.

➤ October 12, 1999—At noon, there was a moderate steam and ash explosion at the Colima Volcano. Ten minutes prior to the explosion, the Red Sismologica Telemetrica de Colima notified the Colima Civil Protection System about the increased activity. The column rose 2,000 meters over the crater. Villagers of La Becerrera (12 kilometers to the southwest of the crater) heard the explosion and reported a light ash fall. Ground reports told of an eruption estimated at 1,700 gross metric tons of material on October 12, with an ash cloud to 20,000 feet.

Earthy Language

A **volcanic dome** is a steep-sided mass of viscous lava extruded from a volcanic vent and often round on top. **Volcanic bombs** are fragments of molten or semi-molten rock, 2½ inches to many feet in diameter, which are blown out during an eruption.

➤ October 6, 1999—Light ash fell on the village of La Yerbabuena (8 kilometers southwest of the Colima Volcano). The ash fall lasted only a few minutes.

Villagers reported hearing "jet" sounds coming from the volcano's crater. The Red Sismologica Telemetrica de Colima warned civil protection authorities that nearby villages needed to remain alert.

➤ **July 26, 1999**—A strong explosion occurred at the Colima Volcano. The pyroclastic flows and rockfalls ran 5 to 5.5 kilometers along the La Lumbre gully (the volcano's west flank). Following the explosion, a relatively intense ashfall occurred on the village of La Yerbabuena. More intense ashfall was noted at some towns located on the south and southeast sectors of the volcano. A light ashfall was noticed in the city of Colima.

➤ **July 19, 1999**—A block and ash flow occurred on the Colima Volcano due to a collapse on the south flank. A hot lahar (4 kilometers in length) was caused by heavy rains a few hours after the flow.

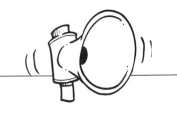

Sound the Alarm

Just because a volcano has been silent for 500 years does not mean that it will remain so. Civil defense units trying to evacuate the area surrounding Pinatubo were challenged by local disbelief that it could erupt. If civil authorities say your friendly local mountain may explode, believe it and leave.

➤ **July 17, 1999**—The Colima Volcano erupted on July 17 and sent a 4-mile plume of smoke into the sky.

➤ **February 11, 1999**—Toxic gases released during an eruption of Colima forced the evacuation of 118 people from the town of San Marcos. Volcanologists detected sulfur dioxide in the volcano's emissions. An eruption plume from the event reached heights of 3 miles (5 kilometers). No injuries or property damage were caused by the eruption, but grass fires were started from a small lava flow.

The difference between now and 79 C.E.? Warnings.

Mount Pinatubo

After Mount Saint Helens, the volcano to get the most press in the modern age was Mount Pinatubo in the Philippines. Why? Possibly because the United States had to evacuate an Army base in the bargain.

On the afternoon of June 15, 1991, Mount Pinatubo erupted and devastated more than 400 kilometers, blanketing most of southeast Asia with ash. This was the first eruption of this size to be monitored in detail. Earthquakes were known to precede eruptions, but quakes were magnified at Pinatubo. Startlingly, geomorphic changes that might be expected over many millennia occurred within years, or even days, of the eruption.

World's Biggest Blowouts

There are well-known volcanoes all over the world—Mexico, Russia's Kamchatka Peninsula, Indonesia. But the United States has three of the most infamous.

The biggest eruption in the twentieth century was in 1912 in Alaska. That explosion produced 15 cubic kilometers of magma in just 60 hours, beginning on June 6. (That equals 230 years of eruption of Hawaii's Kilauea, or 30 times what Mount Saint Helens produced.)

Still, the May 18, 1980, Mount Saint Helens eruption was the most destructive to valuable property and lives; the Alaska blow didn't cause as many problems because no one lived near it (fortunately).

But the United States has no. 3, too—the largest active volcano. Mauna Loa takes that title; including its base below sea level, the mountain is higher than Mount Everest. Not only that, the huge volcano makes up half the land mass of the island of Hawaii.

So, does the United States take the title for greatest number of volcanoes, too? Thankfully, no. It is third, behind Indonesia and Japan, in number of historically active volcanoes. Ten percent of the more than 1,500 eruptions in the last 10,000 years have been in the United States, mainly in Hawaii, the Alaskan Peninsula, and the Aleutian Islands.

Research Findings

Mount Saint Helens spewed forth only one-tenth of the material Pinatubo delivered, although it thinly blanketed an area as great as that covered by Pinatubo.

To Ensure Preservation

It ain't necessarily over when it's over. Since 1991, heavy rains continue to remobilize large volumes of deposits, which still batter the city of Luzon, near Mount Pinatubo.

What follows is a list and chilling statistics for the rest of the world's biggest blowouts, including place, year, fatalities, and cause of death (in that order).

Location	Year	Fatalities	Cause of Death
Nevado del Ruiz, Colombia	1985	25,000	Mudflows
Mount Pelee, Martinique	1902	30,000	Ashflows
Krakatau, Indonesia	1883	36,000	Tsunami
Tambora, Indonesia	1815	92,000	Starvation
Unzen, Japan	1792	15,000	Volcano collapse, tsunami

continues

continued

Location	Year	Fatalities	Cause of Death
Lakagigar (Laki), Iceland	1783	9,000	Starvation
Kelut, Indonesia	1586	10,000	Unknown
Mount Pinatubo, Philippines	1991	350	Roof collapse, disease
Mount Saint Helens, Washington State	1980	57	Asphyxiation from ash
Kilauea, Hawaii	1924	1	Falling rock
Lassen Peak, California	1915	0	
Mount Vesuvius, Italy	789 A.D.	3,360	Ashfall

Mount Saint Helens erupting.

Pliny the Younger wrote about them. Movie moguls shot them, or at least reasonable facsimiles of them. Folk-rocker Jimmy Buffett sang about them in his song, "Volcano": "Ground she's movin' under me, tidal waves out on the sea, sulphur smoke up in the sky, pretty soon we learn to fly." About the only thing he had wrong was the part about learning to fly. You're much more likely to learn to duck the "bombs"— right before you suffocate, or are buried by ash.

The Least You Need to Know

➤ The United States is one of the top three volcano zones in the world.

➤ Volcanoes are caused by rising magma and steam that pushes up and sometimes breaks the earth's surface.

➤ Famous recent eruptions occurred at Mount Saint Helens, Mount Pinatubo, and the Colima Volcano in Mexico.

➤ The biggest eruption in the twentieth century was in the United States, in Alaska in 1912.

Chapter 7

Byproducts of the Big Blast

In This Chapter

➤ Rising from the ashes: food and drink

➤ The many hazards of volcanic soot

➤ Hot time in the old town tonight: geothermal power

➤ Household goods from Vulcan's forge

➤ Precious metals, precious stones

As the old candy bar ad jingle said, sometimes you feel like a nut.

Sometimes that's a macadamia nut. Did you know we wouldn't have so many of those without volcanic ash? Nor so much sugar, coffee, or abundant pineapple. All of these—and much more—grow on the volcanic slopes of Hawaii.

Many of humankind's most extravagant desires are fulfilled only because of the work of volcanoes. Some valuable commodities and many precious metals owe their existence to volcanic action within the earth, or above it. Above it, volcanoes also contribute to some negative events. In this chapter, we'll take a look at both.

Sound the Alarm

The most common gases associated with active volcanoes are water vapor, carbon dioxide, sulfur dioxide, hydrogen sulfide, hydrogen, helium, carbon monoxide, and hydrochloric acid. Smaller amounts of hydrofluoric acid, nitrogen, argon, and other compounds are commonly associated with active volcanoes as well. People with respiratory or heart diseases are especially susceptible to volcanic gases, although such gases rarely reach populated areas in lethal concentrations.

Homegrown Land, with a Price Tag of Danger

The Hawaiian Islands, formed of volcanoes rising from the floor of the Pacific Ocean, show how new land—with all its benefits—is formed by volcanoes.

Research Findings

The largest eruption of modern time in Hawaii occurred in 1790. The explosion produced pyroclastic surges of molten material moving at speeds of 30 to 200 miles per hour. A band of Hawaiian warriors going from Hilo to the Ka'a district to do battle with Chief Kamehameha was overtaken by one. About 80 of them died. The blast created about 30 feet of new soil on the rim of Kilauea's summit caldera.

Today, there are three active volcanoes in Hawaii: Kileuea, active since 1983; Mauna Loa, which last erupted in 1984 and is poised to erupt again; and Lohi, which erupted in 1996. (There are two dormant volcanoes also: Hualalai, which last erupted in 1801; and Haleakala, which last erupted in 1790.) Mauna Loa is the largest active volcano on Earth. Kilauea is presently one of the most productive volcanoes on Earth in terms of how much lava it emits each year.

Although the island of Oahu, with state capital Honolulu atop it, is made of two volcanoes, they have not erupted for more than a million years. Aside from high prices and high waves, Oahu may be the safest place in the islands!

Fumes, Smog, and Gas

While volcanic byproducts can be very good for crops, there is a downside. Volcanic fumes—often present in a volcanic region long after the ash settles and the area returns to cultivation—can damage the very crops that the mineral-rich soil helps to grow.

During the 1969–1974 eruption at Kilauea's Mauna Ulu vent, the South Kona district (think Kona coffee, and you'll begin to see the interconnections) experienced long periods of eruption-based smog. But it was the tomato crop that was damaged. Other Kilauea eruptions caused problems for growers of flowers and other vegetables in the district; they weren't damaged by smog, but by volcanic gases that blew over their fields.

Ash and Sunlight

When Mount Pinatubo in the Philippines erupted in June 1991, it tossed about 20 million tons of sulfur dioxide into the stratosphere up to about 15 miles. While the gaseous products of most volcanoes are localized, the SO_2 (sulfuric acid) from Pinatubo was carried by stratospheric winds and was transformed by sunlight into sulfuric acid. A scholarly publication of the National Geographic Society published in the spring of 1993 said that it resulted in a "global layer of small droplets (aerosols)."

According to that report, "the stratosphere aerosols scatter sunlight back to space and absorb terrestrial heat radiation, thus cooling the lower atmosphere and warming the stratosphere."

The global climate impacts of the Pinatubo eruption are believed to have peaked in late 1993, about two years after the eruption occurred.

To Ensure Preservation

Despite the fact that 80 percent of the Earth's volcanic activity takes place in the oceans, you don't have to worry about danger from volcanism on the high seas; water is a better cushion than air.

Research Findings

Some of the earliest civilizations (for example, Greek, Etruscan, and Roman) settled on the rich, fertile volcanic soils in the Mediterranean-Aegean region.

Ash and Planes

It's bad enough to imagine a prolonged winter because of reduced sunlight from volcanic ash clouds—although the presumed 1°F decrease in global temperature after Pinatubo did little except imperceptibly mitigate the global warming going on at the time. It may be worse yet—especially for white-knuckle flyers—to think about what white clouds of ash do to airplanes.

The U.S. National Oceanic and Atmospheric Administration maintains two sites to monitor these deadly conditions—one in Anchorage, Alaska, and one in Camp Springs, Maryland. NOAA's clinical assessment is this:

Accidentally flying through an ash cloud is sufficient to severely damage critical aircraft components including lift surfaces, wind screens, and engines. This damage endangers passengers and crew through the potential loss of aerodynamic lift, engine power (by ash ingestion), visibility, and by hampering communications between the flight crew and air traffic control centers.

To deal with this, NOAA issues Volcanic Ash Advisory Statements. The information NOAA develops is provided to the Federal Aviation Administration, the USGS, Meteorological Watch Offices, climate analysts, and scientists in other countries.

Houston, We Have a Problem

The space program is also useful in averting volcanic-ash induced air disasters. After the eruption of Kliuchevskoi Volcano on Russia's Kamchatka Peninsula on October 1, 1994, astronauts aboard the Endeavor Space Shuttle saw a spectacular cloud shoot almost 20 kilometers into the atmosphere. As it fell to the ground, it formed a curtain of ash that threatened any aircraft that entered into it. And that could have been a large number of planes; the ash was falling over the Pacific Ocean toward some of the busiest air routes between Asia and both Europe and the United States. One Boeing 747 encountered some ash at 11 kilometers up but was able to climb fast enough to 12 kilometers to escape it.

Volcanic ash can cause an airplane to lose power in all engines in less than a minute. Pilots sometimes also have a tough time distinguishing eruption clouds from weather clouds.

What Can Volcanic Ash Do to Aircraft?

Lots, depending on the skill of the pilot, the construction of the aircraft, and the magnitude of the volcanic ash cloud. Here's a list of ways that ash assaults aircraft:

To Ensure Preservation

If you visit an area of high volcanic activity, drink bottled water. While acidic water generally doesn't pose a health hazard in itself, the acidic water can leach lead from roof flashings and nails and solder in older plumbing systems, causing lead levels in drinking water to become unsafe.

Sound the Alarm

Hawaiian eruptions commonly produce sulfur dioxide (SO_2), which combines with water to make sulfuric acid. The acid can attack skin, cloth, and metal. Or, it can become acid rain. Acid rain can retard growth of plants downwind of fumaroles and vents that produce sulfur dioxide over long periods.

➤ Ash ingested by jet engines may lead to the immediate deterioration in engine performance and engine failure. Possible result: Crash.

➤ Glass from melting volcanic ash can coat fuel nozzles, the combustor, and the turbine, which reduces the efficiency of fuel mixing and restricts air passing through the engine. This causes surging, flameout, and immediate loss of engine thrust. Possible result: Crash.

➤ Ash may also seriously erode moving engine parts, including the compressor and turbine blades, which reduces the efficiency of the engine—a problem which may not even appear until some time after the event. Possible result: Crash.

➤ Volcanic ash contains abrasive sharp rock fragments that easily scratch glass, plastic, and metals; cockpit windows may become so abraded in a short time that pilots have difficulty seeing the runway to land. Possible result: Crash.

➤ Air that enters a plane's cabin—where all those white knuckles are already gouging the armrests—enters through the engines. Even if it doesn't clog the engines, small amounts may clog air-filter systems or even the plane's electronic systems, including power generators and navigation instruments. Possible result: Crash.

➤ Of more economic and visual impact than safety concerns, the ash entering the plane can also damage carpeting, seat covers, and cushions. Possible result: Discomfort. Whew! (As if the shrunken seats—hey, maybe it's from ash!—didn't cause enough of that.)

Sound the Alarm

Flying toward an eruption can be hazardous to your flight safety. The cloud accompanying the little-heralded Kamchatka Peninsula volcano extended more than 800 kilometers downwind and covered an area of 150,000 square kilometers.

Research Findings

More than 80 commercial aircraft have unexpectedly encountered volcanic ash in flight and at airports in the past 15 years. Seven of these encounters caused in-flight loss of jet engine power, which nearly resulted in the crash of the airplane.

And Now the Good News

Remember, though, that volcanic materials and processes provide all sorts of benefits, including these:

➤ Rich soil

➤ Building materials

➤ Cleaning agents

➤ Heat and power

➤ Industrial metals

➤ Precious metals

➤ Gems

To Ensure Prevention

Don't hunker down in low places if you're in the vicinity of a volcano letting off vapors from fumaroles or vents. Carbon dioxide is heavier than air and tends to collect in depressions, where it can occur in lethal concentrations and cause suffocation. Also, don't drink the water without having it tested. On occasion, toxic concentrations of fluorine from hydrofluoric acid have been absorbed into ash and have been ingested by livestock or leached into domestic water supplies, affecting humans.

Rich Soil

For coffee lovers everywhere, it is fortunate that the plants like a little overcast sky so that the effect of volcanic ash doesn't drive the growth down and prices up. Indeed, Kona coffee finds an ideal greenhouse environment on the Big Island in Hawaii—sunny mornings with cloud cover and light rains in the afternoon. Kona is the only coffee grown in the United States on a commercial scale; the first seedlings didn't arrive in Hawaii from Brazil until 1928.

The fertile volcanic soils in many prime agricultural regions in the western continental United States don't give us coffee—the region is too dry and too cold—but they do give us grains. And they provide one answer to the question, "Where's the beef?" It's on the hoof, grazing atop volcanic debris.

Digging Deep, Building High

Building materials? Chunks of lava have been used for centuries to create interesting landscapes in gardens. Volcanic cinders also can be used to make roadbeds.

Ash is the size of soot and can be used in beauty preparations. *Lapilli,* bits the size of small stones, can be used in building and for garden paths and other ornamental uses. *Bombs,* the big hunks of volcanic debris, can also be used decoratively.

And the stuff is decorative all by itself. Lava clots, after hitting the earth, form various shapes depending on their temperature at impact and what they land on. Interesting names like spindle, fusiform (worm-like), ribbon, bread-crust, and cow-dung are used to describe these rocks. The name for all volcanic airborne material, in general, is *tephra.*

Dirt Devil

As for cleaning supplies, in addition to the venerable Lava Soap, designer soaps are also getting some volcanic help. Bruce Shoenfeld, of Bloomberg Personal Finance, says that Musgo Real Pedra Pomes Pumice Scrub Soap is the real deal. Indeed, he says it is "one of the world's best shaving creams!" The manufacturer says, "Pedra Pomes contains coconut oil to create a rich, creamy lather, while pumice, a light lava, provides a gentle abrasive action to thoroughly clean dirt and grease. From crankcase oil to tree sap, Pedra Pomes is ideal for use on the hands and feet after any outdoor job."

But Not a Drop to Drink?

Below the earth, ground water heated by large magma bodies can be tapped for geothermal energy, as is done extensively in Iceland. Even where it is not used for heating and other energy needs, volcanically heated water is often a boon to humankind.

And, yes, you can drink it. In fact, water from warm and hot springs is sold as "designer water," specifically because of the mineral content it derives from contact with the magma.

Earthy Language

Tephra is a general term for all airborne ejecta from volcanoes. **Ash** is the size of soot; **lapilli** are pieces the size of small stones.

Sound the Alarm

Until Mount Saint Helens, the only volcanically related human fatality in the Cascades occurred in 1934, when a climber exploring ice caves in Coalman Glacier melted by fumaroles suffocated in the oxygen-poor gas. So don't spelunk without a gas mask in volcano country.

Hot springs often offer relief to suffers of arthritis and other ailments who come to bathe in them. Geysers and hot springs depend on surface water percolating downward. The water is heated by the magma, becoming less dense, and rises back to the surface along fissures and cracks in the rock.

Of course, geysers are more spectacular—and more dangerous. How they work is not completely understood, but it is assumed that surface water percolates down into an underground chamber. The water is then heated; when a portion of it flashes into steam, it is ejected through a small, distinct opening. Often this happens on a very predictable schedule; the Old Faithful Geyser at Yellowstone National Park has erupted on an average of every 65 minutes.

Earthy Language

The **water table** is the depth in the Earth below which the ground is saturated with water.

Research Findings

The concept of running steam through pipes to heat cities is most feasible when the source is free, a gift of the Earth, courtesy of a geothermal region. But some cities, notably Baltimore, have borrowed the idea, creating condensed steam with conventional means and delivering it to midcity buildings through pipes, not unlike those in naturally heated Reykjavik, Iceland.

Hot springs occur in many thermal areas where the surface of the Earth intersects the *water table*. The temperature and rate of discharge of hot springs depend on factors such as the rate at which water circulates through the system of underground channel, the amount of heat supplied at depth, and the extent of dilution of the heated water by cool ground water near the surface.

As pleasurable as both of those byproducts of volcanism might be, geothermal power is also the most economically valuable.

Both active volcanoes and geologically young inactive volcanoes can provide heated water or other liquids that can be harnessed to drive turbines and generate electrical power. These are called hydrothermal waters if they have been heated by contact with magma. But these or any other heated water coming from within the earth are all geothermal waters.

The lower-temperature fluids can be used directly for space-heating, greenhouse and industry purposes, and, of course, as hot or warm springs at spas.

Geothermal heat warms more than 70 percent of the homes in Iceland, and The Geysers geothermal field near Santa Rosa in Northern California produces enough electricity to meet the power demands of San Francisco. The Geysers area is the largest geothermal development in the world.

Besides providing energy, some geothermal waters also contain sulfur, gold, silver, and mercury that can be recovered as a byproduct of energy production.

In other places, that heated ground water contains concentrated valuable minerals—gold, silver, copper, lead, and zinc—into deposits large enough to be mined.

Precious Stones, Precious Metals

Sometimes rising magma doesn't reach the surface of the Earth and doesn't heat water. Instead, it cools slowly and hardens beneath the volcano to create a variety of crystalline rocks. Some of these are huge and spectacular, producing landscapes like the one at California's Yosemite National Park; once the softer rock has been eroded away, the giant granitic forms—volcanic plugs—stand alone, like some cosmic sculpture.

Earthy Language

From the Latin for bringing together, **convection** means the transferring of heat or electrical impulses or other very tiny particles in mass movements.

Other flows of magma circulate until, finally, *convection* concentrates small amounts of various minerals, depositing them as mineral veins in the spaces the magma once surged through.

Much of this happened eons ago, of course, and the mineral deposits are found under land that is extinct volcanic earth. Or sometimes, they are found under land that is still active but thought to be quiet—like, for example, Mount Saint Helens.

Mining claims for copper, gold, and silver were staked in the district north of Mount Saint Helens as early as 1892. About the turn of the century, hundreds of claims were staked in the Spirit Lake area. Copper ore was the target; in 1905, 14 tons were hauled to Tacoma to create the bronze statue of Sacajawea for the 100th anniversary celebration of the Lewis and Clark Expedition.

Prospecting was also carried out for gold and silver, but the veins did not prove to be rich enough or easy enough to work to be commercially valuable. Small amounts of lead, zinc, and molybdenum were also found. Tourmaline has been associated with the copper veins as well.

The Clear Lake Volcanic Field in California has long been a heat source, but it offered up large amounts of gold at one time and still boasts mercury deposits. Active volcanic vents in the spreading midocean ridges continue to create abundant ore minerals—iron, copper, zinc, and nickel.

On rare occasions, such deep-sea ore deposits are later exposed in remnants of ancient oceanic crust that have been scraped off and left ("beached") on top of continental crust during past *subduction* processes. The Troodos Massif on the Island of Cyprus is perhaps the best-known example of such an ancient oceanic crust fragment. Cyprus was an important source of copper in the ancient world, and Romans called copper the "Cyprian metal"; the Latin word for "copper" is *cyprium*.

Earthy Language

Subduction is the process when one huge land mass, or tectonic plate, slides beneath its neighbor; see Chapters 1 through 4 for more details.

These days, we don't just monkey around with picks and axes on Mediterranean islands looking for volcanic metals and gems. Rather, we bring a chimney—a solid formation—created by a black smoker aboard a research vessel to see just how much these subocean volcanic vent extrusions contain.

A black smoker is sort of like a Yellowstone geyser, except that it happens under the ocean and that the stuff that comes out is not water with minerals mixed in, but magma—virtually pure mineral goop. The black smokers are apparently laced with gold, silver, and other precious metals, although not in commercial amounts because of the expense of retrieving the huge things from the ocean floor. So why do it?

Geologists like to say that the present is the key to the past. Dissecting the black smokers allows us to sneak a peek at the processes that formed the mineral deposits that are commercially valuable. By extension, perhaps it will let us figure out where new commercially valuable ones might be hidden.

The Least You Need to Know

➤ We wouldn't have such abundant exotic edibles as coffee and pineapples without volcanoes.

➤ Gases vented from volcanoes and ash can disturb plant growth.

➤ Volcanic ash is a serious danger to air travel, so much so that both NOAA and NASA monitor explosions.

➤ Water heated by volcanic magma can be both beautiful and healthful; water affected by atmospheric volcanic sulfur can be deadly.

➤ You can heat whole cities with volcanic water and steam.

➤ Precious gems and metals are provided by volcanic activity.

Chapter 8

It's Mudslides, Slim

> ### In This Chapter
>
> ➤ Most slide-prone places in America
>
> ➤ The rest of the story: more unhappy landslides overseas
>
> ➤ Why slides are underrated
>
> ➤ What to do if you face mass wasting

Mudslides, landslides, slumps—and a few less common-sounding words—technically define what kind of solid material is shifting from one place to another on the surface of the Earth. But they all connote something else: death and destruction, with little or no warning. Most slides, of any sort, are over in an instant.

In the United States alone, slides cause about $1 million to $1.5 million in damage and kill between 25 and 50 people a year. Every state can have landslides, as can our island territories. The places you are most likely to experience a slide, though, are California, West Virginia, Utah, Kentucky, Tennessee, Ohio, Washington, and Puerto Rico.

We're lucky. Worldwide, the toll is much higher.

Making New Horizons: Landform Alteration Through Mud

Police departments hunt for mass murderers. Some economists deplore mass consumption (while the Coneheads of TV's *Saturday Night Live* golden era, on the other hand, celebrate when they "consume mass quantities"). A bad play will cause the audience to engage in a mass exodus.

Geologists don't want to be left out. Their favorite mass is mass wasting, under which they group rockfalls, avalanches, *mudflows,* landslides, and any earthly process in which gravity moves stuff from higher ground to lower ground or to a river or sea in large quantities.

In the Zone

Compared with other geological hazards, landslide zones are very narrow, very specific, and relatively easy to avoid. Unfortunately, they're often also attractive places to live. The Puget Sound lowlands are a good example. Born of mud and ice, these unstable hills of sand, silt, and gravel were bulldozed and compacted by glaciers that obliterated much of the geological record. That jagged shoreline abuts some of the newest hot real estate in the country. A third of it—660 miles along the islands and mainland—is composed of steep bluffs continually subject to collapse.

The wealthy who can afford to erect substantial buildings on coveted land will, of course, have a lot to lose if geologic push comes to shove. Alternatively, the scrabbly earth in some slide zones dictates that poorer buildings be constructed there, as is often the case in less developed nations where homeless people erect shelter on any ground they can find. The inhabitants don't have as many possessions to lose, but the flimsy nature of the structures just about guarantees that they will lose the most precious possession they have—their lives.

Research Findings

The biggest and most expensive slide in U.S. history happened in the spring of 1983, in Thistle, Utah. The slide was anywhere from 1,000 feet to 1 mile wide and racked up costs, in damage and loss of use, exceeding $500 million.

Earthy Language

Mudflows (or debris flows) are rivers of rock, earth, and other debris saturated with water. They develop when water rapidly accumulates in the ground, such as during heavy rainfall or rapid snowmelt, and change the earth into a flowing river of mud or "slurry" that can travel several miles from its source, picking up trees, cars, and other materials along the way.

Puget Sound and Fury

In 1997, near Seattle and all around Puget Sound, ground had been slipping. By the third week of January, rainfall since October—the start of the rainy season—had reached 26 inches, 40 percent above normal.

On January 19, a landslide demolished a house beneath a high cliff on rural Bainbridge Island—a house that, when remodeling was finished, would have provided panoramic views of Seattle and the Cascades. It was a house along that very 660-mile stretch of newly desirable acreage.

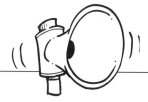

Sound the Alarm

Brenda Bell reported on the economic impact of such disasters in *The Atlantic Monthly* in 1999: "Landslides and other 'ground failures' cost more lives and more money each year than all other natural disasters combined, and their incidence appears to be rising. Nevertheless, the government devotes few resources to their study—and the foolhardy continue to build and live in places likely to be consumed one day by avalanches of mud."

The house belonged to a popular high school biology teacher who lived there with his wife and two young children. As rescuers tried to dig the family out of the mud, it was still raining. The top floor of the house was on its side, and newly framed windows and the roof lay on the beach, lapped by the tide. Except for that, the house and everything—and everyone—in it were gone—buried, literally, alive. Dwight Herren, Jennifer Cantrell-Herren, and children Skyler and Cooper were killed instantly by the weight of their own house and the weight of an entire cliff face.

Reports said that the Rolling Bay slide, as it became known, took about 3 seconds. It scooped out only a 3-foot track down the cliff face, but the weight of it was estimated at 2,000 tons. The neighbors, relaxing in their hot tub, heard only a giant exhalation, a "whoof!" of major proportions, as the air was squeezed out of the Herrens' house. After that, it was so quiet that other neighbors taking a look outside thought that the slide must have happened the night before, while they slept. At first, they didn't realize that there was a house under all that.

Puget Sound house, one of the lucky ones, after the 1997 rainy season.

Days later, as grieving neighbors who walked the shore put rusting toys and other small treasures of life reclaimed from the sea, sand, and mud up on a concrete bulkhead for Dwight Herren's father to keep, a bulldozer uncovered the family's dog, a Labrador named Henry, as if asleep in his usual spot, yards and yards beneath the solidifying earth and mud.

Research Findings

The Herrens—and other Washingtonians—had had fair warning, if not government warnings. In the rainy season before the Herrens were killed, newspapers ran an article about a man riding his slide-ravaged house into the water like a boat captain; about a slide throwing a freight train into Puget Sound, whole, having missed an Amtrak passenger train by only two hours; and about an almost $1–million expenditure by Seattle to stabilize a bluff that was slowly sliding several houses toward the sea.

Other houses still look out to sea beneath the cliffs, landforms that can betray in a noise-filled instant the trust of humans who shelter beneath their solid-looking brows.

Types of Flows

Landslides and mudflows come in various sizes, all of which can be seen at Mount Rainier.

In December 1963, one the USGS called a small landslide traveled to within 0.6 miles of White River Campground. It didn't change to a debris flow and was of most interest to geologists who could use the slide deposit to study variations in rock types, from hard blocks of unaltered lava to soft, highly altered rock. They could actually see the *banding* recording the various lava flows that had formed the rocks in the slide.

Intermediate flows, both in size and frequency, also occur. One example occurred on October 2–3, 1947. A park road was buried for half a mile, and the former channel of Kautz Creek was buried under 28 feet of boulder gravel. This flow was caused by water surges during a heavy rain; others have historically begun by melting of ice and snow by volcanic activity from about 200 to 700 years ago.

Earthy Language

Banding, in geology, can mean two things: the visible differences in a single rock caused by deposition of various minerals in different densities underwater (in sedimentary rocks), or different minerals extruded from a volcano during different eruptions and laid down one atop the other. The resulting rocks have a banded appearance, showing the times of either deposition or flow.

Of these, the best and biggest is The National Lahar, a large, distinctive example with yellow, sandy deposits that are best seen in roadcuts along the Nisqually River outside the park. The flow can be traced 59 miles to Puget Sound.

Debris flows are distributed over time like floods. The largest ones are also the rarest. Although the largest flows recur with the lowest frequency, planners may consider their potential for widespread impact to impose too high a level of risk for certain types of structures and development in some downstream areas.

Finally, the USGS categorizes some Mount Rainier flows as large but infrequent. Thank goodness. By far the largest flow in the history of Mount Rainier is the Osceola Mudflow. About 5,000 years ago, a huge landslide removed 3 cubic kilometers (0.7 cubic miles) from the summit of Mount Rainier. Another one, called the Paradise Lahar, overran the area around the visitor center, probably at about the same time, geologically speaking.

These and other landslides were not directly associated with volcanic activity, so such activity won't be useful in warning of future flows—which scientists say have occurred every 100 to 500 years during the past 6,000 years. Most northwestern U.S. triggers—earthquakes, rain, meltoff, and increased underground movement of molten material—can happen without warning. One could happen tomorrow.

Research Findings

The Montana Bureau of Mines keeps tabs on what's shakin' and what's slidin' in that state. On August 17, 1959, the state experienced the largest seismically triggered rock slide in North America in modern times. The slide descended 1,300 vertical feet down the south wall of Madison Canyon and buried an area of 130 acres. The 28 million cubic yard slide mass weighing 60 million tons dammed the Madison River to form Earthquake Lake. Twenty-six people camped near Rock Creek Campground were killed.

Other "Ker-Chunk" Experiences Worldwide

In December 1999, 10 days of unseasonably heavy rains set rocks, dirt, and water—mud—in motion in Venezuela. After gargantuan mudslides, the Foreign Minister of Venezuela said that fewer than 10,000 were dead. But UNICEF, the United Nation's Children's Fund, said that at least 15,000 had been killed, and another 30,000 were missing. Another 150,000 were homeless; it isn't tough for a cardboard shelter in the country's many shantytowns to be swept away when a large slide makes matchsticks of palaces. "There are bodies in the sea, bodies buried under the mud, bodies everywhere," the minister said.

Several days into the rescue operation, tens of thousands were still trapped in buildings surrounded by up to three stories of mud and water. Helicopters were used to rescue some. President Hugo Chavez, a former paratrooper, directed a 1,000-man platoon delivering food, water, and communications devices to stranded areas.

Research Findings

Landslides first appeared in written records in 1767 B.C.E.; then, earthquake-triggered slides dammed both the Yi and Lo rivers in China.

The Sarno Slide

A year and a half earlier, on May 5, 1997, mudslides covered Sarno and other towns in Campania, in southern Italy. In that case, many believe that if geologists' warnings had been heeded, the toll would not have been so high. At least 147 were killed.

Take a look at part of this May 21, 1999, report by Rosa Ieropoli for the World Socialist Web site:

For the past half-century geologists have warned about the construction of towns and housing in the region, declaring it a "risk zone," prone to mudslides. During the past 70 years, 631 landslides have hit this region near Naples. Since 1945, 3,800 people have been killed in Italy from mudslides. The majority have been in southern Italy. On average this means six deaths every month from mudslides. The authorities have ignored scientists' consistent warnings rather than regulate construction and furnish money that could have prevented the tragic deaths and destruction.

Research Findings

The poorest housing areas with the worst construction were on the most unstable ground in Italy's Campania region. Unfortunately, so was Sarno's hospital, Villa Marta. It was completely destroyed, with six of the staff killed. More would have died if workers had not carried out 60 patients on the second floor. A new hospital, almost completed but with work stopped because of budget cuts, survived the slides. A middle school was also destroyed, trapping many teachers and students whose bodies have still not been found.

That part of Italy is made up of sedimentary mountains that geologists say will eventually fall into the Tyrrheanian Sea, no matter what. The soil tends to crumble with the area's frequent rain and wild fires. Building more roads and houses—digging into the earth—has made it even more unstable. Add to that the removal of ground-holding chestnut trees in favor of planting the less sturdy but more profitable hazelnut tress, and slides are all but inevitable.

Other Stories

August 4, 1999, brought to news wires everywhere several stories of landslides and mudslides.

In Manila, Philippines, a hillside collapsed after a wave of severe storms that had killed scores elsewhere in Asia. Rescuers searched the ruins of 50 houses for survivors. Officials said 24 were missing in the housing estate, bringing the death tolls from mudslides in Manila to 32. There was fear that the toll would be far higher. Squatters refused to leave, fearing that looters might take whatever they left behind.

To Ensure Preservation

The Japanese spend more than $4 billion each year trying to control gravity—or, at least, the slides that gravity causes. The beautiful pictures tourists can take of Japanese scenic rivers are possible partially because of hundreds of dams that keep mud and rocks from sliding down into them, disturbing the silent sentinel evergreens and sinuous, sonorous rivulets that form the charming basis of Japanese landscapes.

Earthy Language

Terracing is the appearance of land that has had multiple landslides. Each one may not slide as far as the one before it. They are vulnerable because the initial slide, the lowest "terrace," was likely unstable, with material still needing to settle. Subsequent slides layer more unstable land over that, and so on.

Besides the mudslides, the homes of more than 60,000 people were flooded; half of those had been evacuated to higher ground. There would likely be other fallout from the floods and slides; two major rice-growing areas near Manila had also been affected.

The same weather pattern caused landslides in Seoul, South Korea, killing at least 119, leaving 53 missing, and submerging thousands of homes, according to the Associated Press. Ten of the dead were vacationers whose cabin in Hwachon, about 60 miles northeast of Seoul, was buried under a landslide. "Witnesses saw mud and rocks tumble from the mountainside, sweeping away a bungalow where the missing tourists were taking their morning coffee," said an official at the South Korean disaster agency, cited in a Reuters report at the time.

Prime Causes of Mudslides

Landslides, mudslides, and slumps increasingly impose threats in most nations, developed as well as less developed. In developed nations, the financial damage is extreme, with costs caused by slides running into the billions annually, especially in the United States, Italy, India, and Japan. In less-developed nations, the cost is more often greater human injury and death, and less property loss.

Either way, scientists say that the increase in slides is attributable to the same causes: increasing development of vulnerable *terracing*, global climate changes causing severe weather, and deforestation.

And the toll may be even worse than anyone thinks. Because slides most often occur in tandem with other disasters—earthquakes, volcanic eruptions, and flooding—casualties are usually not counted separately but are included in the statistics of the major causative event.

An example is the earthquakes in Afghanistan in 1998. Most victims were killed when their homes were crushed by avalanches of debris, but they were classified as earthquake victims.

No matter what precipitates it, a mudslide requires a certain set of conditions to occur.

Steep hills and mountains are needed for the slide to slide down. The integrity of the slopes must have been weakened by something: *erosion* by rivers, glaciers, or ocean waves; fires that leave them bare; heavy rain and meltoff of snowpack; volcanic eruptions; earthquakes; blasting operations; digging and drilling; heavy machinery; and even thunder.

Once a slope is weakened, it's easy to start a slide. If the hillside is dry, dirt and rocks tumble down, making a landslide. If it is saturated with water, the dry material turns to mud, a much more destructive flow that can then pick up debris, from rocks to cars, and become even more damaging. If that flow moves into a river or stream bed, it can block the flow of water and flood neighboring areas behind the temporary dam.

Earthy Language

Erosion is the wearing or carrying away of earth by wind or running water.

Not surprisingly, mountainous areas are ripe for slides. In the United States, the Rocky Mountains, Appalachian Mountains, Pacific Coastal ranges, and mountainous parts of Alaska and Hawaii experience slides.

But even gentle hills can produce them, so you're not safe just because you can easily bike up the hill to your house. Be aware of the possibility of a slide if you live in an area with a history of slides, if you live at the base or top of a steep-cut slope (from building, quarrying, or mining operations), or if you live at the bottom of a low-lying area.

FEMA says these signs will alert you to a possible landslide:

➤ Doors or windows stick or jam for the first time; the same forces that create the landslide—shaking ground and/or humid conditions, and especially those together—will alter the set of the window and door openings of your house.

➤ New cracks appear in plaster, tile, brick, or foundations.

➤ Outside walls, walks, or stairs begin pulling away from the building.

➤ Slowly developing, widening cracks appear on the ground or on paved areas such as streets or driveways.

➤ Underground utility lines break.

➤ Bulging ground appears at the base of a slope.

➤ Water breaks through the ground surface at new locations.

➤ Fences, retaining walls, utility poles, or trees tilt or move.

➤ You hear a faint rumbling sound that increases in volume as the slide nears. The ground slopes downward in one direction and may begin shifting in that direction under your feet.

Avoiding the Slipping Slopes

Remember, mudslides can happen virtually anywhere there's dirt and a slope. So, you either have to live on flat land and never travel, or face the fact that you might experience a mudslide.

FEMA says you can take some measures, though. For instance, before you buy property, get a ground assessment from a county geologist or planning department. If you think there are problems, consult a geotechnical expert for any corrective measures that might help.

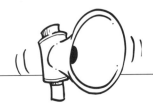

Sound the Alarm

Observers of recent landslides in California report they didn't drag, roll, or tumble. The land was "gone in one second," an eyewitness reported after one Anaheim, California, slide. Experts attributed the slide to a combination of a developer grading for home sites at the toe of a previous landslide slope and the effects of El Niño rains. Upshot: no time to sound an alarm. Just don't build in slide country.

Plant ground cover on your slopes. In mudflow areas, build channels or walls to direct the flow around buildings. (Don't divert it onto a neighbor's property, though, unless you want to risk liability.) In the end, make evacuation plans—and hope that your "event" doesn't happen in the middle of the night and isn't so big that it covers your entire house.

If you are caught in a landslide or mudslide and are inside, stay inside. Take cover under a sturdy desk or table. If you're outside, run like mad to get out of the way of the flow. Run to the nearest high ground away from the slide's path. If escape is not possible, curl into a tight ball and protect your head.

If the slide has come and gone, and you're able to stand upright and look around, leave the area; it may be ripe for other slides. Beware that flooding might follow a slide. If the slide was caused by an earthquake or an eruption, there might be more.

If your house is still standing, replant damaged ground as soon as possible, and consider other corrective techniques.

The Least You Need to Know

➤ The United States has several significant slide zones.

➤ Avoid real estate hot spots if they are also geological hot spots.

➤ Volcanoes, earthquakes, and flooding are often accompanied by mudslides.

➤ If you're caught in a slide, stay inside (if you're already inside) and take cover under a sturdy desk or table. If you're outside, run like mad to the nearest high ground away from the slide's path.

Chapter 9

Sinkholes

In This Chapter

➤ What lurks below beautiful landscapes

➤ Florida, Missouri, and Kentucky: sinkhole states

➤ Interesting tidbits about karst topography

➤ Tips to help you deal with disappearing land

Consider this scenario:

NewsCenter Six in Mitoun, USA, is on the scene live, where a six-year-old child has been swallowed up by the earth.

Just a few hours ago, little Samantha Summersby was playing in her yard with her dog, Smartie. When Mrs. Summersby looked out the kitchen window to check on Samantha, she saw Smartie with his hind end in the air, barking at one of the holes he digs for bones. Or so she thought, at first.

But, said Mrs. Summersby, there was a quality to his bark that she didn't like, so she ran out. There, in her yard, was an opening about a foot wide. She bent over and looked in, but all she saw was darkness. Samantha, crying softly, was down there.

Fire-Rescue came within minutes. Within half an hour, they'd widened the hole to 5 feet across, and discovered a 12-foot-deep cavern—and little Samantha, curled up crying in a shallow stream running through the bottom of the hole.

Samantha suffered only a badly twisted ankle, bruises, and the loss of her favorite doll. The doll was carried away by a swift underground stream. The cold stream might have caused Samantha real harm if her mother had not called for help as soon as she did.

And her mother wonders: Is the rest of her yard safe to play in? Will her basement fill with water? Who will pay for this?

This is the fourth sinkhole to open in the county in less than a month. NewsCenter Six is wondering, what's going on?

This is Kelly Youngblood reporting live.

Yes, it's fictional, but not an unusual tale over the centuries. Many of the world's great tourist caverns were discovered by people who fell in. Aillwee Caves in the west of Ireland was discovered when a farmer kept losing his sheep.

Sinkholes, as well as caves and caverns—all sorts of openings in the Earth—happen in karst topography. They can be beautiful and fascinating—and scary.

Earthy Language

A **sinkhole** is a collapsed portion of bedrock above a void. The collapsed portion may open into a cave or may be a shallow depression of the ground ranging from a few feet to many acres in area.

Karst Topography: The Good, the Bad, and the Ugly

When you're talking about karst topography, you might say that a river runs through it. Or, you might say, "Oops! There used to be a river here; where did it go?" Or even an entire lake.

The Lake Jackson Story

That's what happens about every 20 years at Lake Jackson, Florida. The lake goes dry. Not from drought, usually, but through one of many *sinkholes* that open in the lake, draining the water in a matter of hours. One commentator wrote, "It's an awesome sight to see a lake there one day and a mud pit the next."

It is probably the collapse of an underground cavern, opening new channels in the limestone below, that lets the water escape. The whole surrounding area is like a giant sponge; collapse could happen anywhere the water seeps and overlying rock is weak.

When Lake Jackson is intact, it is beautiful. Because *karst* topography is anything but flat, it is beautiful. Although it makes for great scenery—as in the rolling, horse-dotted green slopes of eastern Kentucky, for example—karst topography is not without its genuine risks.

Streams disappear underground. Holes open in the Earth and swallow homes and businesses without warning. A landowner's well dries up. A family dies of radon poisoning. All of these happen in karst regions. And 10 percent of the earth, by estimate, is karst.

Earthy Language

The term **karst** comes from the Karst region of Slovenia, an area on the Adriatic coast, where geologists first noted the striking and characteristic features of the landscape—rolling hills, streams, springs, caverns, and caves.

Earthy Language

Carbonate rocks are typically transparent in part and have white streaks. They are soft and somewhat soluble in acidic solutions, which includes rainwater percolating through the topsoil. They are most prevalent in sedimentary areas, where eroded matter has been laid down for millennia. **Dolomite** rocks too are commonly found in sedimentary areas, where rock has been formed by deposition over the eons. While dolomite does not form on the Earth's surface, it did at one time, in vast beds. So far, there is no explanation for why it no longer forms at the surface of the Earth.

Karst Defined

So what is this sometimes dangerous stuff with the name like an eastern European pastry? Most karst topography is based on a layer of soluble bedrock, usually *carbonate*, such as limestone or *dolomite*. Those two types of rock create slightly different landforms; karst landscapes near the sea appear quite different from those where mountain uplift has turned the layers of rocks on their side, or where volcanism has

Research Findings

It is not a genuine risk to breed horses in Kentucky karst. Of 125 Kentucky Derby winners, 93 are Kentucky horses, including the 1980 winner, a filly named Genuine Risk.

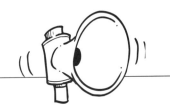

Sound the Alarm

Radon is a gaseous, radioactive element that was discovered in 1899. Colorless and highly radioactive, it has been used in treating cancer. However, it has also been blamed for *causing* cancer. Radon can infiltrate homes and other structures built on ground where radon is present. Radon-detection services are available to determine whether your karst-region house is collecting radon.

contributed its part. But caves and caverns will underlie both.

Erosion of the soft rock layers might have been caused either by carbonic acid seeping in from above, or by sulfuric acid welling up from below. The carbonic acid is made by rain filtering through decaying organic material; the sulfuric acid happens when water leaches sulfur out of rocks in the Earth.

To make it easy to remember, here's a recipe for karst terrain:

> Take carbonate rock, a few to a few thousand feet deep. Add about 45 inches of rainfall a year. Cover with vegetation (oak-hickory forest and grasslands are nice) and their debris—humus, mulch. Create a hole or two in the basic mix (the carbonate rock) for the water to mix in, and subject the whole batch to temperature extremes. Voila! Give it a few millennia, and you'll have a nice, fully formed Missouri, Kentucky, Florida, or Tennessee! Serve with side orders of spelunkers and geologists.

Despite these variables, all karst topography has one thing in common: It can be dangerous to life and property.

Karst systems are very sensitive to pollution. As it is estimated that as much as one-quarter of the world's population is supplied by karst water, it is essential not to pollute in areas where karst serves mankind so essentially.

Karst water supplies are subject to instability. The supply varies as water seeps down into lower chambers. Water quality varies, too; water in the caves may incorporate radon gas, which can be released back into the air. The changing underground conduits through the soft rock—eroded day by day—can distribute both pollutants and radon unpredictably.

Karst topography, being notoriously unstable, can change at sometimes catastrophic rates. In populous areas, it is essential to locate buried cavities and monitor their potential for collapse through *geophysical surveys,* exploratory drilling, and *dye-tracing.* Without determining how thick the overlying layer of rock is now—and comparing it to prior measurements—it is impossible to predict when collapse might occur.

Earthy Language

Dye-tracing dates back to 1871, when fluorscein, a green fluorescent dye, was developed. As early as 1877, it was used to trace sinking portions of the upper Danube River. Dye is dumped into the water upstream and followed downstream. If it disappears, it can be located by observing any streams containing dye where they surface. The technique is also used to measure stream flow speeds by measuring how long it takes the leading edge of the dye to reach a predetermined spot.

Florida—and You Thought Pink Cadillacs Were a Problem

Florida offers some serious sinkhole scenarios. The *St. Petersburg Times* reported in November 1998 that Andrew Peterson lost the back half of his electronics sales and repair business to a 150-foot sinkhole the previous April. He was suing the Florida Water company, claiming that it had ignored several signs of an impending sinkhole.

Earthy Language

Geophysical surveying means mapping the sorts of rock in an area, and then taking samples of the rock and analyzing them for various qualities.

In his lawsuit, Peterson claimed that pumping from four wells on Florida Water's adjacent property had drained underground water and caused the ground to collapse. Water quality tests of a nearby well had revealed a too-high bacteria count, closing it. The day it was put back in service, Peterson said, his property collapsed. Cost: His business, in many respects. He was seeking redress and payment for the devaluation of his property (who would buy it after that?), and for the part of his building that didn't fall into the hole (it was declared by the government to be unsafe). That's not to mention the cost of relocating his business.

This experience is typical of karst topography. Although water is abundant, it picks up contaminants easily because it doesn't filter through earth as in other areas, but simply drains right through it, keeping most of the contaminants it came with or even picking up more. Because the water is not distributed through dense soil but is collected in underground hollows, when the water is removed, there's nothing holding the roof up. Bingo! Sinkhole.

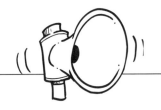

Sound the Alarm

Don't let those animals eat too much grass! Overgrazing in Europe several centuries ago caused severe soil erosion. That exposed the fissured rock surfaces of the karst terrain to even more water, leading to more frequent collapses than might have been expected from nature.

Earthy Language

Three kinds of sinkholes exist. A **subsidence sinkhole** forms where the layer of earth over soluble limestone is thin. **Solution sinkholes** occur when there is no layer of earth over the limestone, so the soluble rock is exposed and is worn away directly by water flowing over or standing on it. A **collapse sinkhole** happens when the layer of earth above the limestone is thick, but a layer holding it up is breached or absent.

Sinkholes were also caused during 1998 by severe storms, high winds, tornadoes. and flooding that struck the state starting on December 25, 1997. At the end of April 1998, disaster recovery operations were still underway and state officials cited sinkholes as a remaining problem. Orange County officials reported a sinkhole 5 feet wide by 4 feet deep in the parking lot of an apartment complex. As of April 27, 1998, 7,097 Disaster Housing Assistance checks had been disbursed for a total of $5,995,800.

Missouri—Show Me

Missouri possesses textbook karst. It has well-eroded rolling hills, deep hollows, springs, caves, natural bridges, and tunnels. And sinkholes.

Although the state is on the country's central *plateau,* it is more like a minefield than the table that a plateau is supposed to resemble. The state also has its own peculiar version of karst topography. It has *karst windows,* where one may look into a cave or a water-filled sink below (getting down there is another matter entirely).

Missouri has abundant natural springs and, frankly, has had fewer problems with karst terrain than other places. Indeed, Missouri's karst has made it a tourist showplace, with at least 20 large springs. So it isn't surprising to learn that more than 70 percent of all water in the Ozarks goes underground via a karst process.

Kentucky—But the Lime Is Good for Horses

Most horse owners worry about their animals stepping in a chuck hole and breaking a leg. In Kentucky, they can worry about the entire horse stepping into a sinkhole and vanishing. The part of the state most hospitable to horses is also most hospitable to sinkholes.

The *Lexington Herald-Leader* reported in 1997 that two city residents had been suffering from a sinkhole problem for seven years. It all began with a storm. A city storm drain emptied into the backyard of Pat and Marty Gruggs and drained into a sinkhole.

The sinkhole problem was long-standing in the Stonewall community, where they lived. "It's been an ongoing thing," said Urban County Councilwoman Jennifer Mossotti, whose 9th District includes Stonewall. "One gets fixed, and another gets filled by water."

The sinkholes are related to a vast network of limestone caverns under the city, said Phil Meador, deputy director of the city's sanitary sewers division.

The Gruggs's sinkhole was about 8 feet across and depressed only about 6 inches, but it was a collector for debris from other storm drainage. It was unsightly, as well as slightly frightening in its implications.

Another hole, 20 feet across, sits right behind their property line. Neighbors just don't think it's safe to go digging about, filling them with soil from other parts of the property. Who knows what effect that would have, or where another one would pop up? (Or down, as the case may be.) Indeed, perhaps removing top-soil from one place to fill another would be all that's needed to start another shallow sinkhole forming.

Earthy Language

A **plateau** is a large, elevated expanse of more or less level land between the coastal plains and mountains. It's also called tableland. A **karst window** is a small hole in the earth through which the cavern below may be glimpsed.

Research Findings

Meramec Caverns is the largest commercial cave in Missouri. Missouri claims the title Cave State, being home to more than 6,000 surveyed caves.

There's more: Apparently, the Gruggs's property is in an active sinkhole area; the basement fills with a foot and a half of water after heavy rains. That's a pain in the neck, but it's nothing compared to the pollution disasters lurking behind every stalagmite.

Ground water pollution in cave country is serious, more serious than surface pollution. If sewage enters karst ground water systems, it can seriously deplete the amount of oxygen dissolved in the water. Without this oxygen, aquatic life will die of suffocation. When serious oxygen depletion occurs, the underground waters exude offensive odors.

To Ensure Preservation

It's little wonder that humans have had trouble with karst; since early days, they have built settlements around springs in karst country. The springs provide water for livestock and humans, as well as summertime bathing opportunities. Because the water bubbling out of the ground is cooler than the summer air, most farms (and even some rural and suburban homes) previously boasted spring houses, where butter, milk, meat, and watermelons were kept in or near the cooling waters.

Hidden River Cave, in Horse Cove, Kentucky, is a case in point, and a warning to Lexington folks of what could happen. Hidden River Cave was once a popular show cave. But urban growth happens, and large amounts of household and industrial wastes were dumped into sinkholes upstream. Terrible odors wafted out the cave entrance. The unique eyeless fish in the cave's waters began to die off. In 1989, a new sewage treatment center was put online, and the odors disappeared. Enough fish remained to begin to rebuild the population. But it was certainly a tourism—and piscean—disaster for a few years.

Research Findings

Kentucky geography includes the Lexington Plain, or Bluegrass Region, and the Highland Rim in the central plateau. The Lexington Plain is atop the oldest rocks in the state, with limestone soils that make excellent row crops and pasture grasses. The Highland Rim is also called the Pennyroyal (Pennyrile) Plateau. It's atop limestone, too, under which many sinkholes and caverns, including Mammoth Cave—355 miles long—have formed.

How to Live, Well and Safely, in Sinkhole Territory

The Florida Office of Emergency Management is the default agency for responding to sinkholes reported in that state. Its role in sinkhole investigation is to determine whether there is a threat to public safety, to provide guidance to property owners, and to refer them to more appropriate agencies.

Here's the office's Action Checklist for handling sinkholes:

1. If a sinkhole forms on a street, mark and secure the sinkhole, and notify the agency responsible for maintenance.

2. If a reported sinkhole is located on private property, mark and secure the area and determine whether any structures are in danger. Indications of possible structural damage include cracks in walls, floors, and pavement, and/or cracks in the ground surface.

3. If it is determined that a sinkhole is on private property and no structures are in danger:

    ➤ Ensure that the sinkhole is marked and secured. Make sure that the sink is fenced, roped, or taped very clearly. Usually, the property owner will be liable if someone is hurt in the sinkhole.

    ➤ Keep children away!

    ➤ If lake or river levels are affected, or if you think groundwater quality is endangered by a sinkhole, please report it to the Southwest Florida Water Management District at 352-796-7211, extension 4347.

    ➤ If your home is threatened, contact your homeowner's insurance company.

    ➤ Check carefully for signs of the sinkhole enlarging, especially toward buildings, septic tanks, drain fields, and wells (flowing water into a sinkhole will continue or accelerate its growth). This can be done with a thin, hard metal rod that can be pushed into the soil. Areas near the sinkhole will offer less resistance to the rod than the unaffected soil.

    ➤ Do not throw any waste into the sinkhole. Do not use the sinkhole as a drainage system. Pesticides and other wastes seep easily through the sinkhole into the aquifer—your drinking water.

Sound the Alarm

You wouldn't want a nuclear site to sit on top of sinkhole-prone land, would you? Then don't think about Oak Ridge, Tennessee, and its nuclear installation. Hint: All the sinkholes and nuclear stuff are within sneezing distance of populous Knoxville. One might well ask why the government would build there, when tractor manufacturer John Deere declined to build a factory because of the sinkhole danger.

➤ Do not construct buildings between sinkholes that form a line in a northwest-southeast or northeast-southwest direction.

➤ If the hole is small, fill the hole with clean sand or dirt, and monitor it for future growth.

➤ If the hole is large, contact your insurance agent to have a claims adjuster sent out to assess the damage and make arrangements for repairs.

➤ If desired, the resident may make contact with a private contractor to evaluate the hole to officially determine if it is a sinkhole.

If you live on the 10 percent of the Earth prone to sinkholes, make sure that you have sinkhole/karst insurance. If you buy land with an old springhouse, have your land checked for hollow ground. And don't depend on municipalities and government to relieve sinkhole suffering; they don't consider it severe enough to warrant immediate or far-reaching attention.

The Least You Need to Know

➤ Sinkholes are common in areas of karst topography, landscape beneath which a layer of soluble bedrock, usually carbonate, such as limestone or dolomite, is present.

➤ Sinkholes occur when this layer is eroded by filtering rain or underground water to the point of collapse.

➤ Objects from the size of a bullfrog to the size of a building can disappear down a sinkhole.

➤ Missouri, Kentucky, and Florida are states with prevalent karst topography.

➤ Pollution is one of the main dangers with karst topography.

Part 3

Wind

It will huff and puff and blow houses down. It will twirl and swirl and pick houses up—or, at least, what's left of them.

Sure, wind can be a gentle breeze and add some romance to a summer night. But it can also be a ferocious broom gone mad, sweeping up anything and everything in its way.

In short, the wind is nothing to sneeze at. Turn the page, grab a tissue—because its effects are sometimes something to cry about—and turn your face to the wind.

Chapter 10

Tornado!

In This Chapter

➤ How gently swirling air becomes a devilish disaster

➤ The 1974 Super Outbreak

➤ The 1925 Tri-State Tornado

➤ What to do in the event of a tornado

In *The Wizard of Oz*, Dorothy and her little dog Toto were lucky. They lived through a tornado and had a great adventure besides. Best of all, the tornado itself was merely special effects.

Granted, it was nightmarish, even as a special effect. If you are in the path of one (or your house is), it's probably too late to head for the hills. Tornadoes can happen at any time of the year and just about anywhere in the world. However, the unique geography of the United States makes it a particularly safe haven—for the storms, not for people.

First, what is a tornado? Let's find out.

The Tornado Defined

A tornado is a violently rotating column of air extending from a thunderstorm to the ground. These storms might have wind speeds of 250 miles per hour or more. They can cut a path of destruction as much as a mile wide and 50 miles long. And they can carry objects about as far as Dorothy and Toto went. A tornado in Broken Bow, Oklahoma, carried a motel sign 30 miles and dropped it in Arkansas.

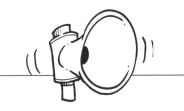

Sound the Alarm

Tornadoes may appear nearly transparent until they pick up dust and debris, making them harder to get away from at first.

Earthy Language

In meteorology, a **dryline** is the boundary separating warm, moist air on the eastern side from hot, dry air to the west.

How Tornadoes Form

The Broken Bow tornado was typical. It formed from a thunderstorm that developed in warm, moist air before an eastward-moving cold front. Tornadoes often are accompanied by large hail as well. Several states can be affected by storm formations along fronts, and many tornadoes may drop out of them.

Tornadoes can also be caused by hot air meeting hot air. A *dryline* thunderstorm develops when warm, most air from the east meets hot, dry air to the west. As the dry air moves east, typically during the afternoon hours, the tornado-dropping storms form.

A third but less common weather condition that spawns tornadoes happens along the front range of the Rockies, in the Texas panhandle and in the southern High Plains. There, thunderstorms frequently form as air near the ground flows "upslope" toward higher terrain. If other favorable conditions exist, these thunderstorms can produce tornadoes.

And there is a fourth possibility, less likely even than the third. Tropical storms and hurricanes moving over land can toss tornadoes out to the right and ahead of their paths as they move onshore. These tornadoes, however, don't possess the destructive power of what Americans think of in terror as twisters.

Whatever combination of atmospheric events causes tornadoes, there are certain hallmarks of tornado genesis.

Before the thunderstorm develops, a change in wind direction and an increase in wind speed occur, accompanied by increasing heights of the wind. The warm air rises up through and over the cold air and then descends the sides of the cold air mass toward the ground again. This creates an invisible horizontal spinning effect in the lower atmosphere.

An early photo of a funnel cloud. (Courtesy NOAA)

When the storm forms, rising air within the thunderstorm updraft tilts the rotating air from horizontal—along the ground—to vertical so that it swarms upward.

About this time an area of rotation between 2 and 6 miles wide emerges, extending through much of the storm. It is in this area that most strong, violent tornadoes form. The area is often rain-free.

Rating the Tornado

Tornadoes are rated with the Fujita tornado scale, devised by Ted Fujita. It can only be used once the tornado has struck; teams of trained meteorologists from the National Weather Service survey the damage and rate it according to the following guidelines.

Scale	Speed in km/h	Damage
F0	64-115	Light—Tree branches broken, signs damaged
F1	116-179	Moderate—Trees snapped, windows broken
F2	180-251	Considerable—Large trees uprooted, weak structures destroyed
F3	252-329	Severe—Trees leveled, cars overturned, walls removed from buildings
F4	330-416	Devastating—Frame houses destroyed
F5	417-508	Incredible—Structures the size of autos moved over 100 miles, steel-reinforced buildings highly damaged

➤ About 69 percent of all tornadoes are classified as "weak" tornadoes. These tornadoes account for less than 5 percent of all tornado deaths and have winds of less than 110 miles per hour.

➤ "Strong" tornadoes make up 29 percent of all tornadoes, cause 30 percent of all tornado deaths, and have winds from 110 to 205 miles per hour.

➤ "Violent" tornadoes are only 2 percent of all tornadoes, but they cause 70 percent of tornado deaths. They have winds in excess of 205 miles per hour—and they can last as long as an hour!

When East Meets West

Tornadoes are nothing to fool around with—although scores of professional and amateur tornado-chasers make a good living and experience lots of excitement (see Chapter 11, "Twister Sisters").

Map showing tornado risk areas in the conterminous United States.

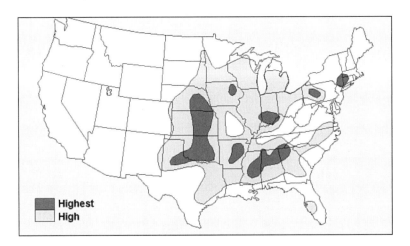

I can tell you firsthand that although there is excitement, not much of it is good. The Super Outbreak of 1974 left 300 people dead, hundreds more injured, and thousands of homes and businesses destroyed. There were 148 twisters in 13 states: Alabama, Georgia, Illinois, Indiana, Kentucky, Michigan, Mississippi, North Carolina, Ohio, South Carolina, Tennessee, Virginia, and West Virginia. It left those who survived unscathed with a lasting set of the jitters during every thunderstorm.

A Firsthand Look at a Tornado

Two years before that Super Outbreak, I—a Yankee—was a writer for *The Daily News* in Athens, Georgia. One of my tasks was calling the National Weather Service each day; before ubiquitous TV/radio/Internet news/weather, people actually read the next day's forecast in the paper. One late afternoon in April, the National Weather Service guy, Elmer Tingle, told me that a tornado watch was in effect for the area.

We'd had those before, and they usually amounted to zippo—usually, that is. But this time the populace of Athens (about 45,000) and I were a little nervous after a funnel frenzy less than two months earlier that had done a great deal of damage. That storm had wiped out whole neighborhoods, killed several people, and injured more. I was only too eager to check with Elmer again about every 15 minutes until the watch was canceled. And it surely *would* be canceled. It wasn't.

Research Findings

In an average year, 800 tornadoes are reported in the United States, most of those east of the Rocky Mountains in the spring and summer months.

Trial by Wind

That night, the watch turned into a warning. The city editor took all of us except one photographer to the safety of the basement press room. (The photographer went out chasing.) We got our marching orders; mine was to go to the hospital. (It was my first year as a reporter—trial by wind, if not by fire.)

One person had died, ripped from the steps of her mobile home as she sought a safer place. A young man had had a branch driven through his leg. Another woman's shoulder had been dislocated by her car door as it was torn from her hands and taken to South Carolina, no doubt.

The death toll probably was so low because the earlier tornado has raised our collective consciousness. This second tornado had followed virtually

Sound the Alarm

Often two or three tornadoes will occur at the same time—sort of in stereo. So don't think it's all clear just because you've seen one come and go. Wait until you hear local radio give you the all clear from the National Weather Service.

the same path, up the interstate, hitting the neighborhoods on either side. People heeded the broadcast warnings, and it was daylight, so they could see it. (I saw it, too. A bunch of us sneaked up the stairs and saw it in the distance, pummeling the west side of Athens as we gawked.)

It hadn't even been a week since a contingent of Eastern Mennonite men had finished helping rebuild a lot of those houses from the first tornado; it looked like we'd see their helpful hands and compassionate faces again.

But we got off easy. Two years later, much of the country—including the South, the Midwest, and the Plains states—suffered the most violent atmospheric season on record.

The Super Outbreak

Whether you're a meteorologist, a survivor, or an observer, the 1974 tornado season is the champ—at least in modern recorded history, since video became common.

The 1974 Super Outbreak spawned 148 tornadoes, the largest number of tornadoes ever produced by one storm system. The tornadoes tore across 2,500 miles of open land, forested land, and built-up land in 13 states. Thirty of the tornadoes were classified as F4 or F5. Of those 148 twisters, 48—one third—were killers, taking the lives of 300 people.

Earthy Language

Unstable air exists, in meteorological terms, when a warm air mass is below cold air. Because the warm air, being lighter, will try to rise, vertical movement and mixing of air layers can occur.

It all started the morning of April 3, with a low pressure area in central Kansas. A warm front was present in the lower Ohio River Valley. South of that was an area of *unstable air* rapidly spreading north. At the same time, a powerful trough high above was spreading strong winds over much of the eastern half of the nation. All this activity caused intense thunderstorms to develop rapidly in the afternoon. And they kept forming until the early morning hours of the next day, April 4.

Six F5 tornadoes developed. One hit Guin, Alabama, killing 20 and wiping the town off the map. Nearby Huntsville was spared; the tornado lifted back up into the cloud at the city limits. In Brandenburg, Kentucky, another F5 tornado killed 30. An F5 in Xenia, Ohio, killed 34, destroyed 300 homes, and damaged 2,100 more.

At the time, National Weather Service forecasters could do little more than watch the green blobs signifying tornadoes form on their radar scopes, long after the "blobs" had begun their deadly work. Since then, a $4.5 billion weather service modernization program has made it possible to issue warnings as much as 11 minutes before a tornado hits. If people have adequate underground shelter at hand, lives should be saved by the hundreds. But are enough shelters in place? Probably not. And there will certainly, say forecasters, be another deadly swarm of tornadoes sooner or later.

The Tri-State Tornado

More than one expert views the Tri-State Tornado of March 18, 1925, as the most devastating tornado ever. It began moving east in Ellington, Missouri, traveling across southern Illinois and into southwest Indiana. It killed 695 people and injured 1,027.

In southern Illinois, 540 people died. Two towns in Illinois—Gorham and Parrish—Annapolis, Missouri, and one in Indiana—Griffin—were almost completely demolished.

Writer Stephanie Winston of Weather.com interviewed a survivor of that rampage, Thelma Davis, who was then a 12-year-old schoolgirl in Murphysboro, Illinois. When the storms hit, she was helping in the principal's office:

> The phone began to ring, and Thelma went to answer it as she always did. But this time, the principal stopped her.
>
> "He says we're going to be going downstairs, meaning the basement," she recalls.

To Ensure Preservation

Tornado Alley is a wide swath of the United States that stretches from Texas north to Nebraska and Iowa. In sheer numbers, it sustains more tornadoes than any other place on Earth.

Thelma and the other children made an orderly procession down the stairs of their two-story school, but as they passed the window on the stairway landing, Thelma could see that something was terribly wrong outside.

The sky had turned pitch black, and menacing-looking clouds were approaching fast. The wind howled, shearing the window into sharp slivers of glass, which began to rain down on the children.

They were relatively safe from the F5 tornado. The rest of the town fared far worse.

Should they have been expecting the tornado? Should Jazz Age weathermen, at least, have been expecting it? Shouldn't a population that lived in tornado country have known that conditions were ripe for a tornado? The week before had been unusually warm, with the forecast of a cold front and a break from the unseasonable heat. The signals were all there, especially for those who live in Tornado Alley. Yet it seemed to catch everyone off guard.

A thunderstorm had developed just behind the cold front. It skipped to the front of the cold air and began pulling the approaching warm, moist air toward it. Fueling its grab at the warm air was the counterclockwise rotation within the storm, a strong low-pressure condition outside it (giving up more warm air easily), and a vertical *wind shear*. One meteorologist likened it to a "skater squeezing

Earthy Language

Wind shear occurs where two wind currents of different speed or direction or both meet. Eddies form at the boundary, creating turbulence—frequent updrafts and downdrafts. The roughness of the surface terrain may increase the effects of wind shear, which can be deadly to airplanes by pushing them forward, up, down, or sideways faster than they can recover.

the arms together, spinning faster." There were no storm weather balloons back then, but kites indicated that the storm would rotate at 67 miles per hour. So some weathermen did know.

But they did not or could not get the word out. There was no national weather warning system in place. Some towns had emergency sirens. But there was no managed effort to issue warnings. In any case, the only weather report issued that day by the U.S. Weather Service called for "rains and strong shifting winds." Prediction, as well as warning, has gotten a lot better in 75 years.

Most storms occur in late afternoon. But this storm developed at 1:01 in the afternoon; by 1:15 it had wiped out Annapolis, Missouri. The next town it demolished, Biehle, Missouri, didn't have a clue that it was coming. The storm did not have the characteristic funnel shape that signaled a tornado, but was a mass of clouds that looked like a typical thunderstorm.

Then the storm moved to southern Illinois, crossing the Mississippi River. At 2:30 P.M., it wiped out Gorham, Illinois. A little girl huddled in the town's schoolhouse was quoted in *The Old Farmer's Almanac Book of Weather and Natural Disasters*:

> "The walls seemed to fall in, all around us. Then the floor at one end of the building gave way. We all slipped or slid in that direction. If it hadn't been for the seats, it would have been like sliding down a cellar door."

Only 20 of 80 houses remained; half of the 500 residents were killed or injured.

By the time the storm got to Thelma Davis's town of Murphysboro, it had started moving at 73 miles per hour, more than twice as fast as the average tornado. The incredible cloud had cut off the town's water supply by destroying some pumping stations, consigning 150 of the town's 200 blocks to fire as firemen watched helplessly.

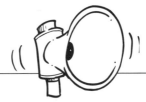

Sound the Alarm

Contrary to popular belief, windows should not be opened before a tornado to "equalize pressure." Opening windows lets damaging winds enter. Instead, forget the windows and leave the structure. If the tornado hits, you'll be safe. It if doesn't, the winds in the surrounding storm won't damage your things as they would if open windows let them in.

Typically, it was not the weather alone that caused grief; it was, as well, the structures of mankind, often pitiably inadequate when nature gets angry. Some who were not killed outright suffered from untreated injuries as the infrastructure broke down; some lost their homes not to the tornado, but to fires that could not be quenched. Whatever the cause, there were few residents in the vicinity of the Tri-State Tornado's path who were not touched by it, one way or another.

Ill Winds: Greatest Twisters in History

Here's a rundown of more bad twisters from modern history:

➤ **The Great Natchez Tornado, May 7, 1840**—This tornado killed 317 people and injured 109. At least 269 of the dead were on boats in the Mississippi River.

➤ **The Great Southern Tornado Outbreak, February 19, 1884**—In a mini-Super Outbreak, more than 60 twisters swept the Southeast. More than 170 people were killed.

➤ **The Louisville, Kentucky, Outbreak, March 27, 1890**—In Illinois, Indiana, and Kentucky, at least 125 people were killed—76 people in the city of Louisville, Kentucky, with 44 of those in one building.

➤ **The St. Louis Outbreak, May 27, 1896**—At least 255 of the 305 killed were in and around St. Louis, Missouri. A thousand people were injured, and $10 million in damage was done in St. Louis alone.

➤ **The Dixie Outbreak, April 23–24, 1908**—Sixteen killer twisters hit from Texas to Georgia, resulting in 320 deaths. Hardest hit was Purvis, Mississippi; the town was destroyed, and 55 people were killed. At one point, this tornado was 2 miles wide.

➤ **April 20, 1920**—Mississippi and Alabama lost 224 citizens to seven killer tornadoes.

➤ **The Poplar Bluff Outbreak, May 8–9, 1927**—A total of 217 died from 17 major tornadoes across Missouri, Arkansas, and Texas. An F4 tornado ripped through Poplar Bluff, Missouri, and killed 83.

➤ **March 21–22, 1932**—Ten violent tornadoes roared through Alabama, Georgia, and Tennessee. Near Tuscaloosa, Alabama, 37 people were killed. The final total for the entire outbreak was 330 dead.

➤ **The Tupelo-Gainesville Outbreak, April 5–6, 1936**—More than 10 tornadoes swept across Mississippi, Tennessee, Alabama, Georgia, and South Carolina, but two did most of the damage. One in Tupelo, Mississippi, leveled more than 200 homes, killed 216 people, and injured another 700 on the night of April 5. On April 6, another tornado in Gainesville, Georgia, killed 203 and injured 1,600.

➤ June 23, 1944—A total of 154 people were killed during a series of tornadoes that hit Pennsylvania, Ohio, West Virginia, and Maryland. A mile-wide funnel killed 72 people in Harrison County, West Virginia.

➤ April 9, 1947—A band of tornadoes played out in Texas, Oklahoma, and Kansas. The worst was an F5 tornado that razed Glazier, Texas; the town was never rebuilt. In all, 181 people died and 970 were injured.

➤ March 21–22, 1952—Tornadoes broke out all over Arkansas, Mississippi, Missouri, and Tennessee. The town of Judsonia, Arkansas, was wiped out. Overall, 177 people died.

➤ The Waco Tornado, May 11, 1953—An F5 tornado smashed into downtown Waco, Texas, killing 114 people. More than 200 businesses were destroyed, and damage reached at least $41 million.

➤ The Flint Tornado and Worcester Tornado, June 8–9, 1953—Flint, Michigan, experienced the last single tornado to kill more than 100, with 115 dead and another 844 injured. The same system spawned another tornado that became the deadliest New England tornado on record, killing 94 in Massachusetts and damaging or destroying 4,000 buildings.

➤ The Udall, Kansas, Tornado, May 25, 1955—More than half the population of Udall, Kansas, was killed as an F5 tornado slammed it. Other tornadoes that day killed 102 in Texas, Oklahoma, and Kansas.

➤ The Palm Sunday Outbreak, April 11–12, 1965—More than 48 tornadoes devastated Iowa, Wisconsin, Illinois, Minnesota, Indiana, and Ohio, killing 256 and inflicting more than $200 million in damage.

➤ The Mississippi Delta Outbreak, February 21, 1971—The Mississippi Delta quaked under the assaults of three major tornadoes. In Louisiana and Mississippi, 119 died and more than 1,000 were injured.

➤ The Wichita Falls Tornado, April 10, 1979—More than 3,000 homes were destroyed and 20,000 people were left homeless in one of the most destructive tornadoes. The death toll was 45, with another 1,740 injured.

➤ The Carolina Outbreak, March 28, 1984—On the afternoon and evening of March 28, 22 tornadoes touched down in South and North Carolina. Fifty-seven people were killed, with one-third of those deaths occurring in mobile homes. Another 1,248 were injured. Damage reached $200 million.

➤ The Pennsylvania-Ohio Outbreak, May 31, 1985—At least 76 died in the United States, with an additional 12 deaths in Canada. The damage reached more than $450 million. This was the region's worst recorded tornado event, with 41 tornadoes in Ohio, Pennsylvania, New York, and Ontario, Canada.

➤ **The Widespread Outbreak, November 21–23, 1992**—A late-season outbreak covered a widespread area from Houston, Texas, to Raleigh, North Carolina, and from the Gulf Coast to the Ohio Valley. In it, 94 tornadoes killed 26 people and injured 641. Total damage was more than $300 million.

➤ **The Palm Sunday Outbreak, March 27–28, 1994**—All afternoon and evening, tornadoes ravaged Georgia and South Carolina, killing a total of 42 and injuring 320. A devastating mid-morning tornado struck the Goshen United Methodist Church in Piedmont, Alabama, during Palm Sunday services, killing 20.

➤ **The Arkansas Outbreak, March 1, 1997**—At least a dozen tornadoes ravaged Arkansas. Other tornadoes touched down in Tennessee, Mississippi, and Kentucky. Twenty-seven people were killed. Arkadelphia, Arkansas, was particularly hard hit, as were the southern suburbs of Little Rock.

Don't Let the Door Hit You as You Leave

The best way not to get hurt in a tornado is not to be there. But few can leave town each time conditions are right for tornadoes to form. Basements and cellars, though, provide good shelter—as Dorothy knew as far back as 1936. Some tornadoes also bear watching more than others.

The Storm Prediction Center in Norman, Oklahoma, and formerly the Severe Local Storms Unit (SELS) in Kansas City, Missouri, have had the responsibility of forecasting tornadoes since SELS was established in 1953. They do it by issuing a tornado watch.

While a watch was a watch was a watch for many years, in 1982, it was decided that more violent possibilities would be denoted by a line that said, "This is a particularly dangerous situation (PDS) with the possibility of very damaging tornadoes." The philosophy has been to reserve these PDS tornado watches for primarily the "tornado outbreak" situations in which widespread damaging tornadoes are predicted.

Research Findings

During the 14-year period between 1982 and 1995, only 557 intense tornadoes—ratings of F4 and F5—occurred in the United States. The annual total varies greatly from only 15 in 1987 to as many as 65 in 1982 and 62 in 1983.

Earthy Language

A **supercell** is a dangerous atmospheric condition hallmarked by strong winds, hail (often very large), a continuous feed of warm, moist air, and frequent and prolonged tornadoes.

Before 1988, the possibility of detecting intense tornadoes in PDS watches was generally less than 10 percent. Since then, there has been a tremendous increase in the understanding and diagnosis of the tornadic *supercell* and the environment in which it forms.

To Ensure Preservation

NOAA is the National Oceanic and Atmospheric Agency, and it wasn't created until 1970. NOAA is responsible for issuing weather, water, and climate warnings and forecasts. To do that, the agency has the cooperation of every other agency which deals with the natural world, from the Marine Fisheries Agency to NASA. The information it provides is important to heed, especially if you live in an area of the country prone to violent weather of any sort.

Because the United States experiences about 1,000 tornadoes a year, averaging 70 deaths, the National Oceanic and Atmospheric Association (*NOAA*) suggests that these safety tips be followed during tornado months and in tornado-prone areas:

1. Listen to NOAA Weather Radio, or local radio or television, for tornado warnings and instructions.

2. If you hear a tornado warning, or if a storm threatens, seek shelter immediately.

3. If you are in a building, go to the designated shelter, the building's basement, or an interior room, such as a bathroom or closet.

4. If you are in an automobile, do not try to outdrive a tornado. Abandon your vehicle and seek shelter in a ditch or depression.

5. If you are in a mobile home, leave it for a more substantial structure.

6. Protect your head and body from flying debris.

It doesn't matter what kind of tornado is threatening. You won't know until afterward anyway, because the F scale is based on damage as well as storm characteristics. But these days, you can be forewarned. People who live in Tornado Alley should begin every spring with making sure sufficient NOAA radios—dedicated units tuned always to the NOAA frequency—are on hand. Or, at least, they should listen to weather reports hourly. More than that, though, they need to ensure that they and their loved ones have sturdy undergroud shelter available within the 11-minute warning period NOAA strives to provide.

The Least You Need to Know

➤ Tornadoes are usually formed by thunderstorms in which a violently rotating horizontal column of air becomes vertical and extends downward to the ground.

➤ Deaths and injuries from tornadoes are not caused by wind, but by what the wind delivers.

➤ The 1974 Super Outbreak spawned 148 tornadoes, the largest number of tornadoes ever produced by one storm system, and killed 300 people.

➤ The 1925 Tri-State Tornado killed 695 people and injured 1,027.

➤ These days, tornado warnings are reliable; listening to them can save your life.

Chapter 11

Twister Sisters

In This Chapter

➤ We are not alone: funnel clouds in foreign lands

➤ Tornadoes on the water: water spouts

➤ Tornadoes' tiny little cousins: dust devils

➤ The chase is on

In this chapter we'll examine other tornadic winds, including the cyclone, the water spout, and the dust devil, and conclude with a brief look at the wild world of tornado chasing.

Cyclones: The Tornado's Foreign Cousin

You might be surprised to learn that the Indian Ocean spawns the second greatest number of tornadoes on Earth (after the United States' Tornado Alley). There, and in other tropical and subtropical regions where swirling storms develop, tornadoes are often called cyclones, although they may also be called tornadoes, dust devils, or a number of other local twister names.

Cyclones are rated differently than tornadoes: Wind speeds are used. Maximum winds of a tropical cyclone are usually based on a 10-minute average, except for the 1-minute average used by the Joint Typhoon Warning Center (JTWC) in Hawaii. So, the estimated maximum winds by JTWC may be higher than in other countries.

Fujita, the same man of F-rating fame, also rates international tornadoes and produced a map showing the areas most vulnerable to tornadic activity. What foreign nation experiences the most cyclonic excitement? Bangladesh. And its tornadic political situation probably means that the cyclones of Bangladesh are underreported in U.S. media.

The Other Tornado Alley

India and Bangladesh combined have suffered more tornado, or cyclone, fatalities than anywhere else in the world, including Tornado Alley. On April 26, 1989, a single storm north of Dhaka killed 1,300 and injured 12,000. In April 1995, another one killed 30; in 1996, 1,000 were killed near Tangail.

To Ensure Preservation

In Tornado Alley, most deaths are caused by flying debris. Many people escape injury and death by hiding in bathtubs with something solid pulled over them if they lack a basement.

Like our tornadoes, cyclones tend to appear in the spring—March, to be precise. Like ours, they are most often late-afternoon events. They tend to develop as thunderstorms—nor'westers, as they are called locally—along the Ganges River basin in northern India, and they then track east or southeastward into Bangladesh, bringing rain, high winds, and occasionally tornadoes.

Most fatalities and injuries associated with nor'westers occur in kutcha houses, temporary shanties built of thatch that easily collapse in high winds. Other deaths are caused by falling trees and flying debris, usually from corrugated iron sheets used for kutcha roofing.

A Cyclone Is Born

The birth of a cyclone is very like the birth of a tornado; one observer says you could think of Dhaka, India, as Dallas, and Patna, India, as Amarillo.

There is often a dryline west of Bangladesh. The winds aloft come from Iran/Turkmenistan and are forced around the Himalayas, bringing lots of disturbances to the region and helping set the stage for the cyclones.

The Tangail, Bangladesh, cyclone of May 13, 1996, was typical. A large tornado coming out of a nor'wester lasted 20 minutes, killed more than 1,000, injured 34,000 more, and left 100,000 homeless. Worse yet, the government, in as much disarray, took more than 24 hours to organize relief. The state-run evening news originally reported the death toll at 22.

Fortunately, nor'wester outbreaks are less frequent than Great Plains tornadoes.

Water Spouts

You will most often find the tornado's cousin, the water spout, in the Florida Keys. The Keys, says Joseph Golden, a scientist with the National Oceanic and Atmospheric Association (NOAA) who has studied the phenomena extensively, "are the greatest natural vortex lab in the world. Water spouts probably occur more frequently in the Florida Keys than anywhere in the world."

From Marathon, a city about halfway down the Keys from Miami and located on Knight's Key (a key that may get as high as 10 feet above sea level in spots) to Key West, this is spout-spotting territory—and that doesn't even take into account the outlying keys, where a road *doesn't* run through it. The Barracuda Keys, for example, form a 200-square-mile area of flats, channels, and tiny mangrove islands; this is a water spout–hunter's paradise.

In all, the area stretching from Marathon to Key West, and on westward 70 miles to the tiny outcrops in the ocean known as the Dry Tortugas, experience 400 to 500 water spouts a year. Most go unreported because so few cause damage. That's not because they aren't severe; it's because the area is sparsely populated except for sharks and dolphins. The abundant water spouts form there because the weather and the landscape supply all that's needed to make them.

Research Findings

The seven little keys making up the Dry Tortugas were discovered in 1513 by Ponce de Leon, who named them after the legions of turtles living there. The U.S. acquired them from Spain in 1821 and built Fort Jefferson there on Garden Key—despite the lack of fresh water. The fort was never used in battle, but did become a prison, housing the famous Dr. Samuel Mudd, who set John Wilkes Booth's broken leg, and later served valiantly in a cholera epidemic at the fort. Today, the islands are a national park, reached by boat and plane by 70,000 visitors a year.

While water spouts are often described as tornadoes over water, scientific work during the last 30 or so years has revealed both similarities and differences. Water spouts and all the different kinds of tornadoes do have a similar basic structure, with upward-moving air.

Here's the recipe for making a spout:

Start with low-lying islands and shallow water, which helps heat the air. Add temperatures in the mid 80s to low 90s in summer. The air will rise, heated from below. The humidity then will get so high that little droplets form, making clouds. As the water vapor in the clouds condenses—being sent farther aloft against cold air by the still-rising hot air off the water—it releases more heat, making the air rise still faster.

Research Findings

Beginning in the late 1960s, Joseph Golden became a water spout hunter when a friend flew him in a single-engine Cessna 172 into the heart of a spout. During 12 days in September 1974, he flew into 16 Florida Keys water spouts, one of them 26 times, in a modified North American T-6. The spouts he flew into had winds blowing at more than 60 miles per hour around the vortex; those winds were also moving upward at 20 miles per hour.

So much for the first half of the recipe: a rising area of warm air, bumping up against colder air aloft. Then what?

"Bake" it in the conveyor-belt oven of the Trade Winds, which blow right up the Keys, lining up the clouds as they go. It is known that lines of clouds encourage water spouts to form. How? That is still a mystery, but the correlation is there.

Says Golden, clouds that spawn the Keys spouts usually are from about 18,000 to 22,000 feet high, and the spouts develop as the clouds form upward. If spouts will occur, they will usually form between 4 P.M. and 7 P.M., with a secondary possibility between 11 A.M. and 1 P.M.

While spouts are most likely to form in the Keys, moving up the coast from Homestead to Stuart, Florida, will give you another pretty good chance of seeing a spout. Tampa Bay has had a great number of spouts, too. But other spots on the Atlantic coast northward to Chesapeake Bay have also seen spouts form. On the West Coast, weak spouts have formed from islands off Washington state to San Diego, California. Every so often, the Great Lakes and the Great Salt Lake see spouts. (If one formed on the Great Salt Lake, would it look like a pillar of salt?)

Florida spouts are the strongest, investigation shows. Studies of videos show speeds in the range of 190 miles per hour. Dangerous? Yes. Some researchers believe that a significant portion of the so-called Bermuda Triangle incidents are actually disasters caused by water spouts; over the open ocean, they wouldn't leave a trace.

Spout Signs

From the air, you might see the formation of a dark spot on the ocean. That's fine. A lot of those just disappear. But if one begins to show spiral patterns of dark and light water, look out. In a boat, you might be able to see these from the water's surface, or you would feel the wind suddenly shift and increase. You might also see a funnel coming from a cloud nearby.

You will definitely see the next stage. A vortex reaches the ocean surface from the cloud. When the wind reaches 40 miles per hour or so, it kicks up spray in a circular pattern, and you may see the funnel pointing out of the cloud into that frothy ring.

Finally, you'll see the funnel reach all the way to the water, and usually you will be able to see through it. Waves are kicked up, and a bubbly wake follows the spout as it moves across the water.

The funnel then collapses in one direction or another, moving out from under the cloud and getting skinnier at the bottom. When rain begins to fall, the spout is doomed; the cooling rain shuts down the updrafts of water-warmed air needed for the spout machine to remain operational.

Sound the Alarm

You might also encounter land spouts, columns of rotating air similar to water spouts but on land. These differ in their formation from tornadoes and are not as severe. The rotation begins in unstable conditions under a cloud over the land.

This might be nice to see, but it's a little dangerous. How do you avoid water spouts? Stay informed; a NOAA weather radio will tell you if conditions are right for spout formation. Have a radio on your boat, and stay tuned when you're on the water.

Water spouts tend to come from clouds with a dark, flat bottom when there is just the first hint of rain. If one heads your way, try to escape by going at right angles to its path. If it's about to hit your boat, the best bet might be to dive overboard. Flying debris is the big killer in tornadoes and water spouts.

Has anyone ever done this? Not that anyone else knows about. After all, there are spooky things under the tropical waters, too: sharks, rays, barracuda. And no one really knows what the water is doing right under a spout; maybe it's twisting and twirling, too, or maybe it has a current that will drive you into the depths. Even the best water spout researcher, Joseph Golden, doesn't know whether this tactic is safe. It's far better just to avoid them.

However, in the Keys and elsewhere, a water spout can damage things on dry land, although damage usually is minimal. A March 3, 1999, storm in western Washington left 250,000 people on Puget Sound without electricity, damaged the Evergreen Point floating bridge and the Fauntleroy ferry dock, and produced water spouts. Who knows whether it was a spout, and not just strong winds, that did the shoreline damage?

In fact, water spouts, for all their dangerous attributes, are about as elusive as rainbows, and they usually don't even last as long as a rainbow. They aren't as beautiful. They also aren't deadly, despite the mayhem they are known to have caused. So what good are they? Something for sailors to talk about, and for NOAA weather radio to put on otherwise boring midsummer radio "air" in the Florida Keys once in a while.

Mini-Tornadoes

We have exported a weaker version of the great American tornado to Canada. We send them across the border from Windsor, Ontario, to Barrie. How many? About 25 to 30 a year. On May 31, 1985, we sent a system across that produced an F4 or two, the worst Canada has ever had.

Generally, most Canadian tornadoes that touch down are weak and do only minor damage. Most happen in July, and the time period for the return of damaging ones is about five years.

To Ensure Preservation

It's a popular concept that tornadoes don't cross water. Unfortunately, it's also wrong. In fact, the ones crossing the Great Lakes to Canada are assumed to gain some strength by passing over the relatively warmer water of the lakes.

The Dust Devil

A final sort of tornadic wind some people have to deal with is the dust devil. Sounds awful, but is it?

They're actually the pussycats of whirling air masses. They can occur in any hot region of the world and can be created by as simple a thing as a large truck passing over very hot pavement. They may develop near thunderstorms, too. These generally are not too terrible, but they can be hazardous to light aircraft and light vehicles on the ground; severe cases can cause damage to houses and uproot trees.

The effects of the dust devil are localized. Typically, these wind masses are only several meters wide at the base and can lift dust and debris only a few hundred meters into the air. They also last only a couple of minutes.

You can observe cyclonic action on a small scale in any leaf-strewn schoolyard—preferably a paved city schoolyard—on warm, windy autumn days. A few leaves will rise and swirl about in a circular pattern. Sometimes, the little funnel will travel a hundred yards. Tame, certainly, compared to the big, bad tornado.

Earthy Language

Whirlwinds are just what the Aussies usually call dust devils—although Americans usually call the Australian ones dust devils. Go figure.

Tornado Chasing for Fun and Profit

Let's round out our overview of tornadic winds with a look at tornado chasing—what it is, who does it, and why.

There's no doubt that tornadoes are a serious problem, especially in the continental United States. But they also provide opportunities for recreation combined with learning.

T.J. Turnage of Midland, Texas, thought that since he lived in the High Plains, where the sky is a dominant part of the scenery, he might as well give tornado chasing a try. Eventually, he became a writer about tornadoes for *Storm Track* magazine.

For his first tornado chase, he went with someone who had been before and who knew where to go, what to look for, and what to expect. Turnage was a meteorologist with the National Weather Service, but that didn't mean that he'd been physically close to his subject. He wanted the knowledge a chase would bestow; he ended up liking the aesthetics of a chase just as well—maybe more.

Indeed, chasing tornadoes gave Turnage an appreciation for the flat, seemingly changeless landscape. "As one passes through, changes in the landscape are often gradual and barely perceived," he writes.

The High Plains certainly demonstrates the order sought by nature. So, then, is a storm—a tornado—lack of order? Is that what makes them so frightening and, to some, so beautiful?

"In weather," Turnage writes, "there is often order, but much of the time it occurs on a scale too large to be appreciated by a single person in one place."

All that aside, what about the chase? How does one know where to look for a tornado? Listening for warnings issued by the National Oceanic and Atmospheric Association and peeking at it from under the bed isn't quite the idea.

But nature gives clues to what she might deliver. Just as there was an ominous calm in *The Wizard of Oz* after Dorothy's run-in with the proto-witch, so there are telltale signs that tornado-chasers can look for. One must be observant and willing to become something of a detective in pursuit of quarry.

Some chasers chase big thunderstorms; others chase only tornadoes. But because you must have a thunderstorm to produce a tornado, the tornado-chasers get treated to both, whereas the storm-chasers may be satisfied with significant flashing and booming and not miss the twirling and whirling at all. Tornado-chasers think of themselves as something of an elite among storm-mongers, though: "If one views storm chasing as the pursuit of order, a tornado is a very reasonable objective," Turnage writes. "After all, tornadoes could arguably be called the highest manifestation of order in a storm, since their rarity indicates the incredible balance and simultaneity of processes needed to create them."

Sound the Alarm

A more organized storm is also more likely to be severe; if a funnel cloud descends and looks just like a movie version, watch out. If it kind of begins and stops dropping from the clouds a couple of times, well, still watch out.

Either way, one can take forecasts as the first hint. You've got to have a weather forecast that says the big storms are possible. You've got to do your meteorological homework and make sure that the upper atmosphere is on the move and that some nice, big clashing fronts are coming your way (and the more disparate, the better). You've got to be sure, in short, that a bit of darkening sky isn't just the precursor of an air-clearing summer shower.

Even so, one may not always get a tornado, nor even a storm. The thing then is to chalk up the tire rubber you've burned and the time spent as a learning experience and an opportunity for a beautiful drive in the country.

"At the end of any stormy day," Turnage says, "there is usually a beautiful sunset."

Giving Chase

Several companies will take you tornado chasing, and set you down gently at the end of the adventure. They don't promise, absolutely positively, that you won't come to harm. But they are experienced chasers, and provide their safety records, as well as their sighting records, for clients.

Tornado Alley Safari

Tornado Alley Safari leads a "quest into passionate skies." They've been featured on CBS *Hardcopy, National Geographic,* NBC Evening News, and in features produced by the Associated Press.

Tornado Alley Safari has been officially chasing since 1996, and has been, since then, within a couple of blocks of tornadoes. They have certainly seen stunning lightning, and towering thunderheads have exploded for the viewers. They've had waterfalls of hail. They've seen St. Elmo's Fire—the natural event, not the movie. And there have been multiple double sunsets on their watch.

Their trips begin in May and June from Dallas. They pick you up at the airport, dine with you and the rest of the tour, and then go chasing. Caveat: "Please note that we cannot guarantee how severe it will get—that's up to Mother Nature. We will do our best to ensure that all of us get to see nature's energy in action and live to tell about it!"

Cost: As of this writing, about $2,000 per person for a 10-day tour. Contact them at: POB 833189, Richardson, TX 75183; Phone: 972-889-0196; or see the Web site: www.tornadosafari.com.

Spacious Skies Tours

Spacious Skies Tours is another vacation/learning excursion, operated by husband-and-wife team William and Lisa Monfredo. They have a beautiful Web site, and they promise an exciting experience. But don't, they add, think of all this as *National Lampoon's Tornado Chase*. They want to know if chasers have medical conditions they need to take into account. They place restrictions on personal items so that there will be room for equipment—not to mention not tripping over stuff if you have to get out of Dodge quick. "Lastly, we expect you to abide by our safety restrictions, including not drinking alcohol during chase hours and not smoking in the vehicles."

Bill is a doctoral student in Environmental Geography and a university instructor at Southwest Texas State University. He teaches Physical Geography, the study of the interrelationships between the atmosphere, land, water, and people. He specializes in natural hazards and the climatology of severe storms. In his Master's thesis, he correlated the phase of the El Niño–Southern Oscillation (ENSO) and the frequency of significant tornadoes, F2–F5 (on the Fujita scale) in the south-central United States, a study he presented at an Association of American Geographers National Conference in Honolulu, Hawaii. Bill also completed a climatological study of southwestern Pennsylvania strong and violent tornadoes. He will focus on Southern High Plains tornadoes in his future research.

Lisa received her Bachelor of Arts degree in English from SWTSU in December. But she also has studied operational meteorology through the Broadcast Meteorology Program at Mississippi State University. Both are certified SKYWARN Severe Storm Spotters.

Contact Spacious Skies Tours at: William and Lisa Monfredo, 1900 Aquarena Springs Dr., Apt. # 12202, San Marcos, TX 78666.

Silver Lining Tours

The Silver Lining Tours site opens with a great clap of thunder. They offer a video, "Stormriders," to allow potential chasers to see what a storm-chasing tour with them is like.

Veteran storm chasers Gene Moore and William Reid guide tours for the company. And this company, too, has been featured on TV, Discovery Channel's "Inside Twister Week."

Although they say you could chase on your own, they ask who you would have to share the intensity of the moment with if you succeeded. And they promise a "stress-free storm-chasing adventure" for not much more than you'd pay for travel and lodging for ten days of doing nothing much.

As of this writing, the tour costs $2,400 per person for the ten-day tour, including all expenses *except* travel to and from the base city, food, and incidentals. It also includes daily snacks and drinks, and, of course, ground transportation during the tour.

From their Web site: "On days when there are no storms expected (we hope those are very few!), we will offer a few optional recreational activities. These will be weather-related whenever possible.

"Examples from last year: toured the Storm Prediction Center/National Severe Storms Lab in Norman, OK; toured three National Weather Service Forecast offices; viewed severe tornado damage in Oklahoma; visited the Twister Museum in Wakita, OK. We have also visited Devil's Tower, Mount Rushmore, and the Badlands (I love South Dakota!)."

Contact them at: Silver Lining Tours, L.C., David Gold, Manager, 2701 Longmire Dr. #1016, College Station, TX 77845. Or see the Web site at www.silverlining.pair.com.

The Least You Need to Know

➤ The cyclone is the foreign equivalent of the tornado and is most prevalent in India and Bangladesh. If you travel to India or Bangladesh in the spring, listen to international weather reports.

➤ Water spouts are caused by a rising area of warm air, bumping up against colder air aloft, and "baked" in the conveyor-belt oven of the Trade Winds.

➤ Dust devils are localized wind masses that are only several meters wide at the base and can lift dust and debris only a few hundred meters into the air. They also last only a couple of minutes.

➤ For some, storm chasing provides opportunities for recreation and learning.

El Niño: Good Name for a Bad Boy

For a while, in the late 1960s and early 1970s, sunspots were blamed for all the troubles in the world. These days, it's El Niño, a weather pattern named after the Christ Child, since it makes its appearance around Christmas. That, however, is the last of the similarities between the weather pattern and Christianity's focus.

The more correct name of the phenomenon these days is El Niño–Southern Oscillation. I'll call it El Niño, though, because it acts more like a naughty child than a neutral scientific concept.

What the Peruvian Fishermen Saw

Back in the 1500s, fishermen along the Pacific coast of northern Peru started noticing changes in fish abundance and species. What did they notice? Sea bird beachings. The birds' food source, anchovies, had disappeared, and they were dying off in great flocks.

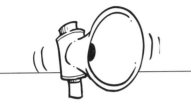

As the birds died, guano gatherers also suffered. Guano, bird droppings, make rich fertilizer. So, farmers suffered.

Nothing has changed, except that now—we are ethnocentrically prone to think—it has gotten more troublesome. In April 1998, the El Niño of 1997–1998 had warmed water near South America's west coast so much that the anchovies moved north once again, following their food supply, phytoplankton. Peru suffered a 78 percent drop in anchovy production, a prime commodity in the country's economy; in fact, the government declared a halt to anchovy fishing.

Sound the Alarm

El Niño episodes usually occur approximately every two to seven years. Recent El Niño events occurred in 1976–1977, 1982–1983, 1986–1987, 1991–1993, 1994–1995, and 1997–1998.

Farmers and Famine Prevention

Ancient fishermen did not have an exclusive on El Niño prediction. For centuries, native farmers living in the high Andes in Bolivia and Peru would look to the heavens to determine what sort of weather they would have in the upcoming growing season. Would they have early, abundant rain, making for a bountiful potato crop?

To Ensure Preservation

Torrential rains, not farm-friendly rains, accompany El Niño in Peru. In the late 1997–1998 El Niño, the Peruvian government spent millions to dig ditches and spread plastic to safeguard prehistoric monuments (including Chan Chan, a major archeological ruin on the outskirts of Trujillo) and to protect adobe relics from El Niño's fury. Chan Chan is 28 square miles and dates from 1000 C.E., so only a small percentage can be protected. Unfortunately, costs of protecting all of it would be prohibitive, so only a small portion will be saved.

Written in the Stars

The constellation they consulted was *The Pleiades*. If it could be seen bright and clear just before dawn, things would go well. If not, then likely they would have terrible weather. In fact, they would have ENSO. Of course, they didn't have our sorts of acronyms for everything from our favorite day (TGIF) to dread diseases (AIDS). They didn't even speak English. But they knew ENSO, El Niño–Southern Oscillation, even if they did call it by a more prosaic name.

They coped with the meager late precipitation, followed by periods of crop-hostile gully-washers, by planting smaller crops.

Earthy Language

Celestial bodies seen from Earth seem to suggest pictures of various objects, if one connected the dots made by stars. **The Pleiades** are also known as The Seven Sisters and have been used as metaphors for poetry about women.

Predicting El Niño

The Andean farmers were not practicing some sort of ancient witchcraft. Recent studies by scientists at the Lamont-Doherty Earthy Observatory of Columbia University have discovered that as long as 400 years ago, the Andean farmers were doing what we have learned to do only in the past 20 years: predict El Niño.

The Andean technique works pretty well, the scientists found. Said researcher Mark Cane, "The method involves a great deal of nuance. I still wonder how they possibly worked it out. It's really quite a feat."

Cane and Lamont-Doherty colleague Stephen Zebiak devised the modern El Niño forecasting technique, not expecting to be shown up by native people who had never been inside an observatory, never mind being connected to one of the world's foremost research organizations.

But in 1995, while on a sightseeing excursion, Cane's guide mentioned a local farmer who looked at the predawn sky during the festival of San Juan to figure out how wet the coming wet season, six months away, would be.

Cane reported in *Nature* magazine: "No other weather phenomenon would present symptoms that far in advance, and Andean droughts are known to occur in El Niño years. It was intriguing."

The El Niño–Potato Connection, and Other Acts of War

It seems now, say many researchers, that the Potato Famine in Ireland can be blamed as much on the disease susceptibility of the almighty spud—imported to Ireland by

English explorers—and the weird weather of the 1845 El Niño year as on the English themselves.

Researchers also think that a drought during a long slump in El Niño activity in the 1920s may be the cause of the American Dust Bowl. In addition, Lewis and Clark may have been hindered by its effects in their exploration. Here are a few other possible El Niño effects through the ages:

➤ Influenza outbreaks in the past 100 years are linked to El Niño, suspects Reuters' Michael Byrnes.

➤ The Black Death (Bubonic Plague) of the fourteenth century in Europe could have been related.

➤ The French Revolution (scarce bread, as in "Let them eat cake") was probably caused by the El Niño–based grain shortages.

➤ The Biblical drought reported in Exodus 9:33 might have been caused by El Niño, which causes more rain in the Middle East, an Israeli scientist thinks.

➤ Hitler's armies were halted in Russia by increased El Niño snowfall there, proposes William Vogt, an early El Niño–Southern Oscillation researcher.

What the Satellites Proved

In case you're not convinced that El Niño is a physical reality on Earth, satellites prove that it is.

Using satellites, scientists found that the sea surface is actually 2 feet higher around Indonesia than it is near the South American coast when El Niño is not operating.

Earthy Language

Trade Winds are any cross-oceanic winds blowing toward the equator. On the north side of the equator, they blow from the northeast, and from the southeast on the south side.

When El Niño is not in effect, *Trade Winds* in the Pacific push water west, away from South America, toward Australia and Indonesia. As the warmer water evaporates in the western Pacific, it creates convection cells that make clouds and bring rains to surrounding regions.

The water blown westward is replaced near the coast of South America by deeper, colder water that rises to take the place of the warmer water that has cruised on out. The fish like that cooler water and provide a good living for South American fishermen—when El Niño is absent, that is.

Is that normal? Sure, when its opposite, La Niña, isn't operating. What is normal in the southern Pacific is change. Hence the additional name, "southern oscillation."

As the warm spot moves eastward, pushed there by Trade Winds blowing from South America toward the Far East, the winds change. One wind's change means that another wind must change, in a sort of atmospheric domino effect. Before long, weather upheavals are taking place all over the world.

Four Degrees of El Niño

The 1982–83 El Niño was the most intense on record, although 1997–1998 gave it some hot competition. In fact, all the records were not compiled at this writing.

Still, the 1980s El Niño was bad. Scientists noticed that the sea surface west of Peru was up to 4° centigrade warmer than average in a southern hemisphere summer.

Here's a checklist of the most obvious havoc it wrought:

➤ Torrential rains occurred in normally arid regions of Peru, and floods were reported in southern California. An estimated 2,000 people died in those two events alone.

➤ Damage estimates ranged from $8 billion to $13 billion, including $2.5 billion from disastrous crops caused by drought in Australia, and $2.2 billion due to flooding in the United States.

➤ Fires scorched 3 million acres of tropical forest in Borneo, and severely diminished the orangutan population living there.

It is very likely that the 1997–1998 El Niño was worse, however. Early in the pattern in 1997, scientists found that the sea water surface was 5° centigrade above normal. Ouch! And that "spot" measured covers an area larger than the continental United States.

If heat drives the weather—and scientists say that it does—it looked as if it would be a wild and bumpy ride. And it was—from Mexico to Borneo, and all points in between.

"When measured by a combination of sea level pressure, surface wind, surface air and sea temperature, and cloudiness, the 1997–98 El Niño approached the intensity of the record 1982–83 El Niño," a report from the National Oceanic and Atmospheric Administration found. In retrospect, that El Niño actually exceeded it.

From Mexico to Borneo

No effects of El Niño are minor. They're either very good or very bad. But perhaps the most chilling effects are those that affect human life.

When the weather pattern first developed, CNN reported that scientists expected El Niño to increase the chance of Bubonic Plague in California, where heavy rains increased vegetation and rodent—and hence carrier flea—populations. Mosquito-borne diseases—malaria, encephalitis, and dengue fever—were expected to increase globally.

Research Findings

Says James O'Brien, professor of meteorology and oceanography at Florida State University, "When a big El Niño happens, everything is blamed on it, but there's a lot of nonsense out there." He says that blaming an increase in snake bites in Montana on El Niño is "bunk." What's more, he argues that an Indonesian jet did not crash because of poor visibility due to the massive El Niño–stoked fires, but because the pilot got faulty instructions from a flight controller.

Hantavirus, which became known during the 1980s El Niño, was supposed to increase in the Southwest, where *peromyscus* populations also respond well to more food being available.

Earthy Language

Peromyscus are a species of mouse, of which the deer mouse is one. The Pinon mouse, a close relative, is described as being quite attractive, with large white ears. Still, a mouse is a mouse is a mouse, and any of the peromyscus can carry the often deadly hantavirus.

NOAA reported the following:

> ... in 1997, a total of 40,249 cholera cases with 2,231 deaths were reported in Tanzania alone (compared with 1,464 cases and 35 deaths in 1996).

> Kenya reported 17,200 cases and 555 deaths, and Somalia 6,814 cases and 252 deaths due to cholera in 1997.

> In the Americas, the current cholera epidemic has been raging for seven years and, associated with a major El Niño, the number of cholera cases started to

increase at the end of 1997. In 1998, Peru has been suffering from a major outbreak and has already reported, for the first three months of 1998, 16,705 cases and 146 deaths. Other countries which are reporting increasing numbers of cholera cases in 1998 are Bolivia, Honduras, and Nicaragua.

NOAA also reported that The Centers for Disease Control and Prevention had confirmed a total of 185 cases of HPS in 29 states in 1997. They confirmed another four early in 1998.

Sound the Alarm

The Centers for Disease Control say that hantavirus is carried by rodents, especially the deer mouse, and causes hantavirus pulmonary syndrome (HPS). You can become infected by exposure to mice droppings; the flu–like first signs of sickness (especially fever and muscle aches) appear one to six weeks later, followed by shortness of breath and coughing. Once this phase begins, the disease progresses rapidly, necessitating hospitalization and often ventilation within 24 hours. While HPS is not generally widespread and chances of contracting it are relatively small, it can cause death.

Globally, here are some more of El Niño's effects:

➤ Thunderstorms with hurricane-force winds thrashed Moscow.

➤ The rain-swollen Yangtze River killed more than 400 as it roiled through central China.

➤ Florida was fried by fires, right after being torn up by twisters. In all, there were 2,000 wildfires, with half a million acres charred to a crisp, and property losses estimated at a quarter of a billion bucks.

We like to think that dramatic upheavals—floods, food fish migrating away from their normal range, and such—are unusual. We like to blame something, some force larger than mankind, for our devastating diseases. El Niño is handy. And its effects are severe. But they are not abnormal. They have been happening since the beginning of recorded time and before; it might be time to prepare for them, since they are not preventable.

Research Findings

Influenza outbreaks between 1557 and 1900 appear to have been associated with El Niño, as were smallpox and malaria. Seventeenth-century El Niño events may have caused 50 percent mortality in Java and other areas from malaria.

Death and Drought

Jude Webber of Reuters reported that the UN's Food and Agriculture Organization (FAO) believed a "near-record number of countries" faced food shortages in the 1997–1998 El Niño; affected countries had increased from 31 to 37. Africa, Asia, Latin America, and parts of the former Soviet Union were hit hardest. Haiti, the Dominican Republic, El Salvador, Guatemala, Honduras, Nicaragua, Panama, China, the Philippines, Thailand, Indonesia, Papua New Guinea, and the Pacific Islands also reported extensive El Niño damage, he reported.

Poisonous Smog and Other "Niño Travel Tips"

Needless to say, tourists would be well advised during El Niño years to avoid places where diseases rage. But you might want to watch out for other "travel advisories" as well. Here's a list of some of the places you would have wanted to avoid in 1997–1998, and the date of the publication from which the information was taken:

➤ **April 18, 1998**—The Associated Press reported that an El Niño–driven drought in Vietnam had destroyed hundreds of millions of dollars of crops. Also, 900 forest fires had killed 10 and burned 35,000 acres in the south and central highlands. As river levels fell, salt-water intrusion threatened rice crops. In Daklak province, only 10 percent of the people had access to sufficient water; only 30 of 230 reservoirs still had any water in them. In some places, there had been no rain since November.

➤ **May 20, 1998**—Nando.net reported that government officials in Nepal linked El Niño to "pre-monsoon rains" that led to avalanches, low temperatures, blizzards, and high winds during the mountain-climbing season. Two climbers died in avalanches.

➤ **November 26, 1998**—CNN and Nando.net reported that arid conditions and strong winds had fanned more than 100 lightning-caused fires in New South Wales, Victoria, and South Australia. Winds reached 60 miles per hour, and temperatures shot to 104°F to 115°F. While fires are normal at that time of year, El Niño had delayed the onset of fall rains.

➤ **November 30, 1997**—The Associated Press reported that highways reopened after more than 3 feet of snow stranded hundreds in the Pueblo area; one death was linked to the storm.

➤ **October 20, 1997**—In the first half of July, strong several-day rains occurred over the Jeseniky and Beskydy Mountains, resulting in the most catastrophic flooding recorded in the Czech republic/kingdom in more than 1,000 years. At least 50 people died.

➤ **November 4, 1997**—The Environment News Service reported that the United Nations World Food Program was trying to deal with the heaviest rainfall in more than 30 years in northeast Africa. The flooding followed a drought. Crops and entire villages were submerged. The heaviest damage was in one of Somalia's more productive farming areas. Thousands were homeless. Nando.net and Agence France-Presse reported at least 100 dead: more than 57 dead in Ethiopia, 17 in the Sudan, and 29 in Kenya. Coastal Mombasa was devastated, and roads were washed out through much of the country.

➤ **September 9, 1997**—Drought and frost devastated agriculture, in Papua New Guinea, especially coffee and palm oil. Mining operations had also ceased for a time because of low water levels. The drought was the worst in 25 years, Reuters reported.

➤ **September 13, 1997**—Papua New Guinea highlanders abandoned their villages as drought and brush fires devastated crops in the worst drought in 50 years, Reuters reported. The people were reportedly eating wild berries and tubers normally reserved for pig feed. The local press claimed that 40 people had died of starvation, but the government denied these reports.

The High Cost of Global Heating

At the time of the 1997–1998 El Niño, Commerce Secretary Daley said, "Last June, we predicted correctly that because of El Niño, the United States would experience abnormal weather patterns during the fall and winter. Providing this type of accurate weather information six months in advance has never been done before and has enabled our communities and businesses to better prepare and protect themselves."

Reuters reported that Daley also warned that the world cost of that El Niño would reach $10 billion, similar to the impact of 1982–1983.

Research Findings

David Fox of Reuters reported that El Niño had restored rain to Lake Nakuru, bringing back almost 1.5 million lesser and greater flamingos to the saline lake.

And here's NOAA's assessment:

> The past two decades are replete with evidence of the significant economic and social costs associated with unanticipated disruptions in weather and climate patterns. For example, estimates of global losses associated with the 1982–1983 El Niño event exceeded $8 billion. Of that figure, U.S. losses associated with storms in the Mountain and Pacific states, flooding in the Gulf States, and Hurricane Iwa in Hawaii were estimated to have cost $2.5 billion. The 1988 U.S. drought resulted in an estimated $2–$4 billion in direct losses to agricultural producers, with total losses throughout the economy estimated at greater than $22 billion. The 1993 Midwest floods were associated with about $15–$20 billion in damages and costs. The 1995 floods in California and the Gulf States resulted in estimated losses of $7 billion. More recently, significant damage and losses have resulted from the heavy rains associated with tropical storms along the West Coast, the Gulf of California, and parts of southern Arizona. Yet these figures alone do not adequately capture the real measure of human suffering, direct losses, and missed opportunities.

Other economic impacts were felt as well. Kenya's coffee harvest fell by 10 percent to its lowest level in a decade. Colombia's National Federation of Coffee Growers also had to trim 2 million bags from its harvest forecast of 12 million bags because of El Niño–related droughts.

Some also thought that the El Niño caused the stock market to fall.

Industrial productivity of Indonesia, the Philippines, and Papua New Guinea all suffered significant setbacks. The Philippines ordered additional rice; Papua New Guinea formally requested Food-Aid; and traces of famine appeared in east Indonesia.

Famine affected Asian wildlife, too. The Associated Press reported that the Indonesian drought had caused orangutans to be killed as they attempted to raid village gardens for food when their natural habitat was damaged by El Niño weather. Tigers, also displaced, had mauled four people.

Millions of people all over the globe, from market gardeners in the Far East to wealthy residents of frequently burning—or, alternatively, landsliding—California hillsides, thought they had been mauled by El Niño. And they had. There are lots of bad things about natural disasters, to be sure. But one good thing—depending on your point of view—is this: They do not discriminate on the basis of race, gender, religion, nationality, or wealth.

The Least You Need to Know

➤ The last two El Niños, in 1982–1983 and 1997–1998, were particularly severe, inflicting $10 billion dollars in worldwide damage each.

➤ Developing countries generally are hit harder than more developed ones.

➤ Traditionally terrifying outbreaks of disease—cholera, malaria, and dengue fever—are linked to El Niño.

➤ Many great cataclysmic social and political events are also linked to the privations caused by El Niño.

Chapter 13

They Call the Wind Mariah ...

In This Chapter

➤ The most damaging winds on Earth

➤ Physical and psychological wind damage

➤ Well-named winds of the world

There is a psychology of winds, as well as a physical science; indeed, some of the most significant effects of winds are those visited upon the human body or psyche.

Think about how deeply winds are enmeshed in our thought patterns. Some people fear the winds of change. Others throw caution to the winds. In England, if someone suspects that something not too savory is going on they are often said to "get the wind up." In Ireland, a blessing invokes good living thus: "May the wind be always at your back." We have even named major weather systems for what its winds accomplished: the Trade Winds, for example.

Winds of strength and power have names the world over. And many of them are far less benign than the tuneful Mariah.

How to Make Wind

Through global winds, the wholesale movement of masses of air across the Earth's surface, the planet tries to maintain her thermal equilibrium. Too hot in one place? The global air masses will move colder air toward the spot. Too cold? The opposite happens. That's simplistic, of course, but better than the fairy-tale picture so many of us have of a puffy-faced, bodiless head pursing his lips and blowing out blue and white lines.

What makes those air masses become so individualized that we give them names? Locally, geography and topography give the moving air—the winds—certain characteristics. Because these characteristics, in turn, seem to interact with the local population for good or ill, the locals give them names, just as they name the mountains, rivers, and so on.

Sound the Alarm

If you're looking at a beautiful cloud that has just blossomed up with the incoming wind, but there are dark places at the bottom and a fan of shiny areas spreading out from the top, watch out. It could be a 30,000-foot monster that will drop rain for several hours. Worse, the temperature drop caused by the rain might bestow a tornado along with its fearsome beauty.

The localized wind patterns that acquire names are formed in one of three ways. They can be caused by the following:

➤ Air that is squeezed between two weather systems

➤ Air that moves up or down the slopes of mountains, depending on whether the prevailing winds in the upper atmosphere are coming off the sea (pushing air upslope) or from the land mass behind the mountains (downslope)

➤ Differences in heating between land and water

The Mistral

The Mistral is an example of a wind that occurs as a result of the position of two weather systems. If there's a high-pressure system over northern Europe and a low-pressure system over the central Mediterranean Sea, air will flow from the high (Europe's land mass) toward the low (the sea).

Then the air is squeezed through the Alps, picking up even more cold air and adding to its velocity through the compression until it brings bone-chilling strong winds to the Rhone Valley in southeastern France.

How It Works

Here's the scientific explanation of how the Mistral works:

The Mistral is a cold, northerly wind flowing into the Gulf of Lyon. The winds are most common during winter and spring, although gale-force events can occur year-round.

The Mistral is characterized by the sinking of cold air generated over the mountains and then funneled through the Garone Valley between the Pyrenees and the Massif Central, and through the Rhone Valley farther east between the Massif Central and the Alps. In the winter, wind speeds can reach more than 100 *knots* off the southern coast of France, posing a shipping hazard. Gale-force winds extend into the western and central Mediterranean, creating high seas throughout the region, especially blowing through the Strait of Bonifacio between the islands of Corsica and Sardinia.

Earthy Language

A **knot** is a rate of speed indicating a ship's movement over one nautical mile, or 6,076.10 feet.

The Mistral is considered the most dangerous of all Mediterranean winds because of its high speeds and persistence. It can kick up windstorms at any time during the year, even in the summer, because of the relatively cold Alps it blows through.

And then there's the effect on humans and their lives, according to Peter Mayle, author of three books about southern France, *A Year in Provence, Toujours Provence,* and *Encore Provence.* Mayle was quoted by Salon.com on March 25, 1997, in a section he called "Undisciplined Weather":

> Provence has been accurately described as a cold country with more than its fair share of sunshine, and the climate can't seem to make up its mind whether to imitate Alaska or the Sahara. There were days during our first winter when the temperature fell to 15° Fahrenheit; in summer, it can stay at 85°F-plus for week after rainless week. The local zephyr is the mistral, which has been known to blow at 110 miles an hour, taking hats, spectacles, roof tiles, open shutters, old ladies, and small unsecured animals with it. And there are storms of quite spectacular violence. It is the meteorological equivalent of a meal consisting of curry and ice cream.

Sailor Take Warning

The U.S. military is a bit less prosaic when describing climatic conditions in Mistral Country, which it does because U.S. ships use French ports. Indeed, the ships need safe harbor in the Mediterranean, often whipped up by the Mistral and its platoon of cousins, whom we will meet later.

Read over this material from a U.S. military weather alert:

Hazardous conditions, autumn:

➤ The autumn season is brief, usually lasting only for the month of October, and is characterized by an abrupt change to winter-type weather.

➤ Northwesterly winds become more dominant as Mistral frequency increases.

➤ Southwesterly winds also become more common during autumn as the extratropical storm track moves southward to the northern Mediterranean Basin.

➤ Average precipitation amount is the highest of the year, with 3 inches the average fall for the month.

Research Findings

When is the Mistral most unwelcome in France? During a soccer match, of course. On Friday, June 12, 1998, it was reported that violent winds, gusting at up to 120 kilometers per hour, were causing havoc in Marseilles ahead of Friday night's Group C match between France and South Africa. *Alors!*

The report goes on to mention that gale-force winds are not uncommon, and that Mistral events are strongest and most common during February to April, with a gradual decrease after that. Records for Toulon for the years 1951–1980 show that a maximum velocity of 105 knots was attained in January 1951.

The military meteorologists also worry about the southeasterly winds, a great problem for the port. These winds, sometimes called "Soufflet Noir" (Black Wind) by local residents because they are associated with dark, cloudy skies and rain, reach 41–47 knots and can be accompanied by 16-foot waves at the anchorage. That's not, one would surmise, a good place for anyone prone to seasickness to put to sea.

The Chinook

The Chinook winds of Canada and the upper Rockies in the United States are downslope winds: Chinooks blow down the eastern slope of the Rockies and, amazingly, are warm winds. The Chinook's name in native Indian language, "snow eater," says it all. Its warmth melts the white stuff. Here's how the Chinook winds work:

Warm, moist Pacific air meets the Coastal Mountains range and begins an upward ascent over the western slope of the mountains. As it climbs, the air begins to expand and cool. Some of the moisture in the air condenses and falls to the ground as rain or snow. As the precipitation falls, great amounts of stored heat are released. The air that descends the eastern slope of the mountain is drier and warmer, warming at a rate that is twice the cooling rate.

As the air moves eastward, it encounters a second set of mountains in British Columbia's interior. This process repeats a second time at this mountain range, so more water has been wrung from the Pacific air. Still warmer air approaches Alberta.

As the air approaches Canada's Rocky Mountains, the process begins a third time. The compression of the air by the mountains raises the temperature by 46.40°F to 50°F over the Pacific air that started out over the ocean, at the same elevation on the west side of the Coastal Mountains.

Research Findings

In January 2000, the American Academy of Neurology proposed that migraine headaches may be caused by Chinooks. A study showed a definite correlation between Chinooks and migraines in some sufferers, said neurologist and study author Werner Becker, M.D., of the University of Calgary. "Previous studies on various weather triggers for migraines show conflicting results," he says. "Chinooks are ideal for studying a link between a weather change and migraine because they have a definite time of onset and are a profound weather change."

The Santa Ana

Another example of downslope airflow is the Santa Ana. It's a warm wind, too. But it's definitely a bigger headache than the Chinook (except, perhaps, when the Chinooks cause avalanches).

Santa Ana winds are named after the city of Santa Ana, southeast of Los Angeles. These winds are common during the fall and are the result of air moving across the Mojave Desert and then over and through passes in the San Gabriel, San Bernardino, and San Jacinto Mountains.

How They Form

How do these devil winds form? When offshore breezes blow—when pressure is higher over land than ocean—the wind is forced through the narrow canyons of the coast and increases in speed. As the air goes through those gaps, wind speeds may reach 50 miles per hour in spots.

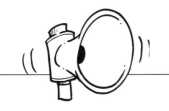

Sound the Alarm

When a Santa Ana fire starts, that's not the worst of it. It feeds off thermal winds produced by the fire itself. Between the Santa Ana and the added thermal winds, Santa Ana fires are tough to contain and can blister everything in their path in a matter of minutes.

The high pressure generally hangs over the Great Basin, the high plateau east of the Sierra Mountains and west of the Rocky Mountains that includes most of Nevada and Utah. Clockwise circulation around the center of this high-pressure area forces air downslope—that is, toward the Great Plains to the east—from the high plateau. The air warms as it descends toward the California coast at the rate of 5°F per 1,000 feet due to compressional heating. Thus, compressional heating provides the primary source of warming. The air is dry because it originated in the desert, and it dries out even more as it is heated.

Frequently, the strongest winds in the basin occur during the night and morning hours due to the absence of a sea breeze. The sea breeze that typically blows onshore daily can moderate the Santa Ana winds during the late morning and afternoon hours.

After a Santa Ana has whipped California for a few days, trees and ground cover are all dried out and even weakened by the wind gusts that reach more than 70 miles per hour. A single bolt of lightning or a careless spark or match acts as a flame-thrower on the new "tinder" the winds have made. The winds are most prevalent between October and February, and often reach speeds of up to 100 miles per hour.

Photo Opportunities, with Teeth

So exactly what sort of havoc can these winds wreak? According to news reports, here's what just one day of Santa Ana winds did in December 1998:

➤ Whipped up dust storms that caused flight cancellations at area airports.

➤ Touched off fires in Glendale, in the hills above Glendale, and in Newport Beach.

➤ Downed power lines and caused power outages; sparks touched off a 10-acre brushfire in Orange County.

➤ Dumped a dust storm on Palm Springs.

➤ Blew boards off an overpass under construction on Interstate 15 in Fontana, closing northbound lanes.

➤ Caused a dozen school closures.

➤ Put motorists in mortal danger; they had to dodge flying debris, including objects the size of trash can lids on the Pacific Coast Highway.

Other Winds

Whether because the name has been adopted by hundreds of French restaurants, or simply because it comes from France, the Mistral is regarded as the most romantic of the winds, even for all its unsettling furies. And it has cousins: the Sirocco, the Levante, and more.

The Sirocco

The Sirocco is any warm or hot southern wind originating in the hot, dry air over Libya and Egypt. It flows into the south-central Mediterranean basin. Because the air flows northward from the Sahara, it produces hot, dry, dusty conditions in North Africa, resulting in poor visibility and damage to navigational instruments and equipment. By the time it reaches Italy and Greece, it has gathered moisture and clouds, causing fog and rain. It can also produce gale-force winds, which are most common in the spring.

The Etesian

Another Mistral relative is the Etesian wind, a monsoonal wind of summer and early fall, which flows into the Aegean Sea and the eastern Mediterranean. It usually brings clear skies and cool, dry weather, but gale-force Etesians are caused by thermal lows over Turkey. Because they are of long duration, the Etesians produce significant seas along the Egyptian and Israeli coasts. (The Turkish name for this wind is the Meltemi.)

The Levante

The Levante, another Mistral relative, is a warm, east-to-northeast wind that flows through the Alboran Channel and is funneled through the Strait of Gibraltar. Gale-force Levante winds can extend to the eastern Gulf of Cadiz. Three things might cause it: high pressure over central Europe and low pressure over the southwest Mediterranean, high pressure over the Balearic Islands (which localizes the Levante to the Strait itself), or an approaching cold front coming from the west. A gale-force Levante often follows a gale-force Mistral.

The Westerly Winds

The Westerly Winds also flow through the Strait of Gibraltar, but in the opposite direction from the Levante. The Westerly Winds come in two types. The Vendaval is a strong southwesterly that precedes cold fronts advancing from the west. It usually brings thunderstorms and violent squalls. The Poniente are northwesterlies flowing off the southeast coast of Spain and into the Alboran Channel, as well as through the Strait of Gibraltar. Gale-force winds are also typical of these.

The Williwaw

Less romantic, but certainly as interesting a name, at least, is the Williwaw. These are also called the Alaskan winds. As with most winds, they know no boundaries and are also known as a type of Siberian storm. They are found in Patagonia and off the coast of Tierra del Fuego at the tip of South America, right down into the Falkland Islands, where at least the sheep in their woolly coats have some protection. The Williwaw are known to blow at more than 68 miles per hour. Other names for this wind, depending on where in its path you live, are Knik, Matanuska, Pruga, Stikine, Takn, Take, and Turnagain.

The Boras

The Boras are another set of cold winds. The Adriatic Bora flows through mountain passages into the Adriatic Ocean east of Italy. Stormy weather, with winds reaching 62 miles per hour, come with it, and the gales can extend well out to sea. The Adriatic Bora also can be produced when high pressure over the Balkans interacts with a low in the Ionian Sea. These, funneled through the Strait of Otranto, can produce storm-force northerlies and associated high seas.

Earthy Language

The **Beaufort scale** is a way to describe the conditions of the oceans. It was devised by British Rear–Admiral Sir Francis Beaufort in 1805 and was based on observations of the effects of the wind. Each observation was given a number and a description. For example, a 1 means that the wind speed is less than 1 knot and that the sea is like a mirror. An 8 means near–gale force; the sea heaps up and creates white foam from breaking waves. Wind is at 28 to 33 knots.

The Aegean Bora flows from the Balkans Peninsula and the mountains of western Turkey, through the Vardar and Dardenelles gaps, and finally into the Aegean Sea. The flow is confined to the Aegean Sea by the Rhodope mountain range to the north of the Aegean Sea, the Boz Daglar to the east, and the Pindus mountains to the west. As the flow moves south, it is channeled, and its direction changes to a northwesterly flow. The gale-force Bora–Aegean Sea can also be produced when high pressure over the Balkans interacts with a low moving across Crete, south of the Aegean Sea.

The Tramontana

Another cold wind is the Tramontana, also known as Garigliano; it brings cold air from the Alps and the northern Apennines to the west coast of Italy and northern Corsica. It reaches as high as Force 8 on the *Beaufort scale* (about 40 knots) and is strongest just before sunrise. It may ease off to 20 knots through the afternoon.

Long-Winded Planet

No population is without its favorite nasty, aptly named wind. Here are a few more:

➤ The Haboob is a wind found in Arizona. Occurring from late April until September, it is really a dust storm moving at speeds above 50 miles per hour and producing a dust wall, a lens-shaped atmospheric structure reaching a height of more than 3,000 feet. The Haboob can also be enjoyed in the Sudan and Egypt from May until September.

➤ The Australian Brickfielder is the same thing as an Argentine Zonda. It is caused by movement of tropical air from the north, brings temperatures above 100°F, and produces clouds of dust.

➤ The Auster is a southerly wind blowing over western and central Europe. Usually it is hot, dry air from North Africa. As it moves over the Mediterranean, it collects moisture and becomes unstable. This wind causes heat waves and hazy conditions, with thunderstorms and often dirty, dusty rain. It happens in spring and fall, when the Sahara is very hot.

➤ The Kharifs are local land winds that occur in June, July, and August in the Gulf of Aden. The winds are worse at night, reaching gale force, and are always full of dust and sand. They can reach up to 30 miles off the African coast.

➤ The Kona is a wind found in Hawaii, usually during January and February, that brings rain.

➤ Papagayos, also called Nortes, happen off the Pacific coast of Mexico. These strong, clear winds, intensifications of the Trade Winds of the Caribbean, are strong and clear and can be felt almost to the equator and Galapagos.

➤ The Solano (also called Leveccio and Leveche) is a hot, dry wind that blows from the south on the southeast coast of Spain. The people of the area are warned of its approach by the strip of *brow cloud* that approaches on the southern horizon and is highly colored with dust and sand. It generally arrives just before a depression that can bring the usual rain and storms. This wind is often compared to the Sirocco.

➤ The Suhaili is the name of the southeast wind in the Persian Gulf. It is a swift wind and was the name Robin Knox-Johnson chose for the boat he sailed in the first non-stop circumnavigation of the Earth in 1969.

Earthy Language

Brow clouds are also called lenticular clouds. They develop when winds blow from 30 to 40 miles per hour, and sometimes resemble flying saucers in shape. They may sit in a ridge, like an eyebrow, above a row of hills or a geographic ridge.

153

The Least You Need to Know

➤ If you live in southern California, a little chill might be better than too much heat.

➤ Europe also has killer winds, the most famous being the Mistral of France.

➤ If you live in Chinook country (Alberta, Canada, and some parts of the northern U.S. Rockies), you might suffer migraines.

➤ The Mistral makes for good reading about flaky Frenchmen; other winds are prime for prose, too.

Chapter 14

Shear Terror

In This Chapter

➤ Winds that wreck planes

➤ How we detect and forecast them

➤ Dropping like flies: a roster of wind-shear crashes

Lots of airplane passengers dread takeoff and landing, despite basically enjoying the flight itself or arriving at their destination more quickly than taking a train or boat. Is there any reason for their terror, aside from the simple facts that, 1) we all know man was not designed to fly like a bird, and, 2) repeat reason one?

Actually, yes. *Wind shear* poses the greatest danger to aircraft during takeoff and landing, when the plane is close to the ground and has little time or room to maneuver. During landing, the pilot has already reduced engine power and may not have time to increase speed enough to escape a downdraft. During takeoff, an aircraft is near stall speed and thus is very vulnerable to wind shear.

Slam Dunks of the Worst Sort

When you've been in a tornado, you don't really care whether the winds that took your house apart were the swirling movements of the twister, or winds that came out of the accompanying showers and thunderstorms. Those winds are known as downbursts.

When downbursts are concentrated in an area extending 2.5 miles or less, they are known as microbursts. Microburst wind speeds can reach more than 150 miles per hour and have been instrumental in dozens of fatal aircraft accidents. Most commercial pilots are trained to avoid them, and detectors are installed in most airports so that air traffic controllers can redirect airplanes.

Earthy Language

Wind shear refers to a variation in wind speed and/or direction over a short distance. Usually, this is a reference to vertical wind shear.

Two varieties of microbursts exist: "Wet" microbursts form in the humid eastern portion of the United States; "dry" microbursts form out West.

And these twins have kinfolk, too, called derechos.

It Was a Wild and Stormy Night

If it *was* wild and stormy, chances are that you experienced derechos. That's especially true across the Midwest, where windy squall lines of rotten weather reaching for miles do a lot of damage.

Earthy Language

The term **derecho** was coined in the 1880s by Gustavus Hinrichs, director of Iowa's Weather Service. Pronounced "day-ray-cho," it comes from a Spanish word meaning "straight ahead." Hinrichs meant it to contrast with the Spanish word for "turn"—*tornado*.

Derechos form when warm, humid air near the ground meets cool, dry air aloft to create thunderstorm clouds, lightning and thunder, and also strong winds that blast down from the storm.

As the storm front moves, usually to the east, more warm air flows upward, cooling as it rises and condensing into cloud droplets and ice crystals. The droplets and crystals fall, becoming all rain in the warm atmosphere below the clouds.

As this moisture drops out, cooler air from above rushes in and then begins "falling" toward the ground as winds, filling in the hole—with a mighty whoosh— left by the descending rain. Those winds can top 100 miles per hour. The whole shebang—line thunderheads moving like a line of Rockettes, with their "kicks" (the downbursts), and the rain, of course—is a *derecho*.

To qualify as a derecho, a storm must produce winds above 58 miles per hour and spread damage across an area at least 280 miles long. Damage reports will—and must, to obtain the classification—show damage in a straight line.

If you want to hunt one, look across the Midwest and east into the Ohio Valley in late spring and summer. Don't go unless there's very humid weather. You also might check for strong winds aloft, at about 10,000 feet.

Although one observer counted at least 70 bad derechos in the 1980s, one of the most destructive ever happened at the end of that period, on June 19, 1990, in Wichita, Kansas. Winds of at least 116 miles per hour struck Wichita and Sedgwick County, toppling trees, ripping apart small structures, and knocking down more than 1,000 power poles.

Sound the Alarm

It isn't bad enough that derechos are another form of wild, wicked weather. They often will take on the very characteristic Hinrichs meant to distinguish them from, spinning out small tornadoes here and there.

Big Winds and Small Planes: A Bad Combination

A report from NOAA indicates that "strong, concentrated downdrafts from convective showers and thunderstorms [that would be wind shears and derecho winds] have caused a number of commercial passenger jets to crash on attempted takeoffs and landings."

But don't think that just any member of the downdraft family of winds can do the job on an airplane. T. Theodore Fujita, the same man who defined intensity in tornadoes by their effects as observed afterward, defined an aircraft-hazardous microburst as one that extends no more than 2.2 miles over the surface—about a runway length. The NOAA report makes reference to the smaller spatial scale of a microburst converting into tighter wind shear gradients that are experienced in the aircraft as more rapid changes in wind vector, perhaps well in excess of the inertial capabilities of the aircraft.

To Ensure Preservation

If you are piloting a small sailboat or fighting a forest fire, you should know that microbursts can be important to you, too. Small sailboats can be capsized by the suddenly shifting strong winds; fires may change directions when a microburst appears, engulfing the firefighters. For firefighters, then, there is a possible downside to the arrival of otherwise fire-quenching rain.

Say what? In short, the winds are so wild and intense that the aircraft is not engineered and built to withstand them—nor, probably, could the pilots react quickly enough to overcome the buffeting, no matter how well-rested and well-trained they are.

The only defense is a good offense, which, in this case, means flying away. And that means someone has to be able to predict the microbursts and shunt aircraft around them to land on other runways or even in other cities.

Earthy Language

Austrian physicist Christian Andreas Doppler (1803–1853) proved that sound waves from a moving source are compressed or expanded, or that the frequency changes, making sound useful in determining distances to objects on earth. **Radar,** short for radio detection and ranging, first was used to locate enemy aircraft during WWII. When it was noted that radar didn't work in storms, a new kind—**weather radar,** meant to bounce off the storm rather than penetrate it—was invented.

Research Findings

On August 1, 1983, Air Force One landed at Andrews Air Force Base while a microburst was in the process of building. Minutes after the presidential jet landed, winds greater than 120 knots were clocked, with tree damage marking the wind's path. Less than 2.2 nautical miles to the left of this track, winds were negligible.

Taking the Measure of the Wild Weather

Doppler *radar* is a good tool in helping identify the intense, sudden, wind-shifting downdrafts that are the plane wrecking microbursts. But physical, observable factors are also important if more deadly plane disasters, like those discussed later in this chapter, are to be avoided.

Mechanical measurements of air speeds can provide data that suggests that a micro-burst is in the air, too. There is a point in the downdraft at which a horizontal wind flows outward from the point where the downdraft hits the earth. These sharp-impact, high-pressure areas are about half a mile in diameter. These days, they are measured by a grid of sensors.

And then there's the pressure nose. Lasting only a few minutes, these small areas of intense pressure are only about 4.3 miles in diameter. These areas of intensity occur at about the mature phase of the growth of a thunderstorm cell, which is about when rain first reaches the ground. These, too, are mechanically measured on approach paths to airports. For good or ill, better instruments are revealing that these pressure noses often are actually fiercer and tighter than anyone originally thought they were.

Pressure drops also are noted in microbursts. One observer reported a low-pressure ring surrounding a high-pressure nose; no doubt, the juxtaposition of the high and low pressure areas in a very tight weather cell might make it tough to stabilize an aircraft. Another observer noted a pressure drop within a downdraft itself.

To Ensure Preservation

With Doppler radar, meteorologists can now not only see the rain coming before the naked eye can, but they also can see the winds inside the storms. New Doppler weather radar can even track insect swarms and dust particles. More important, it can tell forecasters what the wind is up to where there is no rain. When a tornado develops, the new Doppler radar can see the raindrops going in all directions at once and can help track the path of the twister. So, listen when your TV weatherman makes reference to Doppler radar; he probably "sees" a lot more in the sky than you do.

But the wild weather isn't done yet. Some observers have suggested that a vortex is also in action within the downdraft. Some have suggested that there is downward circulation of air at the center of the downdraft (not just plain downward, mind you, but circular), reinforcing the down-ness of it all, but with a twist. But there's a return updraft on the periphery—more "mutually exclusive" turbulence to contend with.

Egad! Still other observers noted a certain instability in these areas, especially in the areas where they impinge on each other.

So now we have, what? Air rushing down, air rushing outward from the downward-rushing air, contiguous and unstable areas of high and low pressure, and swirling winds that are also unstable. Sure, fly that plane through the atmospheric Cuisinart!

Add a vortex rollup with a precipitation curl (in short, the swirling winds sort of climb back up the outside of the downdraft, bringing pelting rain at you from a couple directions—think big kahuna wave), observed through curling plumes of dust or precipitation spray, and you've got a recipe for a plane crash.

Vortex Rings

Unfortunately, that's still not the end of it. NOAA researchers say there is evidence that several vortex rings—small tornadoes—may organize at the base of a severe downdraft, making the already dangerous downdraft/microbursts/rain twisters more deadly still. The researchers think that may have been the case in the crashes of Eastern Flight 66 and Pan American Flight 759. At the time of each, periodic, separate microbursts were observed several minutes apart.

In the Eastern Flight 66 crash, three microbursts occurred along the landing approach within about nine minutes. In the crash of Pan American Flight 759, two microbursts occurred in approximately the same location within about seven minutes. Delta Flight 191, which crashed at Dallas-Fort Worth, encountered a huge microburst lasting five times longer than the one that destroyed Pan American Flight 759.

Research Findings

You think the expression "pelted by rain" is a sort of poetic way of describing a soaking? Hah! Scientists have found that strong downdrafts convey rain to Earth at a much faster rate than it falls through still air. To be precise, as a downdraft approaches the ground, it loses speed, which sort of parks a heavy load of water to hang in just above the ground— and pelt you in bigger-than-normal drops.

The flight recorder of a commercial airliner that crashed after encountering a microburst on its final approach gives credence to the scenarios. The plane apparently got successfully through the downdraft at about 650 feet above the surface, only to encounter several strong vortices lower than that. Those caused the crash.

Ring of Wind

So, if you find out where the vortex rings are and avoid them, you're safely in the terminal, right?

That's easier said than done. The vortex rings are unstable, with most being short (plus or minus five minutes), although some can last as much as six times longer. In a small downdraft, a short, intense vortex might kill off the downdraft's power in just a few minutes. For larger ones, several vortices might develop, all short but of varied duration, before any dissipation in the storm occurs.

Forecasting Microbursts

Once a plane is in a microburst, chances are that it will be tough to survive. So, the trick is to forecast them.

Experts already know that the two main causes are extremely dry and extremely wet environments. In the wet environments, microbursts are often embedded in heavy rain. A telltale sign in dry environments is the development of cumulus clouds—the fluffy, white ones kids like to see pictures in—with very high bases.

Evaporation in the air below the clouds is capable of producing a microburst (as you recall, the moisture going up, freezing, coming down, and so on), but the area's absolute humidity can produce very heavy rain as well. There may also be hail from the cumulonimbus clouds (appearing after the cumulus). That icefall in itself could enhance the power of the downdraft.

What is an aviation weather forecaster to do? Pray, perhaps. Do an anti-rain dance. Take Valium; aviation forecasting is a stressful job. There is no sure index to estimate ahead of time the potential downdraft strength from surface data. There is no sure way to estimate downdraft strength from Doppler radar—only that it probably exists.

Aviation forecasters must use not only science, then, but also art. They must possess a keen perception of size and distance. They must observe numerous microbursts and then compare what they've seen with the data so that they can judge what they're seeing next time.

Sound the Alarm

Towering thunderstorms with heavy rain are particularly suspect in air safety. Why? They provide a lot of mixed-up air, usually a high "lapse rate" (in short, they change fast and furiously), and plenty of rain, which further cools the area and contributes to even stronger downdrafts. The Dallas-Fort Worth disaster was caused by one of these big, high storms, about 1.6 miles high, producing a monster wind shear.

Earthy Language

Ever hear of a **gustinado?** It's a cute term meteorologists have coined to describe cases in which high-based cumulonimbus clouds producing light rain at the surface raise clouds of blowing dust in the path of an approaching airplane.

161

To Ensure Preservation

It's a good thing that someone provided observational tools and standards for microburst forecasting, because almost nothing goes according to the book. A storm with moderate to heavy rain may produce them just as readily as a storm with light rain. A telltale sign of an embedded microburst is a curved plume of dust ahead of the shower over dry ground. But in wetter conditions, the ground may not have dust to kick up, so the weather observer will have to depend on raindrop spray in a similar pattern.

Twenty Years of Downdraft Air Disasters

Here, from records kept by AirSafe.com, are a few statistics culled from about 20 years of fatal accidents that are, or might be, attributed to wind shear:

➤ **April 27, 1980; Don Muang, Thailand, Thai Airways; 53 aboard, 40 fatalities:** "The aircraft entered a thunderstorm, was caught in a downdraft, and struck the ground 8 nautical miles northeast of Bangkok International Airport. The pilot directed the aircraft into a thunderstorm in an early dissipating stage. The aircraft was severely affected by a downdraft and lost altitude rapidly."

➤ **May 7, 1981; Rio de la Plata, Argentina, Austral Lineas; 32 aboard, 31 fatalities:** "... crashed into a river bed after two missed approaches and while in a holding pattern. Severe turbulence and thunderstorms were occurring in area. Wind shear."

➤ **July 10, 1981; Moerdijk, Netherlands; 17 aboard, 17 fatalities:** "Shortly after takeoff, the aircraft entered an area of severe thunderstorm activity. The aircraft apparently had a catastrophic in-flight structural failure due to severe turbulence because it was seen to emerge from the clouds with one of its wings broken away."

➤ **February 5, 1982; Island of Cheju, South Korea, Military—Republic of South Korea Air Force; 53 aboard, 53 killed:** "... crashed into Mt. Halla while on approach to land in poor weather. Possible microburst."

➤ **July 9, 1982; Kenner, Louisiana, Pan American World Airways; 145 aboard, 145 killed:** "The aircraft crashed during a thunderstorm, 29 seconds after taking off from New Orleans International Airport. The plane reached an altitude of 95 to 150 feet and then began to descend and crashed into trees and houses bursting into flames. Microburst-induced wind shear."

➤ **January 16, 1983; Ankara, Turkey, Turkish Airlines (THY); 67 aboard, 47 fatalities:** "The flight originated in West Germany and stopped in Istanbul before beginning a 40-minute flight to Ankara's Esenboga airport. The aircraft crashed short of the runway in fog, snow, and poor visibility. Wind shear."

➤ **August 2, 1985; Ft. Worth-Dallas, Texas, Delta Air Lines; 163 aboard, 134 fatalities:** "While on a flight from Fort Lauderdale, Florida, to Dallas/Fort Worth, the aircraft crashed while making a landing attempt in thunderstorm activity. The plane touched down 6,000 feet short of the runway and 360 feet to the left of the runway centerline, became airborne again, struck a car (killing the driver), crossed the highway, and crashed into two water tanks. Microburst-induced wind shear. Flight into known adverse weather conditions. Lack of adequate training in avoiding wind shear."

➤ **April 4, 1987; Medan-Polonia, Indonesia, Garuda Indonesia Airlines; 45 aboard, 27 fatalities:** "The aircraft crashed on approach during heavy rain after hitting an antenna. Wind shear."

➤ **February 7, 1994; Charlotte, NC, USAir; 52 aboard, 37 fatalities:** "The aircraft encountered heavy rain and wind shear during approach at about 3.5 miles from the runway. The crew attempted to go around for another landing attempt, but the aircraft could not overcome the wind shear."

What More Can Be Done?

About 500 fatalities and 200 injuries resulted from wind-shear crashes involving at least 26 civil aircraft between 1964 and 1985. Since 1985, wind shear also has caused numerous near-accidents in which aircraft recovered just before ground contact. Since 1993, all U.S. aircraft have had to be equipped with wind shear detection systems.

Three prediction systems can be used, all of which are designed to give pilots at least 10 to 40 seconds of warning. (Less than 10 seconds is not enough time to react effectively; more than 40 is too long. Microbursts can change dramatically in 40 seconds.)

➤ **Microwave radar**—This is meant to pick up "ground clutter" as an airplane descends. It works best in wet rather than dry conditions. NASA's Langley Research Center developed the signal-processing algorithms needed for wind shear detection.

➤ **Doppler LIDAR**—A laser system called Doppler LIDAR (light detecting and ranging) reflects energy from "aerosols" (minute particles) instead of raindrops. This system avoids picking up ground clutter—which may include moving cars and so forth—and so has fewer interfering signals. It does not work well in heavy rain.

➤ **Infrared**—An infrared detector measures temperature changes ahead of the air-plane. Specifically, it monitors the thermal signatures of carbon dioxide to look for cool columns of air, a characteristic of microbursts. This system is less costly and not as complex as the others.

Of course, ground-based radar, the Low-Level Wind-Shear Alert System, has been installed at major U.S. airports. The system uses directional sensors and wind speed sensors, linked to a central computer, so controllers can alert pilots when wind shear is detected. However, it cannot predict the wind shear's approach. The newer Terminal Doppler Weather Radar can, though, and it is now used at most major airports. Still, most experts agree that detection systems on the planes themselves are necessary; not every airport in the world will spring for the cost of the most sophisticated systems available at any moment.

The Least You Need to Know

➤ A derecho is a storm that produces winds above 58 miles per hour and spreads damage across an area at least 280 miles long in a straight line.

➤ A wind shear is any variation in wind speed and/or direction over a short distance.

➤ Once an airplane is in wind shear conditions, the pilot has 10 to 40 seconds to correct the problem.

➤ Some of the worst crashes in history were caused by wind shear.

➤ The dynamics of microbursts, which cause wind shear, make tornadoes look simple.

Part 4

Fire

You know, of course, that it isn't Smoky the Bear. It's Smoky Bear! As if the furry fire-fighter were a real person. First name: Smoky. Last name: Bear.

He's wrong about one thing, though. When he said "Only you can prevent forest fires," he forgot about lightning. And volcanoes. And, believe it or not, meteors. You can't prevent any of those.

You could have prevented the Great London Fire; supposedly, a careless bakery assistant burned that city down. You could have prevented The Triangle Shirtwaist Factory Fire, the one that changed fire laws all over the country; it began in a pile of rags.

Did Mrs. O'Leary's cow get a bad rap? Did Nero fiddle while Rome burned? Douse your curiosity with these incendiary tidbits.

Chapter 15

Lightning: Nature's Firebug

> ## In This Chapter
>
> ➤ How lightning is made
>
> ➤ Where to find it, how to avoid it
>
> ➤ The costs and statistics
>
> ➤ Pyrotechnics plague plants and trees

Few natural phenomena are as exciting and as frightening as lightning. It regularly strikes tall buildings around the world. It regularly strikes just about everywhere; few adults don't know of a close call, either firsthand or in the retelling by a family member, neighbor, or friend.

In fact, there are so many lightning strikes at any given moment that if you could hang the Earth up against a black background, it would be hairy with spikes of electricity.

In the United States alone, an average of 20 million cloud-to-ground flashes have been recorded each year since 1989 by the National Lightning Detection Network. Covering all the continental United States, the network became operational in the 1970s. Magnetic sensors detect the massive electrical discharge whenever lightning hits the ground. A computer network then locates the strikes on national maps so that meteorologists can track thunderstorms.

Between 1940 and 1991, lightning killed 8,316 people in the United States. Today, the average number of lightning-related deaths in the United States is 85 a year; many more people are injured.

Chances Are, if You Wear Those Silly Pants ...

What are the chances you'll be struck by lightning? Do you play golf?

Seriously, though, it depends on where you live. In the United Kingdom, your chances are fairly slim; the nation has a low lightning-strike ratio: only .2 deaths per million people. The United States is fairly strike-intensive, with .6 deaths per million. But even so, South Africa, at 1.5 per million, beats us; Singapore, the lightning capital of the Earth, also boasts 1.7 deaths per million per year.

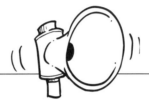

Sound the Alarm

Fame won't render you immune from Mother Nature's tantrums. Golfer Lee Trevino found that out on June 27, 1975, the hard way. He and another player, Jerry Heard, decided to sit out a rainstorm in Chicago by sitting on their golf bags at the edge of the lake on the course. They got hit. Two weeks later, they were all right, but Trevino probably thought that his heart had stopped at the time of the strike.

Research Findings

Roy Sullivan, a forest ranger in Virginia, was listed in the *Guinness Book of World Records* for surviving seven lightning strikes. He was first hit in 1942; in that strike, he lost his big toenail. Subsequent strikes burned off his eyebrows, seared his left shoulder, set his hair on fire, struck his legs, injured his ankle, and burned his stomach and chest.

But in this age of high-stakes games of chance, you might want to know how good the odds are that you'll become the ground wire for a bolt from the blue. An analysis of the problem by the Louisville *Courier-Journal* determined that the odds of being struck by lightning in the United States are 1 in 709,260. That's pretty low, but still better than the odds of winning the Kentucky Lottery, which were 1 in 5,245,786. If you'd just like to win something, you'd have a better chance of getting zapped by Mother Nature's high-voltage son.

How to Get Struck

Aside from moving to South Africa or Singapore, here are some other good ways to improve the odds of getting struck:

➤ Use daylight to your advantage: Statistics show that people are struck more often during daylight hours. This is because people spend more time outdoors during daylight hours. That stands to reason—the more you stay outside in daylight, the better your chances of being outside in a storm and getting struck.

➤ Play golf, preferably on a course located in prime lightning country with shelters at great distances. Remember: The metal clubs pointed at the sky help give the lightning a nice target to pull it to the Earth through you.

To Ensure Preservation

If you want to lessen your odds of becoming a lightning statistic, move to the Pacific northwest, which has the least cloud-to-ground lightning in the nation.

➤ Move to the area between Tampa and Orlando, Florida. While the whole state could be called The Lightning Capital of the United States, that section is particularly prone to thunderstorms.

➤ Move to the Rockies. There the updrafts are almost as good at making lightning as the high temperatures and strong sea breezes in Florida.

How does lightning compare to other natural perils for causing deaths in the United States? Here's a table compiled by the National Weather Service in a "not unusual" weather year.

Weather Deaths in 1994

Type of Event	Deaths	Injuries
Flash flood	33	139
River flood	32	14
Lightning	69	484
Tornado	69	1,067
Hurricane	9	45
Extreme temperatures	81	298
Winter weather	31	2,690
Thunderstorm wind	17	315
Other high wind	12	61
Fog	3	99
Other	6	59
Totals	388	5,165

Looking at the totals for 51 years paints a much bleaker picture for lightning. Here are figures the National Weather Service developed in 1992 for typical U.S. natural events.

Year	Lightning	Tornado	Flood	Hurricane
1940–1949	337	154	144	22
1950–1959	184	135	79	87
1960–1969	133	94	121	59
1970–1979	98	99	182	21
1980–1989	72	52	110	12
1990–1991	73	46	102	8
Total	8,316	5,731	5,828	2,031

Lightning-death statistics abound, and experts differ on how many Americans die from lightning each year. Lightning injury/death expert Dr. Mary Ann Cooper (who is also an associate professor of emergency medicine at the University of Illinois-Chicago) says that as many as 300 Americans are killed by lightning each year. The National Oceanic and Atmospheric Administration puts the figure at a more conservative 106. The National Safety Council gives an average of 100, the National Center for Health Statistics says it averages 80, and the National Climatic Data Center brings the total way down to 41 (perhaps not wanting to believe that our climate is capable of greater carnage).

However many deaths you want to attribute to lightning, it's certain that it does kill. But what causes lightning in the first place?

Bolts from the Blue

Lightning comes from cumulonimbus clouds, thunderstorm clouds that are formed wherever there is enough upward motion of air and moisture to produce a large, tall cloud that reaches up to about 15,000 to 25,000 feet above sea level. The raindrops at that height are converted to ice. In the mixed water and ice area, a lightning flash originates, although scientists cannot agree on exactly why that happens.

The electrical charge itself—the lightning—then moves downward in 50-yard sections called step leaders. It keeps moving toward the ground in these steps, producing a channel along which charge is deposited. Eventually, the charge encounters something on the ground that is a good connection (a tree, the top of the Empire State building, a golf club swinging skyward, and so on). The circuit is complete at that time,

Research Findings

Although no one expects to be able to harness lightning for electrical power, the average flash could light a 100-watt bulb for longer than three months.

and—zap!—the electrical connection from sky to Earth is cracklingly completed. All this is accomplished in a half-second or less.

Of course, because the average thunderstorm lasts half an hour, that's lots of time for lots of charges to make their trip to Earth. Worse, there are nearly 1,800 thunderstorms worldwide at any moment, or about 16 million a year.

Cloud-to-ground lightning can kill or injure people directly or indirectly. The lightning current can branch off to a person from a tree, fence, pole, golf club, or other tall object. Worse yet, flashes may conduct their current through the ground to a person after the flash strikes a nearby tree, antenna, or other tall object.

Sound the Alarm

Who is at greatest risk for lightning strikes? Children and young men (ages 10–35) out playing or working make up 85 percent of lightning victims.

Earthy Language

Not all electrical charges reach the ground. Those that remain in the clouds are called **cloud flashes.** They may happen totally within a cloud, traveling from one part of the cloud to another. Or, they may travel from cloud to air. As a small consolation, cloud flashes outnumber cloud-to-ground flashes by about 5 or 10 to 1. If you're in an airplane within a storm cell, though, that may not be comforting news.

Close Encounters

As I said, most of us have some real-life lightning-strike stories to tell. I have two.

The first, which happened when I was about 9, convinced my mother that any time she heard a storm forecast, we should go to the movies. (I saw many movies as a kid growing up on Eastern Long Island!)

My mother had always been nervous about storms; if my father was working late, she generally asked our neighbor to come over and keep her company. The neighbor wasn't terrified of storms at all and left the front door open during a downpour with lightning. Lo and behold, a bolt came through the screen, zipped by the chair the neighbor was sitting in, and disappeared down a heating grate across the room.

Research Findings

The majority of those struck by lightning live through it, though very few recall the event; the electrical event disrupts circuits in the brain, too. Some people even live better after being struck than before; there are cases of blind people regaining their sight as the result of a lightning strike.

So, I saw approximately every single movie showing, except the R-rated ones, for the rest of my childhood. Dad worked late a lot. We didn't want to hear it, but Mom reminded us that she had been right all along: She wasn't paranoid. One should keep all openings to the house closed during a thunderstorm. (That's what FEMA, the Red Cross, and everyone else recommends, too. Okay, Mom?)

The second lightning strike I witnessed actually did some damage—slight, but real. A friend of mine went into a field to bring her horse in just as a storm sprang up. The field, however, was already soaked—it was a quick, drenching rain. She attached the lead rope by its metal clip to the halter. Just then, lightning struck the ground nearby, or maybe first a big tree not far away at the field's edge. The electrical current traveled across the puddly ground and zapped the horse, who reared and ran, knocking the rider to the ground. She got up, dazed, caught the horse, and came inside. The horse was never the same.

The current also may travel through power or telephone lines, or plumbing pipes to a person who is in contact with an electric appliance, telephone, or plumbing fixture. When objects are struck, the current doesn't necessarily exit and seek yet another victim. Sometimes the object itself will burn or explode.

Striking It Poor

Lightning destroys homes, sparks massive forest fires, and ruins electrical and communications systems, causing millions of dollars of damage.

Research Findings

Each year in the United States, lightning causes 10,000 forest fires and causes about $100 million in property damage.

The National Fire Protection Association (NFPA) reports that direct annual structural lightning losses to public buildings averaged $138.7 million between 1989–1993. NFPA got its information from the nation's fire chiefs, who reported 20,000 lightning-caused residential fires during that period.

Other organizations turn in equally chilling figures. An analysis of lightning claims in Utah, Wyoming, and Colorado in 1995 revealed 307,000 separate claims totaling $332 million. Another source, the Insurance Information Institute, believes that national lightning damage equals about 5 percent of all paid insurance claims, with residential claims maxing out at more than $1 billion in 1990 alone.

Commercial claims costs are higher. Even without lost work time and lost production factored in, the Factory Mutual System reported 2,926 lightning claims between 1973 and 1982, for a total cost of about $385 million. Claims averaged $13,000 each.

Burning Down the House ... of Badgers, Bears, and Bobcats

All that is small potatoes next to the huge conflagrations lightning starts in the forests. In Alaska and the western United States more than 15,000 forest fires in a single decade were started by lightning strikes. More than two million acres were lost, at a cost of several hundred million dollars each year.

Misty Oregon's Baptism by Fire

On August 6, 1999, the Associated Press reported more than a dozen fires in central Oregon, all caused by lightning.

➤ One 350-acre fire burned on private land north of Clarno, Oregon, but didn't threaten homes. Because it was on the John Day River, firefighters also cleaned up the perimeter to control pollution.

➤ A 216-acre fire burned near Santiam Pass, producing such huge volumes of smoke that residents of Redmond thought the fire was closer than it was.

➤ Rugged terrain hampered efforts to douse 10 other fires, ranging in size from a quarter acre to 1 acre, burning along the Crooked River.

Judy Wing of the U.S. Forest Service told the Associated Press that more than 30 small fires broke out: "In most cases, a tree got hit by lightning, blew up, and may have started a little fire," she said.

But trees were not the only things burned in the series of thunderstorms. Two bolts, coming 20 seconds apart, struck KBNC, KTWS, and KLRR radio stations. Computer systems and satellite receivers were damaged. The stations' general managers reportedly said that the whole building sizzled.

Saving Yogi Bear's Home

In August 1994, *Yellowstone Journal* carried a long article about the aftermath of the summer of 1988, a summer unlike any in the park's history. As writer Shelli Johnson wrote:

> Lightning struck. Fires sparked. Persistent winds blew, fanning the blazes into infernos through August and September. These winds were so high they pushed fires at a rate of 2 miles per hour; advances of 5–10 miles in a day were common

To Ensure Preservation

You don't want to even be near something that is struck by lightning; the air near the strike is heated to 50,000° Fahrenheit, hotter than the surface of the sun.

To Ensure Preservation

Area communities were concerned that the fires would diminish tourism in the coming seasons and that their livelihoods would be adversely affected. In fact, there was an increase in tourism as visitors sought to see for themselves the effect of the fires on the park.

for some blazes. One fire traveled 14 miles in just three hours. Smoke swelled 10 miles into the air, leaving the park in an eerie, mysterious pall.

On June 23, lightning struck at Shoshone at Yellowstone's lower end, and from then until the first snow in the fall, fires consumed some part of the park every day.

At least 1,000 miles of fire line were built. Thousands of firefighters (9,500, to be precise) and military units pitched in. There were spotter planes and aerial tankers—117 aircraft in all, plus 100 fire engines from all over the nation. In short, Yellowstone had the largest forest fire fight in its history on its hands. And it cost $120 million.

Still, the fires scorched almost a million acres in the park and 400,000 more outside its boundaries.

In the summer of 1988, lightning started 49 of the fires. Fourteen burned themselves out. Twenty-four were contained or suppressed, and 11 natural starts burned together.

Despite the great economic cost and danger to humans, the fires were less problematical to wildlife. Some small animals didn't escape, of course. But others can run for cover, especially those that can seek shelter in burrows underground. Large animals—elk, deer, bear, and bison—usually simply walk away from the flames. Johnson reported that elk could be seen grazing during the 1988 fires while blazes consumed forest just beyond them.

Some fatalities of large animals occurred, though: In 1988, 5 bison, about 245 elk, 1 black bear, 2 moose, and 4 deer died. The grizzlies felt little impact, except perhaps some short-term food shortages.

Zap-Protection Maneuvers

Unless you're a grizzly bear, it would be wise to know how to stay safe when lightning threatens.

Despite the great personal and economic effects of lightning, neither FEMA nor the Occupational Safety and Health Agency (OSHA) offers much in the way of personal lightning hazard education, standards, or training.

Here's a checklist, gathered from various sources:

➤ When you're outdoors in spring, summer, and fall (although there can be lightning even in winter in northern climates), know where safe shelter is located; if you see a storm approaching, head for it fast.

➤ The safest shelter is a building that is lived or worked in. A very unsafe one is a building without any plumbing or wiring—in other words, no grounding.

➤ A vehicle is better than nothing, but most experts say it's not much better. Don't touch the metal parts, particularly, during the storm. And don't think that a convertible will do it—it must be a hard-topped car with the windows closed.

➤ Don't take shelter under small sheds or isolated trees.

➤ Get out of boats and away from water.

➤ If there's no shelter around, find a low spot away from trees, fences, and poles. Lie down, as long as the area isn't subject to flooding.

➤ If you're in the woods, find shelter under the shortest trees you can find.

➤ Unplug appliances not needed for obtaining weather information.

➤ Avoid using the telephone or electrical appliances. (Use the telephone only in an emergency, and don't yak.)

➤ Do not take a shower or a bath, or even wash your hair in the sink.

To Ensure Preservation

About half of all flashes strike ground at more than one point, for a total of at least 30 million contacts on the ground each year in the United States.

➤ Turn off air conditioners. Aside from the danger of the appliance conducting a strike to you, at the very least, a power surge related to the storm can overload its compressors and cost you money to fix it.

➤ Get to higher ground if flooding or flash flooding is possible. But don't drive through flooding; most flash flood deaths happen in automobiles.

➤ Go to the movies whenever the weatherman says there might be thunderstorms and you're home alone with the kids. Make it a double feature if the forecast is early so that you won't get out before the storms have actually passed. (Don't take this one seriously; my mother did that, and I'm still a movie addict to prove it.)

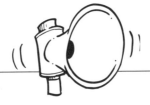

Sound the Alarm

No matter where you are, if you feel your skin tingle or your hair stand on end, squat low to the ground on the balls of your feet. Place your hands on your knees, with your head between them. Make yourself the smallest target possible, and minimize your contact with the ground.

NOAA weather radio is the best way to get warnings about approaching lightning storms in the United States. The National Weather Service broadcasts updates continuously, and those can be heard on NOAA weather radios, which are sold already tuned to NOAA. You can even get them with a tone alert that goes off if a watch or warning is issued in your listening area.

The Least You Need to Know

➤ Singapore is the lightning capital of the world; Florida is the lightning capital of the United States.

➤ Lightning is a lot more common than you might have imagined.

➤ While lightning kills, many people do survive a strike.

➤ Lightning is incredibly expensive in terms of insurance claims for homes and businesses it damages.

➤ Forest fires begun by lightning are frequent and fearsome, not to mention costly.

➤ You can take steps to avoid being struck, even in lightning country.

Man-Made Misery

When you think of ghost towns, you probably think of the American West. Long, dusty streets with vacant saloon fronts looking less menacing than in their heyday. The broken windows of the general store. The caved-in plank sidewalks. And somewhere, in mankind's memory, Liberty Valance shooting it out for the final time with a boy-faced sheriff who unaccountably marks "Paid" to the bad account of a major desperado.

Well, you can think that. But put some coal into it. Ghost towns often began as boom towns surrounding some mining venture, from glittering gold to humble, useful coal.

The Centralia Story

This is a story about coal—and more particularly about the coal belt most people think of when they think about coal, Pennsylvania. It's about the tiny town of Centralia and its sad story as a human disaster of staggering proportions (not to mention stupidity), but one that has been repeated all over "Pennsyltucky" and other areas as well.

The "You Gotta Be Kidding" Department

People who drive regularly on Route 81 through Pennsylvania have known about it for years—the problem of the burning earth beneath Scranton. Smoke often pours over the roadway as one approaches that aging industrial city. But the smoke isn't from Scranton; it's from Centralia, a tiny town about 7 miles west of Scranton.

If you were to go to Centralia today, this is what you'd find:

➤ Route 61 into town possibly closed. It was closed for years, reopened in 1999, but might close again depending on the state of the underground fires.

➤ Signs that say pleasant, inviting things, such as "Gases considered dangerous. Proceed at own risk."

➤ Heat-buckled roadways—in the dead of winter.

➤ Stands of maples that look like birches; the rising sulfuric gases bleached them.

➤ Petrified log piles, mostly white and bleached.

➤ Piles of scorched trees, burned up by flames from below, toppled and rotting on the smoke-swept hillsides.

➤ Hillsides pockmarked with vents for rising smoke and gases.

➤ Hillsides scattered with man-made pipe vents for more steam and gases—explosion prevention 101.

➤ A few remaining row houses, usually unattached to the ones they once held sway with—because some of the abandoned ones swayed so much, the state took them down.

➤ Sudden appearances, out of the ground, of exposed flames, with black coal (anthracite—the good, hard stuff that burns a long time) exposed around it.

Dante imagining his *Inferno* couldn't have created a more frightful setting than that created in Centralia, Pennsylvania, by the simple act of burning trash—back in 1961—on the face of an old open-pit coal mine. Gas venting from beneath the surface ignited and carried the fire to the Buck Mountain coal vein.

One observer found it unnerving to see flames shooting up over tombstones in the old cemetery when he visited the town early into the big burn. He didn't much care for the air quality, but that visual really got to him.

Earthy Language

Pennsyltucky is an area that includes Pennsylvania and Kentucky. They share some features: karst topography and coal underground. But also sharing in the nom de travail are West Virginia (coal), southwest Virginia (coal), and even parts of western New York State (coal) and eastern Ohio (coal, proximity, similarity of culture, history, and so on).

How Long Can This Go On?

Holy smoke, Batman! Could anyone be so dopey as to burn trash on an old coal seam? The trash man displaced 2,200 people, give or take. The trash man spent $40 million of the state's money, give or take. The trash man set a goodly part of the state of Pennsylvania on fire from below—if not permanently, then at least for several generations.

To date, the fire has ruined only about 500 acres. If it took 40 years to do that, how long might it be before the 3,000 acres that overlay the seam in question are burned? Do the math: divide 3,000 by 500. Answer: 6. Multiply 6 by 40. Yup. It will be 240 years before a huge hunk of William Penn's historic grant is safe for human habitation again. And that's assuming that the Department of Environmental Protection (DEP) is right, and that the fire will stop when the seam outcrops—that is, rises above ground. And that's only if it hasn't already started an adjacent or intersecting seam on fire, somewhere deeper in the earth.

The Centralia disaster easily could have begun offshoot fires; combustion of anthracite happens at 752°F. If enough oxygen is present (and the area is laced with the shafts of old mines bringing oxygen in), fire can accelerate through anthracite at temperatures as cool as 176°F, not even the boiling point for water. In March 1996, the DEP measured underground temperatures ranging from 617°F to 772°F, and that's just the acreage near the houses the few residents still lived in. Normal underground temperatures range between 55°F and 60°F. What, then, are the chances that the Centralia fire hasn't started other coal seams aglow?

To Ensure Preservation

On May 3, 1998, reporter Lynne Glover profiled Lanna Mervine, one of only 42 residents remaining in Centralia, Pennsylvania, at the time. Glover quoted Mervine as saying, "It's nicer now than it ever was .... It's like a big park." Possibly she meant Jurassic Park, with the flames bursting out of the earth; huge sinkholes sucking down homes, trees, and roadways; and the stench of sulfur permanently tainting the winds. Be careful that your peace and quiet in the coal fields isn't bought at the cost of dangerous gases, deadly fires, and fatal sinkholes.

Staying Put

Despite the constant smoke outside, the toxic fumes coming up through backyard vents and basements, and the streets ripped open by rising heat and flame, 1,300 of the original 2,200 residents still lived in Centralia in 1985. At that time, the Pennsylvania Department of Environmental Protection estimated as many as 350 acres might be sitting on top of burning coal; the total in 1998 was believed to be closer to 450 acres.

In 1985, the federal government bought the homes of anyone who wanted to move; that erased all but about 30 of the original 540 homes and businesses of Centralia.

Earthy Language

Subsidence is the college-educated word for sinkhole. In coal country, subsidence occurs when the weight of the earth over a mined area causes the surface to collapse into the mine. An added attraction in coal-fire country is that the fire is likely to burn away coal pillars left to hold up the mine roofs when the mines were being worked. These days, this means that subsidence is more likely in mined areas than in seams that are burning but had never been mined.

Although a handful of people still live in Centralia, and although the intrepid can still get in for a look—whether Route 61 is open again, or whether they have to park elsewhere and hike—the Pennsylvania DEP staff doesn't go there alone, for safety reasons, they say. But still, they monitor conditions quarterly.

Meanwhile, eminent domain has been exercised, and Lanna Mervine and her husband Lamar don't really own their home anymore. Of course, they don't pay taxes, either. Perhaps they shouldn't, living as they do with the specter of fires, sinkholes, and toxic fumes. In 1998, Lanna's husband said he thought it was something other than smoke, fumes, and *subsidence,* though, that made the government eager to remove them and the few others still in town. Glover reported Lamar Mervine as saying, "There's 40 million tons of coal still under this town, and Centralia Borough still owns the mineral rights. I think (the government) wants to go back and mine it out. The coal companies are probably pushing to get in here."

Seems like a lot of trouble to go to, especially when coal is still abundant all over Pennsyltucky in places where dealing with infernos is not part of the job description.

What's the Bottom Line?

No one knows. Some history, though, is instructive. Here's a partial list of goings-on in and about Centralia:

➤ Between 1962 and 1978, state and federal governments spent $3.3 million on unsuccessful efforts to control the fire.

➤ In 1983, a study estimated that it would cost $663 million to extinguish the fire.

➤ The state stabilized the roadway of Route 61—temporarily—at a cost of half a million dollars. Route 61 had been a vital transportation link until then, according to state reports.

➤ In 1984, the U.S. Congress appropriated $42 million to acquire and relocate businesses and homes affected by the fire's dangers.

➤ Between 1985 and 1992, 545 homes and businesses were acquired and the residents were moved.

➤ In January 1992, the state used condemnation procedures to acquire remaining properties and relocate remaining residents due to increased threat from noxious gases and subsidence.

➤ Property owners filed legal objections to the condemnation.

➤ Route 61 was closed indefinitely due to fire damage.

Sound the Alarm

As sickening as the stench of sulfuric acid is, and as annoying as the smoke can be, the real danger is the production of hydrogen by the underground burns. Production of hydrogen, a highly explosive gas, increases as the temperature of the fire increases. So does the production of deadly carbon monoxide.

Since 1993, the fires have continued to spread; a revised estimate of spending in 1995 dollars rang in at $53 million and counting; the State Supreme Court ruled against the remaining property owners; and, amazingly, Route 61 once again gave access to Centralia in 1999.

Misery Loves Company

Centralia isn't the only town sitting on top of a flame pit. In Youngstown, Pennsylvania, an underground mine has been burning for more than 30 years. It's called the Percy Mine Fire.

The Percy Mine Fire

Unlike the die-hard Centralians, the residents of Youngstown want to leave. They are worried that the fly ash–based substance being used to plug openings to the fire is dangerous to inhale. It has exploded off those openings sometimes, so how good a sealant can it be?

The residents also worry that the fire-fighting foam pumped by the boatloads into the mine has contaminated their water and their soil. They worry that subsidence will break natural gas lines and cause an explosion—if, indeed, the hydrogen produced by the fire doesn't do it first.

The Percy Mine Fire involves about 60 homes, paltry next to the Centralia problem. But the Percy Mine Fire is a lot worse, in terms of human misery, than most of the 45 other fires burning Pennsylvania from the underground up.

To Kill a Fire

In 1984, the federal government spent $2.4 million to excavate 7 acres of land and extinguish part of the Percy Mine Fire. It then installed a clay barrier underground between the remaining fire and the community. In 1999, researchers discovered that the fire had burned around the barrier. Another $2 million was being spent to divert—note, one doesn't hear the term *douse*—the fire again. The goal was to entrap the fire and let it burn itself out. But where does the coal end and just plain dirt begin?

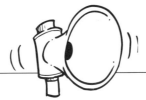

Sound the Alarm

The worst thing you can do is poke a sleeping bear. Apparently, the same is true with a smoldering mine fire. A resident of Youngstown had this reaction when officials uncapped a plugged bore hole to assess what was going on: "When they flipped the lid off of that pipe cap, the heat, stink, smoke, you name it, that came out of that mine fire hole was a shock to us. We were not expecting this. The smell and the sight of it alone is horrible, re-pulsive, like rotten eggs. It scared me."

Then, too, there's the hope that this fire isn't aiming for a college degree; it could burn up to and under Penn State's Fayette campus all in the same vein. Of course, that would alleviate the need for the school's Nittany Lions teams to build bonfires for victory.

Rings of Fire

Pennsylvania has more than 250,000 acres of abandoned mine lands, which also give it more than a third of the nation's mine-related geological problems. Allegheny County alone has five underground mine fires. There's one in Westmoreland County, and four in addition to the Percy fire in Fayette County.

The DEP estimates that the state's coal mining heritage has created a $15 billion problem, with fires, subsidence, and acid drainage to correct. DEP also estimates that about 1,300 acres across the state are burning underground.

Allegheny's Boyce Park is one. This area has a relatively small, slow-moving blaze in a barely used wooded area. A DEP spokesman says, "You really have to look for signs of burning. There's only one small area with smoke venting on the 1.5 acre site. It's not a serious fire, and there are no dwellings, so it is unlikely that people will be overcome by gases …." But it is on public land, so it gets priority treatment.

Here's a list of some other hot spots in the burning mines capital of the nation:

Research Findings

As distressing as mine fires are to us today, they aren't exactly new. Around 1772, a mine fire burned for more than a year at the top of what is now called Mount Washington.

➤ The Renton Mine fire, also in Allegheny County, has been burning for more than 15 years, causing gas problems and carbon monoxide in one house. This is considered an unstable area, but it's not a priority because no homes are atop the fire itself.

➤ Two fires are burning in Findlay Township, one of them just several thousand feet south of the Pittsburgh International Airport runways. A dozen years go, there was concern that smoke could obscure vision on the runways, but no more. Did anyone think of sudden subsidence?

➤ The Tepe Pump Station Mine Fire in West Elizabeth is estimated at 100 acres, although there are no surface effects, due to several hundred feet of earth cover. Potential problem: Two major natural gas lines run close by.

➤ Newell and Vanderbilt, both in Fayette County, are atop mine fires, but they apparently pose no significant threat.

Almost Heaven

It can be hellish in Van, West Virginia, despite its location in the center of the area identified as "almost heaven" by the old John Denver song, "Take Me Home, Country Roads."

It seems there is a coal seam on fire below. At times, the smog is worse in Van than in Los Angeles. But cars aren't making the problem here; it's a noxious mix of carbon monoxide, sulfur dioxide, nitrogen, oxide, and other toxic byproducts of burning fossil fuel. The smog covers the narrow valley where Van nestles on the Pond Fork of Little Coal River like a dirty, smelly rug. At the end of 1999, the 400 residents living there could watch flames leap from the ground every so often.

Sound the Alarm

Coal seam fires create a nasty hazard for firefighters. The burning coal sometimes creates an abyss—a sudden, unmapped subsidence—that swallows firefighters who haven't seen the danger because of layers of fallen leaves and branches that can effectively cover many of them.

"This town is just flanked by these fires on all sides," said Mike Richardson, an engineer with the Abandoned Mine Lands section of the state Division of Environmental Protection, in an Associated Press interview in July 1999. "Every year, Van burns."

Sometimes the fires spread to wooded hillsides, especially in dry weather. Then the local ranger for the State Division of Forestry rounds up volunteers who head for the hills to dig firebreaks. He said it felt as if he were "whipping bears with a switch."

Or maybe a whole den of them. At least 80 recurrent mine fires are burning in southern West Virginia, and they start forest fires more than occasionally.

State officials believe that the origin of the fires in West Virginia is a bit more natural than the fires in Pennsylvania. The origin, they think, is probably the ignition of exposed coal seams (outcrops) by lightning. Those then carry the fire down the seam underground, where they can pop out some other place and start more forest fires, which in turn can start more outcrops burning, ad infinitum.

Luckily for West Virginia, its mine fire problem has not been as costly as Pennsylvania's, partially because most of the fires are in remote areas and pose no threat to homes. So, they simply watch and do very little, unless fire literally breaks out.

Ute Oughta See This

Native Americans are not immune from burning earth, despite a historic reverence for the land. In 1998, the *Durango Herald* reported on an underground coal fire on the Southern Ute Reservation.

Two fires, actually, were burning about 20 feet below the surface of the Fruitland coal outcrop, a ridge of coal between Marvel and the New Mexico border, a tribal scientist said in the article. Methane seepage and underground fires are possible anywhere from the southwest corner of La Plata County, through the city of Durango, and south along the Pine River. The area is sparsely populated because the few homes built on the outcrop have been purchased by mining companies to prevent lawsuits.

Unlike the eastern underground burns, the Ute experience is not horrific. Indeed, the problems might not even be noticed, except by a few Bureau of Land Management people and tribal officials who go there on purpose. The nearest home is five miles away and separated from the fires by a ravine, which probably stops the outcrop.

Tribal officials determined that there was a slight possibility that the fires could cause the ground to collapse nearby, and an even smaller chance of starting a forest fire. The most immediate danger would be of someone inhaling sulfur dioxide gas, which can damage lung tissue.

In fact, it was gas that first alerted the tribe to the fire. Gas company employees were scouting for possible expansion of a mining operation when they noticed air rushing from a crack where a sandstone slab had shifted. Then they noticed some sinkholes where sulfur dioxide gas and smoke were escaping; two miles away, they found more gas and sinkholes.

Tribal geologists said the coal seam fire might be due to coal bed methane mining production. To obtain methane, water is extracted from cracks in the coal. If the water is removed too quickly, faster than precipitation can replace it, the coal could dry out and spontaneously combust.

Another possibility is that a natural cycle in the landscape could have caused this: It is almost certain that a burn several thousand years ago was not caused by methane mining, but by natural forces.

To Ensure Preservation

Environmental problems beyond gassing of people and plants need to be considered when an operation that could result in a coal seam burn is begun. On the Ute reservation, near the Pine River ranches north of Bayfield, several 100-year-old trees died a few months after an oil company (Amoco) began extracting water from a well downstream from the trees to obtain methane.

Fighting Fire with ... What?

Underground fires do not succumb to traditional means of fighting fires. You can't deprive the fire of oxygen; there is no way to find all the natural fissures that might be providing air.

Removing the fire's fuel is next to impossible; it's burning coal, after all. However, you can drill holes for explosives behind the area burning, and then blast the burning coal away from the rest of the seam and push it over the side of the mountain. The easiest method, though, is to strip-mine the mountaintop completely.

The situation in Danbury, Connecticut, illustrates the difficulties in putting out underground fires. In April 1997, thermal imaging of Danbury's 47-acre dump site indicated that there were two anomalies in the areas where there had been known fires before—fires that people thought had been squelched, starved of oxygen, and killed.

The fires began in 1996, and officials took what seemed logical steps at the time to put them out, such as pouring water over them. It didn't work. Then they tried suffocating the fires with earth and clay. It didn't work.

Another option, injecting gas (nitrogen, for example) to force oxygen away from the burning areas and suffocating the fires that way was rejected as being too expensive.

The ultimate plan is to cover the whole thing with nearly impenetrable plastic so that residents of homes in Bethel and Danbury, Connecticut, can breathe the air without turning up their noses. The fires below may delay or prevent such action. But at least they can be glad of one thing: There are no coal seams down below. Probably.

The Least You Need to Know

➤ The fire burning beneath the town of Centralia, Pennsylvania, has been burning since 1961 and probably was started by a trash fire.

➤ Once a coal seam catches fire, it is practically impossible to extinguish the burn.

➤ Underground coal fires create noxious, toxic, and explosive gases as well as ground subsidence.

➤ Coal seam fires have been happening for centuries all over the globe. Many are started by natural causes, such as lightning.

Chapter 17

The Great Fires

In This Chapter

➤ Historic city-razing fires in the United States and Europe

➤ Of cows and meteors

➤ The worst industrial fire in U.S. history

➤ When nightclubbing was hazardous to your health

When people think of great fires, the one that springs most often to mind is the Chicago Fire of 1871. Almost everyone knows that it was a certain Mrs. O'Leary's cow that kicked over a lantern and started the whole thing. It's even mentioned in popular songs. According to recent investigations of the heavens, however, the cow got a bad rap.

Those investigations were not conducted by astrologers looking for some cosmic absolution for the lady and her cow. Rather, they were conducted by astronomers who know what the skies—or, more specifically, the reaches of space—were up to at the time: meteor showers.

And this has what to do with a cow in Chicago? Only this: If one cow had kicked over one lantern, it is unlikely that an organized fire department—and Chicago had one at the time—would be overwhelmed by the task of putting it out, even if the fire had, for example, spread to another house or two when they got there.

So what really did happen? To explain the new theory, it might be helpful to look at another big fire, the Peshtigo Forest Fire. And no, you probably haven't heard of it before.

Peshtigo, Peshtigo, That Wonderful Town ...

The summer and fall of 1871 found Wisconsin very dry. Numerous small forest fires had broken out. But on October 8, at night, it seemed as if all of northeastern Wisconsin burst into flame. The flames wiped out Peshtigo and several smaller villages, and spread into the "thumb" section of Michigan.

By body count alone, the Great Peshtigo Forest Fire ranks as the greatest natural disaster in Wisconsin's history. It killed about 1,200 people, 900 more than the Great Chicago Fire (which, as it happens, occurred the very same night). The Peshtigo blaze also destroyed more than $5 million worth of property.

Raining Fire

Coincidence? Some don't think so. What then? Some think that the fires—all of them—were caused by meteors.

To Ensure Preservation

You needn't worry about the Biela comet or its debris: All that remains today is the annual Andromedid meteor shower in November. That's not to say that a different meteor shower might not appear, of course ....

Think about it. Simultaneous fires are burning in Chicago and Peshtigo. The entire central portion of Michigan, from Lake Michigan to Lake Huron, is also ablaze. Quite spectacular—the more so because, like a movie frame in still mode, all the fires began virtually at the same instant. Very unusual and very unlikely, by any earthly means. Who or what could have set such blazes virtually simultaneously and in a fairly well-defined geographic space? Blazing hot meteors, that's what.

Proofs, Historic and Modern

Researchers say the meteors that rained that night were actually asteroid and comet debris from the Biela comet (named after Wilhelm von Biela), which re-appeared every six years. During its predicted re-appearance in 1872, an intense meteor display, with 15,000 glowing missiles an hour, appeared instead; the comet had disintegrated and mingled its debris with the asteroids that had been trailing it. The meteors did far more than put on an extravagant night-sky entertainment that night. Many of them, researchers say, entered the Earth's atmosphere and started fires in Peshtigo and Chicago, at the very least.

Their evidence is this: The fires created a cone-shaped pattern from the shores of Lake Huron to a line running north to south, from Peshtigo to Chicago. This perfectly mimics the ballistic pattern of a cluster of shotgun pellets, suggesting an asteroid cluster of hundreds or thousands of pieces. To reinforce this belief, there were *no fires at all* west of the north-south trajectory line.

The "thumb" area of Michigan suffered the worst of Michigan's fires in 1871 and again in 1881, which points to a cycle approximating the remains of the Biela post-asteroid-collision cycle.

Eyewitnesses claimed that fires were falling from the sky. And Kate O'Leary absolutely denied that there was any possibility of her cow being milked, in the dark or by lantern, at the time the fire started. Indeed, she and Mr. O'Leary had gone to bed, according to testimony she gave the police.

Recently, a 26.5-kilogram *carbonaceous chondrite* meteor was found on the shores of Lake Huron, ground zero for the assumptive astral bombardment—new physical evidence that suggests the meteor scenario is what happened.

Whether a cow or a comet's remains caused the Chicago conflagration, it was truly horrendous for those caught in it. Dry conditions and strong winds fanned a blaze that started at about 9 P.M. and continued for 27 hours, destroying the downtown and the near north side. It ravaged 17,450 buildings, killed 300 people, left 90,000 homeless, and destroyed property worth $200 million.

Earthy Language

Asteroids containing large amounts of water and complex carbon compounds and nitrogen, sulfur, and other elements—in short, the building blocks of life, as we know it on Earth—are called **carbonaceous chondrites** by scientists.

London Bridge Is Burning Down ...

After the Chicago fire, the second fire many people think of is the Great Fire of London in 1666. In fact, considering how buildings were constructed back then, it's a wonder that the city lasted as long as it did before the biggest burn in its history (it had had serious fires in the years 798, 982, and 1212).

Playing with Fire

Houses in London at the time were built on timber frames filled in with wattle (a woven mesh of oak

Sound the Alarm

Some houses in Great Britain still are made of wattle and daub; some houses in Ireland still are made with thatched roofs. Indeed, thatch is making a comeback, after years of slate and tin, because it is more authentic. However, it is also more flammable.

Research Findings

Something was learned from the fire. Less than two weeks later, King Charles II proclaimed that the walls of all new buildings were to be of brick or stone, that streets were to be widened to prevent spreading of fires so easily, and that fewer alleyways were to be built in the reconstruction than had existed before.

Research Findings

Before the fire, Old St. Paul's already lacked a spire: It had been destroyed by one of two direct lightning hits that had put the church into disrepair in other ways as well.

or willow sticks) and daub (a covering of mud, horse hair, clay, and animal dung mixed together). Roofs were of thatch, and chimneys didn't exist, except in stately homes. Houses were packed together on narrow streets and were heated by a central hearth with smoke going out a hole in the middle of the roof. Floors were covered with straw. A fire would have a field day—and did.

The summer had been an unusually dry one. On September 2, 1666, the fire was started in a baker's shop on Pudding Lane. It was thought that a careless maid had caused it. No matter. The wattle-and-daub houses, packed into narrow lanes, quickly caught fire one after another, feeding on the tar and pitch used to make the building materials waterproof.

A View of the Fire

Samuel Pepys, Secretary of the Admiralty and a stunning diarist, had a view of the fire from his perch across the Thames. It was, he wrote,

> … a most malicious bloody flame, as one entire arch of fire … of above a mile long. It made me weep to see it. The churches, houses, and all on fire and flaming at once, and a horrid noise the flames made, and the cracking of houses at their ruin …. Over the Thames with one's face in the wind you were almost burned with a shower of firedrops.

His angst did not prevent his burying the wine and valuable parmesan cheese he kept in his London house, just in case.

The Great London Fire ate the city like a gourmet meal. From Pudding Lane it leapt to Fish Street Hill. Then it devoured the Star Inn. For its next course, it gobbled the warehouses bursting with oil, tallow, and other combustible goods.

Long before that leap from comestibles to combustibles, leather buckets and water were proving wildly inadequate to douse the flames. Ordinarily, houses for some distance in front of the flames would have been hastily demolished to deprive the fire of fuel. But the mayor forbade it, fearing rebuilding costs.

Then the flames became visible from the aptly named Seething Lane near the Tower of London. At first Pepys was not much concerned. But when it continued another day and night, he went out to see for himself how bad it might be. He later wrote:

> … I rode down to the waterside, … and there saw a lamentable fire …. Everybody endeavouring to remove their goods, and flinging into the river or bringing them into lighters that lay off; poor people staying in their houses as long as till the very fire touched them, and then running into boats, or clambering from one pair of stairs by the waterside to another. And among other things, the poor pigeons, I perceive, were loth to leave their houses, but hovered about the windows and balconies, till they some of them burned their wings and fell down.

To Ensure Preservation

There are often saving graces in great disasters. In the year before the blaze, 75,000 Londoners had died of the Great Plague. In the aftermath of the London fire, the plague declined because the rats whose fleas transmit the disease had been killed or displaced in large numbers. Although the flames took 16 lives or so, they may have saved many thousands.

And still it went on, through September 4 and 5. But on the 5th, the wind abated a bit, and the people began again to try to fight the flames, finally bringing the roaring inferno to an end.

When all was over, the fire had burned for four days and had destroyed five-sixths of the city. More than 13,000 houses had been lost, as well as 89 churches and 52 guild halls. Much of the population had no place to live, no place to pray, and no place to work. Even Old St. Paul's Cathedral, the spiritual center of London, was rubble. But amazingly, only 16 people had died.

The Fiddle Hadn't Yet Been Invented …

The old saying goes that the Emperor Nero fiddled while Rome burned. The fiddle—the violin—had not been invented in 64 C.E., so the fiddling referred to must have been Nero's goofing off.

But did he? Nero was only 26 years old at the time of the fire, having ruled for 10 years. However, he had murdered his mother and his wife and had created a Reign of Terror well beyond the walls of his own household. Fortunately, he would deal himself a similar fate, killing himself in 68 C.E. after the Roman Senate declared him an enemy of the state. Did his implication in or response to the fire have anything to do with that declaration?

The Fire That Roamed Rome

The fire broke out during the night of July 18, 64 C.E., in the merchant section of the city. Dry summer winds—possibly the Sirocco—had fanned the flames for six days and seven nights, springing handily across Rome's wooden roofs. The fire destroyed 70 percent of the city.

Despite the tradition that Nero had ordered the city torched while playing his violin at the summit of the Palatine hill, he apparently actually entered the city the first night of the blaze to help. But he was despised enough that the rumors persisted. To offset them, he looked for a scapegoat or two, and the Christians would prove handy.

The historian Tacitus described the fire in this way:

> First, the fire swept violently over the level spaces. Then it climbed the hills—but returned to ravage the lower ground again. It outstripped every counter-measure. The ancient city's narrow winding streets and irregular blocks encouraged its progress.
>
> Terrified, shrieking women, helpless old and young, people intent on their own safety, people unselfishly supporting invalids or waiting for them, fugitives and lingerers alike—all heightened the confusion. When people looked back, menacing flames sprang up before them or outflanked them. When they escaped to a neighboring quarter, the fire followed—even districts believed remote proved to be involved. Finally, with no idea where or what to flee, they crowded onto the country roads, or lay in the fields. Some who had lost everything—even their food for the day—could have escaped, but preferred to die. So did others, who had failed to rescue their loved ones ....
>
> By the sixth day enormous demolitions had confronted the raging flames with bare ground and open sky, and the fire was finally stamped out at the foot of the Esquiline Hill. But before panic had subsided, or hope revived, flames broke out again in the more open regions of the city. Here there were fewer casualties; but the destruction of temples and pleasure arcades was even worse. This new conflagration caused additional ill-feeling because it started on Tigellinus' estate in the Aemilian district. For people believed that Nero was ambitious to found a new city to be called after himself.
>
> Of Rome's fourteen districts only four remained intact. Three were leveled to the ground. The other seven were reduced to a few scorched and mangled ruins.

From the Ashes

Rome arose from the ashes better than ever, with wide streets, marble structures, and lots of water piped in to douse any future blazes. The fire got rid of the mosquito-breeding marshes around the city, too, putting a lid on the malaria that had vexed the city for years. The fire's debris was used to fill the marshes.

Beantown Burns

A year and a month after the Chicago-Peshtigo conflagrations, Boston had a major disastrous fire of its own. The fire, on November 9, 1872, wiped out 60 acres of downtown Boston—or 65 acres, depending on whose account you read.

Exactly where and how it began is open to discussion. Some say it began in a hoop-skirt factory. Others say it started in the financial district. The fire burned on until November 12. "I saw the fire eating its way straight toward my deposits," Dr. Oliver Wendell Holmes later wrote.

Only extraordinary acts by ordinary citizens saved historical Faneuil Hall. Telegraphed reports of that dire possibility had upset people nationwide.

The reports should have upset Bostonians to the max. Since 1866, the fire chief had been pleading with the city government to install more and better fire hydrants with multiple outlets and to improve the city's water supply. When Chicago burned, the chief, John Stanhope Damrell, was sent to Chicago to report. And he did that: He all but predicted a major fire in Boston, and soon.

Boston, which had grown up higgledy-piggledy, with financial offices, stables, and leather factories all crowding each other for space around the former residences of luminaries such as Daniel Webster, was ripe for a big, bad burn. The city fathers, however, exercised Yankee thrift and decided to forego Damrell's recommended improvements.

The Great Boston Fire leveled 776 buildings, killed 13 people, and caused $500 million worth of damage in today's dollars.

The Triangle Shirtwaist Company Fire

Few factory fires were as horrible as the March 25, 1911, fire at an apparel company in New York City. The Triangle Shirtwaist Company was located in the Asch Building at 23 Washington Place in the old, jam-packed lower end of the island of Manhattan. Like the sinking of the *Titanic*, it was a disaster that wasn't supposed to happen. The 10-story building was built of "fire-resistive" materials. New York had a fine, well-exercised fire department. So what went wrong?

Human intervention, in part. The natural properties of various man-made materials, in part. And plain bad luck.

Research Findings

A TV movie was made about the fire, *The Triangle Factory Fire Scandal*, starring Stephanie Zimbalist, David Dukes, Tovah Feldshuh, and Tom Bosley.

Sound the Alarm

Never get into an elevator when a fire alarm has been sounded.

How It Started

The fire probably started on the eighth floor, in a rag bin containing combustible cloth. That floor and the one above held 500 workers, mainly young women, working in a classic sweatshop.

The hose line inside the building was rotted, and the water valves were corroded shut, so workers had no choice but to head for the exits. One stairwell was cut off by a wall of fire. Another exit was secured by a locked door that workers couldn't open easily. The door opened inwardly. When it finally gave way, crowd behavior took over; so many people were pushing toward it that they jammed it shut. Some young women preferred to leap rather than be burned to death. A few made it to the roof, and some even crawled over ladders to the roof of the New York University Law School next door.

The Horrible Ending

The day after the fire, the *Chicago Tribune* gave this horrific account:

> Women and girl machine operators jumped from the eighth, ninth, and tenth floors in groups of twos and threes into life nets and their bodies spun downward from the high windows of the building so close together that the few nets soon were broken and the firemen and passersby who helped hold them were crushed to the pavement by the rain of falling bodies ....

> The mangled bodies lay there with the spill of the water which the firemen soon were pouring from water towers and hose into the building, soaking them. There was no time to clear away the dead in the street ....

> In the elevator shaft was a pile of bodies estimated conservatively at twenty-five bodies ....

> Inside the building on the three top floors the sights were even more awful. When Fire Chief Croker could make his way into these three floors he saw a tragedy that utterly staggered him ....

> The floors were black with smoke. And then he saw as the smoke drifted away bodies burned to bare bone. There were skeletons bending over sewing machines, the victims having been killed as they worked. Other piles of skeletons lay before every door and elevator shaft where the sufferers fell in their effort to escape ....

The bolts and bolts of fabric helped the fire burn and move quickly. As soon as fire-fighters could maneuver equipment close to the fire—a problem, with so many bodies littering the sidewalks near the building—it was quickly controlled. But in all, 146 died in about 15 minutes.

Law students Charles T. Kremer and Elias Kanter were heroes on that awful day. They found two short ladders and joined them, making a bridge to the Law School roof, one story higher than the roof of the Asch Building. Kremer crossed to the burning building, lined up the women, and sent them up the ladders, where other law students helped pull them to safety. The two, with other law students assisting, saved 150 women, including one who had fainted when her hair caught fire: Kremer and Kanter carried her up the ladder.

Because of the conditions that had permitted the fire, the company's owners were charged with manslaughter but were acquitted. In 1914, they were ordered to pay damages of $75 each to the families of 23 victims who had sued. But the rest of the families got nothing. As a result of the fire, however, New York City established the Bureau of Fire Investigation, and workers in the sweatshops organized the International Ladies' Garment Workers' Union.

Other Deadly Fires

Other deadly fires remind us that this particular type of disaster can strike anywhere, any time.

The Major Slocum Fire

Seven years before the Triangle Fire was the *Major Slocum* disaster.

At 9 A.M. on June 15, 1904, the excursion steamer *Major Slocum* moved away from the 13th Street Pier on the East River with 1,400 men, women, and children on board. Most of the members of St. Mark's Lutheran Church were on it for a floating picnic.

Shortly after the boat left the dock, fire broke out. The hoses the crew members used to attack the fire ruptured. And it turned out that the passenger life preservers were mainly unusable. Lifeboats, lowered improperly, dumped many passengers into the water. Worse, in a vain attempt to return to shore, the captain turned the ship into a stiff breeze, helping it burn all the more quickly. It couldn't get much worse: 1,021 people died, including entire families.

The Ringling Brothers Fire

Toward the end of another sort of conflagration—World War II—7,000 people in Hartford, Connecticut, went to the Ringling Brothers–Barnum & Bailey Circus on the afternoon of July 6, 1944. It was a great day—the circus had gotten to town late but had added a matinee performance so that citizens would not be disappointed. As it turned out, however, it was no favor. The main tent had been waterproofed in the age-old circus way, with paraffin. In this case, the paraffin had been thinned with gasoline.

Sound the Alarm

It doesn't do any good to install fire protection equipment if it isn't used. On September 3, 1934, the cruise ship *Morro Castle*, which had a state-of-the-art fire detection system then, blazed and sank, taking 137 with it. If a fire door had been closed, as it should have been, the fire that began in a vacant locker most likely would have been contained in that room. Investigators noted that it also would have been a good idea to have trained the ship's crew in the use of the fire protection devices on board.

Just before the second act of the program, a passing policeman noticed a small spot of flame. It traversed the tent top, gaining speed as it ate up the fuel-soaked fabric. Despite the early sighting of the fire, there wasn't much hope. The circus's precautions consisted of three tank trucks holding 1,000 gallons and one holding 800. During performances, two circus hands stood by each truck. Buckets should have been strategically placed as well. But on that day, the buckets had been forgotten.

People ran, animals got loose, and burning tent pieces were falling like confetti. When it was over, 168 had died—more than half of them children.

Supper Club Fires

Among the supper club blazes, three in recent memory—three that affected three different generations—were particularly tragic.

The Cocoanut Grove Fire

The first of them, the Cocoanut Grove nightclub fire in Boston, happened on November 28, 1942, and killed 492. The building was overcrowded; meant to hold 600, as many as 1,000 were actually packed in to celebrate after a Boston College football game. When fire broke out in a basement lounge, most nightclubbers knew only of the main stairway, not the fire exits. Many of the dead—as many as 200—were found trampled there.

Accounts by survivors say that a busboy may have been holding a match while changing a light bulb, inadvertently setting an ornamental palm afire. A hodge-podge quickly put together in a former garage, the club was full of flammable materials and false walls to create the illusion of an island paradise. Investigators also suspected that faulty wiring within the club might have been to blame.

In any case, in seconds the flames had flashed across the dance floor and into a passage. A great sheet of flame rushed across the ceiling, followed by tarry smoke. It is likely the smoke was toxic: Some people were found dead at their tables, slumped over their drinks, looking as if they hadn't risen or made any effort to escape.

Disaster in Beverly Hills

In the heat of the disco era, Southgate, Kentucky, boasted a hot supper club, the Beverly Hills, where popular TV personality/singer John Davidson was to perform on May 28, 1977. That night, about 15 minutes into the first show, at 8:45, a fire was discovered in the Zebra Room. Management delayed notifying the fire department while employees attempted to put the fire out with hand-held extinguishers.

To Ensure Preservation

Henry S. Parmalee invented sprinklers in 1874 to protect his piano factory. Not until after the Cocoanut Grove fire, and fires in the LaSalle Hotel in Chicago and the Winecoff in Atlanta, though, were they generally installed anywhere except factories and warehouses. Finally, it became known that buildings with sprinklers had a much better record for lives saved in fires than those without.

The attempt to keep the blaze quiet worked. Many people didn't know about the fire until they saw others leaving. Still, word of mouth moved people out fairly well until thick, dark, choking smoke blanketed exit areas. In all, 164 people died.

The Happy Land Social Club Fire

In 1990, the Happy Land Social Club in the Bronx, New York, was the scene of a fire that killed 87. Fire experts say that nothing had been learned, apparently, since 1942; overcrowding, inadequate exits, and fire protection helped swell the death toll. In this case, though, an arsonist bent on love-triangle revenge helped it along.

The Least You Need to Know

➤ It is unlikely that one barn fire caused the destruction of Chicago without help. It may have been helped by a meteor shower.

➤ The fire in Rome did much damage but destroyed the marshes that spawned recurring malaria outbreaks.

➤ The Great Fire of London killed few and saved many from the plague.

➤ The Triangle Shirtwaist Factory, *Major Slocum*, and Ringling Brothers disasters remind us that fire can get you while you work, sleep, eat, or play.

Part 5

Water

"Water, water everywhere, nor any drop to drink."

That old ditty could have been written for this chapter. Hurricanes disrupt water supplies, despite dumping a good bit of ocean on the landscape one way or another. Floods and flash floods disrupt water supplies, despite dumping rivers and lakes across the landscape. Frozen water—blizzards—can disrupt the water supply. Worse, it can foul things up so much that you can't even melt some of that frozen water and get a drink.

Is it any wonder that droughts are scary in and of themselves?

With Hurricane Force

In the movie *Key Largo*, a masterpiece in black and white, a disabled hotel proprietor (Lionel Barrymore) and his widowed daughter-in-law (Lauren Bacall) play host during a hurricane to a disillusioned World War II veteran (Humphrey Bogart). The hotel is remote, on an island in the string of overgrown mangrove swamps known as the Florida Keys. But not too remote for hurricanes, or for the stormy arrival of a notorious racketeer on the lam (Edward G. Robinson, who else?). The veteran uses his superior wit and prevails over the gangster. The hurricane shoves off. Bacall wins Best Supporting Actress, 1948. And film noir has perhaps one of its finest hours.

When an actual hurricane roars into the Keys, it, too, often walks away with everything in sight: Oscars, Tonys, and other people/dogs/cats/parakeets of every name and type.

In 1935, a hurricane in the Keys provided terror enough to last forever. Like all hurricanes, it formed off the coast of Africa from complexes of ordinary thunderstorms. When the ocean water is warmer than 81°F., and there is a high relative humidity in the lower and mid-levels of the atmosphere, conditions are ripe for hurricanes to develop. If there are also increasingly high winds upward through the atmosphere ... voila, a hurricane. The high humidity means that the thunderclouds will be moisture-laden. The high winds grab them, whipping them ever higher and creating a vortex, the circular appearance and action of a hurricane. If the winds rotate and there's a lot of rain, and there are also sustained winds within the big, cloudy, rainy weather system, it is called a hurricane.

Map showing hurricane activity in the conterminous United States.

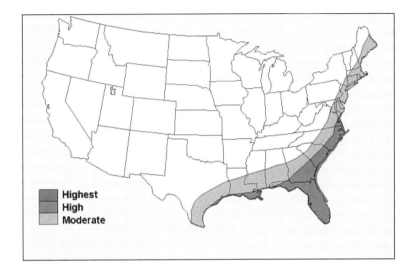

The Labor Day Hurricane

On Labor Day Weekend, 1935, the lowest atmospheric pressure ever recorded in the continental United States—26.35 inches—was posted over the Florida Keys, in the very center of a hurricane. That hurricane joined a small, select group of hurricanes that are remembered to this day even by people who weren't in them.

The "Labor Day Hurricane," as it became known, was also the most severe ever in wind velocity and storm tides. It didn't take the greatest number of lives—the 1900 one in Galveston, Texas, did that. But the lives it took, it took in extreme terror.

A Terrible Beauty—Without the Beauty

In early September 1935, the beautiful Keys turned deadly. The Great Depression was at its deepest point, and the Works Progress Administration had sent hundreds of out-of-work World War I veterans to the middle Keys to help build the road that would complete Highway 1 from Maine to Key West. Matecumbe Key housed most of the workers in flimsy tents and shacks. Not bad, considering the temperature in the Keys is hospitable virtually all year. But tents and shacks make for bad shelter in a hurricane.

In late August, a storm developed in the Bahamas, west of the usual birthplace of hurricanes off the coast of Africa and only a few days from the Keys. It made a beeline for the islands—no skidding around, weakening in an occasional cold area, as other hurricanes might do. Until 30 hours before it struck, it wasn't considered much of a threat, at least to a population that had experienced pretty wicked hurricanes before.

Weather Bureau warnings posted on Sunday, September 1, for south Florida did not even refer to the storm as a hurricane, but rather a tropical disturbance with "shifting gales and probably winds of hurricane force," according to the Weather Channel. The storm struck Andros Island in the Bahamas, but still no one knew how powerful the storm was or would become.

On September 2, that would change. At noon, the WPA camp finally requested a train to evacuate the workers to Miami. The evacuation might have worked, except that red tape held the train up for hours—hours that the storm used to gain speed and water and drop a few millibars of barometric pressure.

Railroad to Hell

When the train finally pulled into the station at the city of Islamorada at 8:20 in the evening, hurricane-force rains and winds were sweeping across Florida Bay. Would-be passengers were clinging to anything they could find to survive the 200 mile per hour winds. Some crawled to the train; it was impossible to stand without holding tight to something very solid—and there wasn't much that was solid to begin with in the Keys back then. Without even substantial cement-block housing to stand in its way, the beach pelted the evacuees with sand, scouring them until they bled and rinsing them with wind-blown brine.

Research Findings

In 1968–1969, when I worked for a sedimentary geologist, I spent several weeks in a small wooden house on Pigeon Key. It is no place to ride out a hurricane, even an average one.

The train crew literally pulled people aboard. But it was too little, too late. As the train backed up into the station, a storm surge 17 feet high rolled over the island like a sponge over a dirty sink, picking up tents, shacks, cars, and the train. It flipped even the train *track* onto its side and deposited 10 of the cars 100 feet away. Some crew members survived, hanging onto parts of the locomotive. Most of the veterans, as well as many visitors to the island, perished.

In an article in *Florida Trend* magazine, Gene Burnett described the scene:

> Objects careened through the air with deadly speed. Sheet metal roofs became "flying guillotines," decapitating several victims, amputating the limbs of others. Whirling lumber became lethal javelins, impaling victims or knocking them loose from precarious grips on poles and trees. Like exploding atoms, pounding sheets of sand sheared clothes and even the skin off victims, leaving them clad only in belts and shoes, often with their faces literally sandblasted beyond identification.

Research Findings

What's it like to be WRONG? In 1878, the U.S. Army initiated the nation's first weather service, the Weather Reporting Office of the National Government, or WRONG. Its thinking was that military discipline would help secure accuracy and promptness in reporting, the unfortunate acronym notwithstanding.

One survivor said that he saw sparks as grains of sand collided with each other; he thought he had died and gone to hell.

A total of 409 people perished; 300 of them were cremated and their remains placed in a crypt in 1937, in front of a monument near U.S. Highway 1 in Islamorada marking the tragedy.

The Long Island Express

The weather wasn't finished with the 1930s. It had yet to produce the Great New England Hurricane of 1938, also known as the "Long Island Express" because it made landfall (struck land) near Bellport, New York, and forever changed the way Long Island looked. And yet, it was only a Category 3 storm, while the Labor Day lady had been at least a Category 5.

It was September 21 when the rains that had been annoying end-of-season swimmers on New York's Long Island finally slacked off.

The U.S. Weather Bureau had forecast a hurricane, but it wasn't supposed to make landfall anywhere near eastern Long Island. Belatedly, forecasters concluded that they had been incorrect in their projection. The hurricane was, in fact, heading toward Long Island. And it was heading there hard and fast—too hard and fast to arrange an evacuation.

The Facts of the Matter

At 2:30 in the afternoon, the hurricane crashed ashore, tearing off roofing and shingles, smashing doors and windows, and snapping telephone poles in half. To bystanders, it appeared that a huge, solid bank of fog was rolling in off the ocean. It wasn't. It was water, a solid wall of water 40 feet high. The surge was so powerful that it tore apart beachfront homes. It was so powerful that it registered like an earthquake on the seismographs at Fordham University in New York City, 100 miles west.

Research Findings

Hurricanes are categorized by the Saffir-Simpson scale.

Category 1: Winds at 74–95 miles per hour; barometric pressure of 29.94 inches; storm surge of 4–5 feet.

Category 2: Winds at 96–110 miles per hour; barometric pressure of 28.50–28.91 inches; storm surge of 6–8 feet.

Category 3: Winds at 111–130 miles per hour; barometric pressure of 27.91–28.47 inches; storm surge of 9–12 feet.

Category 4: Winds at 131–155 miles per hour; barometric pressure of 27.17–27.88 inches; storm surge of 13–18 feet.

Category 5: Winds at more than 155 miles per hour; barometric pressure at 27.16 inches; storm surge of more than 18 feet.

Note: When the wind speed doubles, there's an eightfold increase in the wind's power, making a Category 5 hurricane at least 8 times more powerful than a Category 1.

And then the relief of the storm's huge eye appeared. It offered blue skies and hope that lasted about an hour. Then the *really* fierce winds hit. Even around the ragged edge of the monster storm, in New York City, the winds were described by *The New York Times* as "driving sheets of rain almost horizontally into the faces of the hardy few who ventured into the streets, while many thousands of people remained in their offices after hours rather than venture into the deluge."

At 4 P.M., the storm crossed Long Island Sound and made a second landfall in New England. Unfortunately, the storm had been preceded by a front that had been dropping rain on the region for days. The hurricane deposited another 4 to 6 inches in a hurry. In Hartford, the Connecticut River rose 33 feet above normal.

Sound the Alarm

Coastal areas of New York State rank second to Florida in amount of insured coastal property. Future hurricanes there will be costly, if not deadly.

Ordinarily, meteorologists would project a weakening as a hurricane moves over cooler water, such as Long Island Sound. But the storm was moving so rapidly that it didn't remain over the water long enough to cool its heels, never mind its gales. The narrow sound was not even a hitch in its terrible journey.

When the storm got to the large cities of Connecticut, it demonstrated just how vicious it could be. In New London, on the shore, a short circuit in a building soaked by the storm surge set it afire; winds of 98 miles per hour made sure it did the ultimate damage and took another quarter mile of the business district with it, as firefighters watched helplessly. New Haven also took an immense hit. The next day, the *Hartford Courant* described September 21, 1938, as the "most calamitous day" in Connecticut history.

Roaring into Rhode Island

After its city visits, the hurricane took an early New England leaf tour, roaring into Rhode Island with winds exceeding 120 miles per hour. Narragansett Bay was driven ahead of the winds into the Providence harbor, right at rush hour. Terrified citizens leaving businesses near the waterfront leaped off buses and into water that quickly rose to their chins. Some were saved as workers staying late lowered ropes from second-floor windows. Others were swept to their deaths in the sound that had become part of the ocean.

Sound the Alarm

The Long Island Express was indeed a fast train. It moved its swirling winds forward at an astonishing speed, usually in excess of 60 miles per hour. Even now, it holds the forward speed record for an Atlantic hurricane.

The height of the storm surge was at least 13 feet, 8.5 inches, almost 2 feet higher than the previous Rhode Island record. Still, the storm's itinerary was not quite complete. The Long Island Express then assaulted Milton, Massachusetts, where the Blue Hill Observatory recorded a wind gust of 186 miles per hour.

The Express trekked on toward Montreal, weakening finally, but causing widespread damage even in Canada before losing its tropical characteristics and dissipating. The whole incredible journey took only eight hours from the first hit on Long Island to the last stop at Montreal.

A Dangerous Future?

Long Island was mainly undeveloped in 1938; now it's shore-to-shore homes/malls/offices/schools/hotels/and so on. On a good day, it can take six hours to travel from Montauk Point to New York City on the overburdened highways; imagine an evacuation!

Projections by a NOAA Hurricane Research Division meteorologist suggest that in the future, of the 15 worst possible storms, Long Island would be affected by five of them—and one of the 1938 storm's magnitude would rank only sixth!

Scientists believe that now, after Miami and New Orleans, New York City is the third most dangerous city for hurricane disaster because of some particularly lethal features.

The beautiful Verrazano Narrows Bridge at the mouth of the harbor and the venerable George Washington Bridge spanning the lower Hudson River are both so high that they would experience hurricane-force winds before the winds were felt at sea-level, which is the level that most of New York City and Long Island enjoy. So, they would have to be closed early as escape routes. The two ferry services across Long Island Sound to Connecticut would have to be shut down at least 6 to 12 hours before a storm surge was expected.

Studies say that John F. Kennedy International Airport would be under 20 feet of water in a Category 4 storm. New York City's automobile tunnels under the Hudson and East rivers would fill, as would subway tunnels. Conclusion: A storm bringing low to moderate hazard in the rest of the country would result in heavy loss of life in Manhattan.

Once again, Long Island would be hammered. Amityville Harbor would experience a storm surge of 29 feet; Atlantic Beach and Long Beach, 24 to 28 feet; South Oyster Bay, 24 to 28 feet. Montauk Point would be completely cut off from the rest of the south fork even in a Category 1 storm that was a direct hit, as the 1938 monster was.

Commuter Trips: The Big, Bad Season of 1999

As hurricanes go, 1935 and 1938 offered trips from hell in Hurricane Land. But 1999 offered at least some fairly exciting "commuter" excursions into wet and wild misery. Indeed, according to meteorologists, it was a record-breaking season for the storms themselves.

DisasterRelief.org concluded that the season also holds the record for an unprecedented number of disaster declarations in the United States. Here are the facts:

➤ Hurricane Floyd (September) caused the biggest disaster evacuation in U.S. history. Of the 1999 storms, it also claimed the most lives: between 50 and 80, depending on the source. It affected North Carolina, Virginia, Pennsylvania, New Jersey, New York, Delaware, South Carolina, Florida, Connecticut, Maryland, New Hampshire, Vermont, and Maine.

➤ The 13 major disaster declarations for Floyd are the most for any single hurricane or other event, including the Midwest Floods of 1993. (The East Coast Blizzard of 1996 had 14 major disaster declarations issued, but only for emergency snow removal.)

➤ For the season, the 17 declared major disasters are the most ever for a hurricane season, surpassing the previous historic high of 11 issued in 1985 (Elena, Gloria,

Research Findings

The 1999 tropical storm season included 12 tropical storms, with 8 turning into hurricanes. The average Atlantic hurricane season offers 9.3 tropical storms, 5.8 hurricanes, and 2.2 major hurricanes packing winds of 110 miles per hour or greater.

Research Findings

The period of 1995–1999 had more tropical storms than any other five-year period in history. In 1995, there were 19; in 1996, there were 13; in 1997, there were 7; in 1998, there were 10; and in 1999, there were 12.

Juan, and Kate) and the 10 issued in 1999 (Bonnie, Earl, and Georges).

➤ Hurricane Irene (October) took Florida by surprise, and by flood.

➤ At one point, three storms were simultaneously rolling across the Atlantic Ocean. Highly accurate hurricane predictor Bill Gray, who lives safely at the foothills of the Rockies, says that hurricane activity will become more intense and more frequent over the next few years; he was already accurate in predicting that the 1990s would see more big hurricanes than in the previous 40 quiet years.

➤ Hurricane Bret (August) wreaked havoc in Texas.

➤ Hurricane Dennis (September) drenched North Carolina, Virginia, and Pennsylvania.

➤ Hurricane Lenny got emergencies declared for both Puerto Rico and the U.S. Virgin Islands.

Just Floyd

Floyd may not be the most brawny-sounding name in the world, but the storm of that name was anything but a 98-pound weakling. Here are some stats from Floyd alone:

➤ Relief funds of $420 million have been obligated so far for Floyd, including $223.8 million for North Carolina, $47.9 million for New Jersey, $41 million for South Carolina, and $34.6 for Virginia.

➤ FEMA funding for Floyd surpassed the $292 million for Hurricane Hortense in Puerto Rico (1996) and the $259.7 million for Hurricane Iniki in Hawaii (1992), and approached the $496.3 million for Hurricane Marilyn in Puerto Rico and the U.S. Virgin Islands (1995).

➤ At least 144,854 Floyd victims registered for federal aid in the nine declared states designated for Individual Assistance, including 74,267 in North Carolina. This exceeds the 83,800 registrations for Hurricane Fran in six declared states, including 72,736 registrations in North Carolina.

➤ At least 220 counties were designated for federal assistance because of Floyd.

➤ More than 42,973 homes sustained some damage from Floyd, according to federal/state surveys. Of that total, some 11,779 dwellings were either destroyed or heavily damaged.

➤ Seventy-nine deaths and five injuries are attributed to Floyd, and more than 105,580 people were housed in shelters for some period.

➤ Approximately four million people were evacuated in North Carolina, South Carolina, Georgia, and Florida, making it the biggest hurricane evacuation ever.

➤ Insured losses for Floyd are estimated at $1.35 billion, including $865 million in North Carolina. These figures are expected to rise as unreported losses at the outset become apparent.

How to Survive a Hurricane

The best way to survive a hurricane is not to be there; listen for and heed government evacuation orders in hurricane territory during hurricane season, the beginning of June through the beginning of November.

If you live in an area that is not subject to evacuation orders—you live high enough or far enough inland—there are still precautions you'll need to take to ride out the storm safe and sound:

➤ If you have hurricane shutters for doors and windows, use them. If not, board up openings.

➤ Remove portable structures such as garden sheds and play houses. Secure ornamental objects such as bird baths and garden furniture; when possible, move these items into a garage.

➤ Have on hand and fresh, at the approach of any storm, a week's supply of food and water for the whole family and any pets.

➤ Set refrigerators and freezers to their lowest setting, to help if power goes out for a while.

➤ Unplug small appliances and computers.

➤ Turn off propane tanks and be sure they are secure.

➤ Have ready and in working order survival supplies and equipment such as flashlights with extra batteries; battery-powered radios; credit cards and extra cash; first aid kit and manual; prescription medications in quantities to last a week or more; special equipment such as diapers or sick room supplies.

Most important, don't mistake the eye of the storm for its end. After the initial wind and rain, the eye might move over your location. The sun will come out, birds will fly. But it won't last. The other side of the storm will follow and often is more damaging than the leading edge. Stay inside until the entire storm has passed; listen to a radio for help in making this determination. Keeping your ears to the radio can also help you avoid the small tornadoes that sometimes develop after the storm has passed, in the churned-up air left in its wake.

The Least You Need to Know

➤ The 1935 Labor Day Hurricane killed 409 people.

➤ The 1938 Long Island Express Hurricane still holds the record for the fastest-moving hurricane and forever changed the way Long Island looked.

➤ Escape from New York might not be possible if a really big one blew in.

➤ The twentieth century left with a hurricane bang.

➤ Hurricane Floyd caused the biggest disaster evacuation in U.S. history. Of the 1999 storms, it also claimed the most lives: between 50 and 80.

Rollin' on the River, Part 1: Floods

More than any other type of natural disaster, floods are mythic. From the earliest times, civilizations have told stories of floods and heroes in floods. Noah and his ark are well-known, of course. But other peoples, besides the early Jewish authors of the Old Testament, wrote of floods, too. Modern scientific evidence suggests that the stories have a basis in fact.

Mythic or actual, floods are among the deadliest forces on Earth, killing in greater numbers, on average, than other disasters. In the United States, most people have heard of the Galveston flood of September 1900, which took 6,000 lives. That one was caused by a hurricane. Fewer have heard of the Gros Ventre flood, which took only six lives but was spectacular nonetheless.

Recent years have not seen as much death linked to floods in the United States, but damage has been extraordinary. The Midwest flooding of 1993 was the costliest in U.S. history, with damage estimated at more than $20 billion. About 50 lives were lost.

Research Findings

Despite the great loss of life in some historic U.S. floods, other parts of the world have experienced even greater losses much more recently. Bangladesh lost 300,000 in November 1970, and 130,000 in April 1991. China's Yangtze River flood of 1931 caused more than three million deaths from flooding and subsequent starvation.

Ice Is Nice, Until Spring: Types of Floods

Obviously, Mother Nature has lots of ways to create floods. Here are several ways water wreaks havoc:

Sound the Alarm

Flash flooding occurs within six hours of the rain event.

➤ River floods are what most of us think of as floods. Torrential rain from hurricanes or other tropical systems can fill river basins with too much water too quickly. The deadly combination of winter, followed by spring, when all the snow and ice melts, can do the same thing. If the ice melts too quickly, or if there was a particularly large snowpack, or if early spring is very rainy, bingo: You've got a flood.

➤ Coastal floods are caused by hurricanes or other offshore storms (such as New England's nor'easters) that push ocean water inland, cutting off escape routes from some promontories.

➤ Urban floods are not natural disasters, strictly speaking. Man has had a lot to do with them. Quite simply, as land is removed from agriculture or woodlands are cut down, and roads, parking lots, and big buildings replace them, the earth loses its ability to absorb rainfall to one extent or another. Runoff may increase two to six times over what it had been. For short periods of time, after heavy rainfall, streets can turn into swift, shallow rivers, and basements can become deathtraps.

➤ Flash flooding occurs naturally in areas where there are arroyos—water-carved gullies and dry creek beds—in the western United States. A flash flood in an Arizona arroyo developed in only 58 seconds, a record. In short, there's too little time to heed the age-old flood advice: Climb high or die.

➤ Volcano-related floods also can be dangerous. Many volcanoes are quite high mountains and may keep snowpack at the peak winter and summer. When one of these volcanoes erupts, the snow and ice melt and flow downward, usually carrying large amounts of rock debris. Eruption-caused floods can occur suddenly, and they can be very serious—more serious, in fact, than floods of other causes simply because of the large amounts of debris and sediment they bring with them down the mountain.

A three-step volcanic flood might happen if large masses of volcanic material move suddenly into a lake, causing the water to break over the top of a dam or rise above the usual shoreline.

To Ensure Preservation

When a hurricane pushes a wall of water virtually all at once over a land mass, it is known as a storm surge rather than flooding. Warning of a storm surge will accompany hurricane warnings. Unlike flooding, the waters recede quickly when the hurricane passes.

Research Findings

Boulder, Colorado, at the base of some very high mountains, has long been threatened by flash floods, especially when spring rains combine with melting snow from the peaks. Although we consider the plains to the east of Boulder semiarid, the Continental Divide, on which Boulder sits, gets 40 inches of precipitation a year, mostly snow. The Flood of 1894 was caused by warm spring rains. Barker Dam, on Boulder Creek, was completed in 1910 and was supposed to stop the problem. Still, in 1976, The Big Thompson Canyon Flood killed 139 people.

The Susquehanna River Basin

The Susquehanna River basin is one of the most flood-prone areas in the United States. Its main stem is more prone to ice jams, causing flooding, than any other river east of the Rockies.

Indeed, although its basin fosters a wide, slow flow most of its length, there are places where the water is squeezed into a steep, narrow gorge. Ice can stack up, backing up the river behind it; on breaking loose with the thaw, sudden walls of water can be forced through the gorge. A large melting snowpack and sudden heavy spring rains can accomplish the same sort of destructive event.

The gorges, however, are not the river's only flood-creation mechanism. The river also flows through many areas with very little slope and shallow banks. There, the river levels out and flows slowly. A heavy rainfall quickly swells the river until it overflows its banks. In winter, slow-moving ice causes multiple jams, backing up water for flooding behind the ice; when the water breaks loose, it can cause sudden flooding before it—perhaps not as suddenly as in the gorge areas, but with just as much damage.

The 1936 Flood

A spring trip along Route 17 through Binghamton, New York, where the river is wide, slow, and flat, will demonstrate how easily the shallow banks are overtopped. Most springs, riverside trees are underwater some of the time. But the locals don't really call that flooding. That's just normal behavior for the river.

But in March 1936, the Susquehanna really and truly flooded. It drowned downtown Pittsburgh. It drowned lots of small towns in New York. And it drowned Williamsport, Pennsylvania, at the time a bustling small city where my mother lived.

Sound the Alarm

Native Americans first told settlers of serious flooding along the Susquehanna River; they said the river overflowed about every 14 years. Since its banks became settled in the early 1800s, it has flooded about once every 20 years. Localized flash floods, often on the tributaries rather than the main stem, also occur with little warning.

My mother was seven years old during the Big Flood. She and her mother and two sisters were at home when the flooding began. Her father, a dairy accountant, was out of town, doing what he always did—making sure that everything was shipshape for dairy farmers selling milk in southern New York and Northern Pennsylvania.

My grandmother moved the three girls to the top floor of the house as the waters rose; no one expected that it would be quite so bad, so at first they didn't evacuate.

Finally, it became clear that they, like all their neighbors, would have to be rescued in a rowboat and taken to higher ground. Grandmother told the girls to put on their coats and get ready to leave, as she knew men in rowboats were rescuing people from top floors. My mother, awakening from a nap and hearing the order to leave, put on her coat and sleepily made for the stairs. Had she stepped down two steps, she would have sunk into the murky water filling the house. She likely would have drowned; my grandmother couldn't swim.

Meanwhile, my grandfather was trying to make his way home. When he reached the town a day later, the police stopped him and said he couldn't enter, that in any case the flood waters were still too high and his street was under water. If his family had been rescued, they would be at the high school, they told him. But he couldn't go there, either. It was too dangerous, even if he could find a dry route to get there by.

Really? Grandfather "bought a ticket to the policeman's ball" and caught a ride on the running board of a police car, right to the high school, where he found his family safe—except the cat. That cat, who was not at home when the whole mess started, showed up about six weeks later, yowling for food.

The Extent of the Flood

Williamsport was joined in misery by other towns, small and large, along the river and in surrounding areas flooded by other rivers that overflowed that spring. At least 153 people died in 11 states and the District of Columbia. At least 108 of the dead were in Pennsylvania, and most of those lived on the Susquehanna or its tributaries, and on the Allegheny, Monongahela, and Ohio rivers.

In Pittsburgh, the city waterworks failed. Forty-five people were dead, and 350 were treated for injuries at hospitals. The river had crested at Pittsburgh at 46 feet above flood stage. When it got down to 30.7 feet, restoration work began. One-tenth of normal electricity was restored; hospitals were among the first to get power.

In Etna, Pennsylvania, the Etna Forging and Bolt Company exploded. Fire reached the row houses, and people burned, drowned, or suffocated, with no way to get out, surrounded by raging flood waters. In McKees Rocks, thousands watched from the West End Bridge while two men drowned after a rescue attempt failed. On St. Patrick's Day, 300,000 gallons of oil caught fire and burned well into the night.

Sound the Alarm

Flooding, as opposed to flash flooding, may last for a week or more.

In June 1972, Hurricane Agnes caused the worse recorded flood in the Susquehanna basin. Fewer people were killed than in 1936—only 72—but property damage was estimated at $2.8 billion.

The river has experienced other disastrous floods in 1865, 1936, 1955, 1975, and 1996, with varying consequences for the 1,400 communities in the river's basin. Of those, an astonishing 1,160 have residents living on the flood plain.

Blizzards, Avalanches, and Floods, Oh My!

Although they aren't as famous as the Rockies, the mountains of the East Coast offer lots of winter fun: skiing, snowmobiling, ice fishing. They suffer blizzards, of course, and the occasional avalanche. But they also suffer floods. In 1936, they didn't fare much better than their neighbors in the plateau carrying the Susquehanna to the sea.

In the case of Northern New England, it was the attractive snowpack that caused the problem. The winter of 1935–1936 was particularly severe, with snowpacks reaching about 7.5 inches of water, with 3.5 inches normal.

On March 9, a warm, rainy weather front moved into New England and decided to stay. High temperatures and heavy rainfall March 11–13 got things started. The steep slopes of the White Mountains hurried the extra water downstream.

But it wasn't just the water; it was the ice. Sudden breaking up of river ice resulted in ice jams and dam breaks. In Massachusetts, an ice jam above Holyoke Dam caused the Connecticut River to cut a new channel around it. When the jam broke, it sheared off a 1,000-foot wide section of a granite dam, and a 9-foot wall of water rushed downstream.

That was pretty wicked. But Mother Nature's evil twin had more in store. A few days later, a second rain system moved in. Pinkham Notch on Mount Washington had gotten more than 7 inches of rain in the first soaking. On March 18 and 19, it was doused with another 10 inches.

Almost the entire snow cover of New England melted in the warm rains. The entire length of the Connecticut River was flooded, and flow records were created that still stand. The Merrimack River Basin sustained severe damage. More than 18 feet of water drowned downtown Hookset, New Hampshire.

And it wasn't done yet! A few days later, a third rain storm arrived. It didn't cause any new floodpeaks, but it lengthened the duration of the flood. Between the combination of rain and snowmelt, most places in New England received the equivalent of 30 inches of rain in a two-week period.

Estimates are that 150 to 200 people died in the flooding and that New England damage exceeded $100 million. Although the flooding on the Susquehanna and in New England was the most severe, flooding occurred as far south as the Potomac and James River basins in Virginia.

The Great Johnstown Flood

On May 31, 1889, the South Fork Dam on the Little Conemaugh River near Johnstown, Pennsylvania, collapsed. In less than 5 minutes, a wall of water killed 2,200 of the town's 10,000 residents. Most perished in their small wooden tenement row houses built on the river flats between the Conemaugh and Stoneycreek.

The dam held back Lake Conemaugh, 3 miles wide and 1 mile long, the pride of the South Fork Fishing and Hunting Club that boasted members such as Andrew Carnegie and Henry Clay Frick. The dam had been built between 1838 and 1853 as part of the Pennsylvania Canal system. When the railroads replaced barges, the dam wasn't used and was sold to the club in 1879.

The dam itself looked like a pile of rubble, with trees growing out of cracks in the rock wall. If one stood below it, there was no indication that a lake rocked behind it.

Prelude to Disaster

On May 30, 8 inches of rain fell on Lake Conemaugh, pushing the water to within 2 feet of the top of the dam. The rivers had also been swollen by rain; by the next morning, the lake level was rising by an inch every 10 minutes. When it reached the top, officials feared that the dam finally would break. They quickly tried to add height to the dam and to dig a spillway at the side to relieve pressure. They removed screens from the catch basins. All the measures failed.

Either no one warned the residents, or the townspeople ignored the warnings. By midafternoon, water began to flow over the top of the dam. Shortly, its center began to sink. At about 3:10 P.M., the dam wall collapsed, sending 20 million tons of water toward Johnstown. A wall of rock-and-tree-bearing water 40 feet high roared through the communities of South Fork, Mineral Point, Woodvale, and East Conemaugh on the 14-mile trip to Johnstown. It hit Johnstown at 4:07 P.M., destroying the downtown area completely.

Research Findings

The American Red Cross, organized in 1881 by Clara Barton, arrived June 5th. Clara Barton herself was among those who worked in the first major disaster relief effort in which the organization was involved. The Red Cross built hotels for people to live in and warehouses for the supplies sent to the area.

Thousands of people were swept downstream to the Stone Bridge at the Little Conemaugh-Stoneycreek junction, where debris, houses, train cars, and bodies piled up. The official death toll was 2,209 people; that included 99 entire families, 396 children under age 10, and 777 unidentified victims.

Other towns experienced devastation, too:

➤ The town of South Fork lost four-fifths of its 2,000 inhabitants.

➤ Mineral Point lost 90 percent of its 800 residents.

➤ The town of Conemaugh had 2,500 inhabitants, most of whom perished.

➤ Woodvale, population 3,000, lost most of its residents. The stables of the Woodvale Horse Railroad Company went out with the water; every horse and car in them went also.

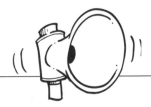

Sound the Alarm

Floods can drain a lake—or make one. In 1925, melting snow in Wyoming's Gros Ventre Canyon caused a landslide that dammed at the Gros Ventre River at Sheep Mountain, creating Slide Lake. But it didn't last. On May 18, 1927, the naturally occurring dam of rock and mud collapsed, draining the lake and pushing a wall of water through the town of Kelly that killed six people. Nine hours later, the water reached the Snake River Canyon, filling it to the rim with water, trees, houses, and dead animals. There's still a small lake behind what remains of that natural dam, but, say geologists, more of Sheep Mountain could slide anytime the conditions are right.

An Eyewitness Account

Here's an eyewitness account by Robert Miller, who lost two of his children and his mother-in-law at the Woodvale tragedy (the account is from *History of the Johnstown Flood* by Willis Fletcher Johnson, published by Edgewood Publishing Company, 1889):

> I was standing near the Woodvale Bridge, between Maple Avenue and Portage Street, in Johnstown. The river was high, and David Lucas and I were speculating about the bridges, whether they would go down or not. Lucas said, "I guess this bridge will stand; it does not seem to be weakened." Just then we saw a dark object up the river. Over it was a white mist. It was high and somehow dreadful, though we could not make it out. Dark smoke seemed to form a background for the mist. We did not wait for more. By instinct we knew the big dam had burst and its water was coming upon us. Lucas jumped on a car horse, rode across the bridge, and went yelling into Johnstown. The flood overtook him, and he had to abandon his horse and climb a high hill.

> I went straight to my house in Woodvale, warning everybody as I ran. My wife and mother-in-law were ready to move, with my five children, so we went for the hillside, but we were not speedy enough. The water had come over the flat at its base and cut us off. I and my wife climbed into a coal car with one of the children, to get out of the water. I put two more children into the car and looked around for my other children and my mother-in-law. My mother-in-law was a stout woman, weighing about two hundred and twelve pounds. She could not climb into a car. The train was too long for her to go around it so she tried to crawl under, leading the children.

The train was suddenly pushed forward by the flood, and she was knocked down and crushed, were my children, by the same shock. My wife and children in the car were thrown down and covered with coal. I was taken off by the water, but I swam to the car and pulled them from under a lot of coal. A second blow to the train threw our car against the hillside and us out of it to firm earth. I never saw my two children and mother-in-law after the flood first struck the train of coal cars. I have often heard it said that the dam might break, but I never paid any attention to it before. It was common talk whenever there was a freshet or a big pack of ice.

Research Findings

The Johnstown Flood's waters amounted to 100,000 tons of rocks, locomotives, freight cars, iron, logs, trees, parts of houses, horses, and cattle, all pushed forward by 20,000,000 tons of water falling 500 feet. It swept downward with a roaring sound at the rate of a mile a minute, putting more than 30,000 people in front of the jaws of death in less than half an hour. So, it became known as the "Avalanche of Death."

Recent Deluges

The floods of 1999 were caused by Hurricane Floyd in mid-September, and they hit coastal areas of New Jersey and North Carolina the hardest. At one point, 1,500 people were waiting to be rescued from rooftops in North Carolina. Floyd had dumped more than a foot of rain, virtually shutting down the eastern coastal plain, east of Interstate 95, and actually closing the road for 170 miles between Petersburg, Virginia, and Benson, North Carolina. In North Carolina, every road east of I-95 was closed.

As in 1936, help often arrived in the form of a rowboat. A man rowing on the Neuse River in North Carolina spent his time rescuing people from trees.

In New Jersey, fire helped the rain create disaster. In Bound Brook, fires raged uncontrolled. Helicopters sporadically dumped water on a blaze that broke out in a cluster of stores, with little effect.

Many New Jersey river valleys experienced all-time record flooding, the National Weather Service claimed. And virtually all rivers, streams and brooks in Bergen, Essex, and Hudson counties in New Jersey overflowed their banks.

Research Findings

Everyone knows the story of Noah's Ark—how he and Mrs. Noah loaded two of every sort of beast onto a huge boat and sailed the world as it rained for 40 days and 40 nights. In recent years, scientists have proposed that there really was a catastrophic deluge on the Black Sea about 7,500 years ago that might have given rise to the story.

In the next chapter, we'll look at the 1927 Mississippi Flood and the 1972 Rapid City Flood as well as some tips on being prepared if you live in a flood-prone area.

The Least You Need to Know

➤ On average, floods kill in greater numbers than other disasters.

➤ There are five types of floods: river floods, coastal floods, urban floods, flash floods, and volcano-related floods.

➤ Learn and heed the most basic flood survival advice: Climb high or die.

➤ In the Johnstown Flood, a wall of water killed 2,200 of the town's 10,000 residents in 5 minutes.

➤ Survival may be a matter of inches.

Chapter 20

Rollin' on the River, Part 2: More Floods

In This Chapter

➤ The 1927 Mississippi Flood

➤ Flash Flood in Rapid City, 1972

➤ Where are you safe from flooding?

➤ How to prepare for property damage

➤ Worst places on Earth for floods

The 1927 Mississippi River Flood might be considered the mother of all floods, not because it took the most lives, but because the Mississippi is one of the longest rivers in the world. Its basin encompasses more territory than most people think, stretching from western New York to Idaho, and from Canada to the Gulf of Mexico.

The Mississippi River Basin is all about levees, and that's how some experts think the flood of 1927 got out of hand in the first place.

When the Levee Breaks

After the Civil War, the Army Corps of Engineers established the Mississippi River Commission and enforced a "levees only" theory to control flooding. In short, the group would simply build higher river banks than Mother Nature had provided.

Problem one: Such a strategy costs money. Problem two: It upsets the balance of nature, eventually making a bad problem worse. How so? Sediments from the levees ran down the slopes into the river, adding to the bed of the river and gradually raising the water. Engineers were forced to keep building the levees higher to hold the same amount of water. Eventually, the Mississippi's bed had actually lifted several feet above surrounding ground level. (A river didn't run through it; it ran above it!)

For example, the original 7.5-foot levee at Morganza, Louisiana, maintained the river in its banks there during the great flood of 1850. By the 1920s, the levee had grown to a height of 38 feet to hold back the water. In 1927, the levee broke, flooding 175,000 acres. Other levees also broke, and the death toll rose as high as 1,000 by estimate. Damage was estimated to be in the neighborhood of $1 billion—in 1927 dollars.

To Ensure Preservation

Perhaps we should have taken some hints from Native Americans. "The north changes the world; in the winter the snow comes, covers the land," says Martin Louie, Sr., elder of the Colville Tribe displaced by the Grand Coulee Dam. "When it breaks in the spring, the mountains and hills will gather all the deteriorated stuff and bring it down to the Columbia, the main channel, and take it away. What goes out in the ocean will never return. And we have a brand new world in spring. The high water takes everything out, washes everything down. That's why we pray to the water, every morning and night."

Here are the thoughts of the U.S. Army Corps of Engineers in their flood post-mortem:

> Heavy rains fell over the mid-Mississippi Valley in April of 1927 ... which flooded down to the lower Mississippi Valley. This caused some widespread flooding that encompassed 26,000 square miles. This triggered the evacuation of a half million civilians from their homes. The river broke through 13 levees along the river. The flooding occurred from April until June ... when the river waters were out of its banks. The lesson learned here was that Flood Control Measures at that time were only as strong as the weakest point. In the flood of 1882, a person could take a boat from Vicksburg to Monroe, Louisiana. This was almost the case in the Flood of 1927.

Flood Stages Along the Mississippi River, 1927

City	Flood Stage	Flood Measurement
Memphis, Tennessee	35 feet	44.7 feet
Helena, Arkansas	44.8 feet	56.7 feet
Arkansas City, Arkansas	48 feet	60.5 feet
Greenville, Mississippi	42 feet	54.6 feet
Vicksburg, Mississippi	45 feet	57.2 feet
Natchez, Mississippi	46 feet	56.1 feet

While seven states were affected, Mississippi, Louisiana, and Arkansas got hit worst. More than 16,570,620 acres were lost underwater. About 162,000 homes sustained great water damage, and 9,000 were lost completely. People of every income, every race, and every age were left homeless. And then, of course, there were the 1,000 who lost their lives.

There have been notable floods and unnoticed ones. Here's a list of the best of the worst in the twentieth century.

➤ **September 1900**—6,000 deaths during extensive flooding in Galveston, Texas

➤ **January 1969**—100 deaths when flood waters swamped southern California

➤ **August 1969**—189 deaths during extensive flooding in western Virginia

➤ **June 1972**—236 deaths during a massive flood in Rapid City, South Dakota

➤ **July 1976**—139 deaths when flood waters swamped Big Thompson Canyon, Colorado

➤ **July 1994**—32 deaths during flooding in Georgia and Alabama

➤ **December 1996–January 1997**—29 deaths during flooding in the Northwest

➤ **March 1997**—35 deaths during the flooding of the Ohio River Valley

Source: The 1998 World Almanac

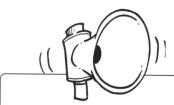

Sound the Alarm

In July and August 1993, 48 people died in Midwest floods.

Sound the Alarm

Even 6 inches of fast-moving flood water can knock you off your feet, and a depth of 2 feet will float your car! Never try to walk, swim, or drive through such fast-moving water. If you come upon flood waters, stop. Turn around and go another way—quickly.

A Flash in the Hardpan

On June 9, 1972, a six-hour deluge poured through the canyons and into the cities on the eastern slopes of the Black Hills.

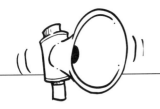

Sound the Alarm

Don't think that dam disasters are things of the past. One could happen again at any time. The United States has 3.5 million miles of rivers. More than 600,000 miles of U.S. rivers (17 percent of total river miles) lie behind an estimated 60,000 to 80,000 dams.

Research Findings

At least 9.6 million households and $390 billion in property lie in flood-prone areas in the United States. The rate of urban growth in flood plains is approximately twice that of the rest of the country. After all, both the shore and the mountain valleys are very pretty and relaxing—most of the time.

That morning was a humid one, with temperatures rising into the 80s as east winds pushed moist air into the hills. A National Weather Service forecast called for thunderstorms to develop, some severe. Huge cumulus clouds began to pile up over the hills west of Rapid City. Between 5 P.M. and 7 P.M., the South Dakota School of Mines and Technology tracked storm echoes on its radar. What they didn't know was that those storms had dumped about 15 inches of rain into the hills.

By 6:45 P.M., water had come over the road in Boulder Canyon. By 8 P.M., there was an organized evacuation in Brookdale, a community along Rapid Creek, and shortly after that, evacuation of all low-lying areas was ordered.

At 10:45 P.M., Canyon Lake dam failed, adding a surge to the spreading flood that lifted homes from their foundations and piled cars one atop another, moving at an incredible 50,000 cubic feet per second.

By and large, residents of Rapid City slept through it—until 12:15 A.M., when the relentless wall of water all but destroyed the city.

Policemen, the National Guard, and volunteer firemen turned out in large numbers to help; some of them were among the 236 who died. Another 3,000 were injured. A total of 1,335 homes and 5,000 cars were lost; damage, in 1972 dollars, mounted to $160 million.

Rapid City learned a lesson the hard way and, since the flash flood, has established a Green Way along Rapid Creek so that water can spill over the banks with minimal effect on homes and businesses. Canyon Lake Dam has been repaired and upgraded, and bridges were rebuilt to make it hard for debris to collect under them, forming impromptu dams during heavy rain and causing other flash floods.

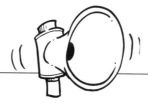

Sound the Alarm

When a vehicle stalls in the water, the water's momentum is transferred to the car. For each foot the water rises, 500 pounds of lateral force are applied to the car. However, buoyancy is the biggest factor. For each foot the water rises up the side of the car, the car displaces 1,500 pounds of water. In effect, the car weighs 1,500 pounds less for each foot the water rises. That means it floats really well—until the inside begins to fill up through breaches in the hull, so to speak. Don't stay in a car stalled in water. As little as 2 feet of water will carry away most cars.

The city has also joined a National Weather Service/U.S. Geological Survey system that monitors stages of rapid stream risings and issues warnings as soon as possible.

Flood–Plain Roulette

If you live in a river basin or near the shore, you're playing flood-plain roulette with more than just insurable property; you're gambling with your life, livelihood, family, and pets, too. Here are some things to keep in mind, gathered from FEMA and the Red Cross, as well as the United States Humane Society; pets make up the forgotten death toll in major floods.

➤ When deciding where to build or buy a home, or even rent one, find out the area's flood risk. Call the local National Weather Service office, the Red Cross, or local emergency management offices.

➤ Find out when the most recent flooding occurred and how severe it was.

➤ If you decide that the risk is reasonable, consider raising your furnace, water heater, and electric panel above the floor if they are in areas of your home that may be flooded.

➤ Consult with a professional for further information if this and other damage reduction measures can be taken.

Naturally, you should prepare a flood emergency kit and keep it updated. It should contain these items:

➤ A portable radio and flashlight with fresh batteries

➤ Candles and waterproof matches

To Ensure Preservation

Just because floods can take several hours or days to develop, don't shut out the warnings.

➤ Reasonable stocks of fresh water (at least 3 gallons per person), and canned food and an opener

➤ A first-aid kit

➤ Strong shoes and rubber gloves

➤ A waterproof bag for clothing and valuables

➤ Emergency contact numbers for your area

➤ Protective clothing, rainwear, and bedding or sleeping bags

➤ Special items for infants, the elderly, or disabled family members

If you hear a flood warning, provided there is time, stack possessions on beds and in the attic. Move garbage, chemicals, and poisons to a high place, and batten down objects that could cause other damage if they float. Check your emergency kit. Check that your neighbors have been warned. Take care of your pets. And seek higher ground.

Hierarchy of Speeds

With apologies to Abraham Maslow, who invented the psychological Hierarchy of Needs, there is a hierarchy of speeds with which you must react to various flood pronouncements.

A flood *watch* means that a flood is possible in your area; make preparations, just in case, and keep listening for further instructions. Move your furniture and valuables to higher floors of your home. Fill your car's gas tank, in case an evacuation notice is issued. Be alert to signs of flash flooding, and be ready to evacuate at a moment's notice.

A flood *warning* means that flooding is already occurring or will occur soon in your area. Listen to local radio and TV stations for information and advice. If told to evacuate, do so as soon as possible.

When a flash flood warning is issued, evacuate immediately. You may have only seconds to escape. Act quickly! Move to higher ground away from rivers, streams, creeks, and storm drains. Do not drive around barricades that are keeping you from dangerous territory. If your car stalls in rapidly rising waters, abandon it immediately and climb to higher ground.

Determine which kind of flood you're being warned of. Flash floods can take only a few minutes to develop, or a few hours if you are farther away from the source. With other flooding, you may have hours and even days to prepare.

Fido and the Flood

In the previous chapter, my mother's cat happily returned after the Williamsport Flood; he could, because he was an outdoor cat and no doubt sought safety in a feral way as soon as he sensed danger. But indoor cats and dogs—not to mention birds and turtles and, yup, fish—need to be considered before a flood begins.

Time after time, Humane Society of the United States rescuers see one of two things: people endangering themselves to return to a flooded home for pets forgotten in the fright of the moment, or pets abandoned to die, miserable and alone. Neither is acceptable to them, or to any pet lover.

"You want to believe that your home's invincible," says Laura Bevan, the Director of the Humane Society office in southeast Florida. "Leaving [pets] behind is part of that denial."

Bevan, who has participated in animal rescue operations in Midwest and Georgia floods, has learned to look at submerged areas with a different eye. Having seen pets tied up and unable to swim or seek higher ground, she has made a habit of checking for small movements as she floats down residential streets, never knowing when a small break in the surface could be a nose straining to stay above water. Of all natural disasters, floods upset her the most. "Once you know how close you were to missing the pet, it just freaks you out forever," she says.

To Ensure Preservation

Shocked by the degree of animal devastation from Hurricane Andrew in 1992, Florida now has 300 volunteers involved in a statewide animal disaster plan. Check to see if there is one in your area; if not, start one.

One pet owner in Winnipeg, Canada, put his two dogs in a shed during spring floods, tying up one of them, a Great Dane. By the time emergency operators got to the shed, the water was three feet deep, too high for the Great Dane to survive. The other, smaller dog was able to perch on its hind legs. It was frightened and stiff from cold, but alive.

Animals have built-in survival instincts and a stronger chance of living through disasters on their own than humans do. One veterinarian made the mistake of blindfolding a horse to move it from one side of a flooding river to another. When the boat started to rock, the 1,000 pound animal panicked and jumped into the water. Unable to see, it swam in circles until the vet himself jumped in the water to remove the blindfold. The outcome? The horse ended up swimming the vet to shore.

The rule is simple: If you have to leave, so does your pet. Find out in advance whether your designated disaster shelter will permit animals; if not, arrange to take them to an animal shelter on high ground or a friend's house out of the danger zone.

The Best Places Not to Be, With or Without Pets

So far we've focused mainly on the United States, but worldwide there are flood-prone areas that have experienced flooding on a far more devastating scale.

A prime flood-prone place to avoid is Bangladesh; it's the Susquehanna Basin of the Far East, only much worse. In the floods of 1995, the homes of Chanpur residents simply crumbled into flood waters.

That's only one way for water to leave Bangladeshis homeless. With 17 million living less than 1 meter above sea level (and, by the way, sea level is rising), and with frequent typhoons and the occasional tidal wave—well, figure it out. In 1971, 20 million people became homeless in a flood; in 1992, 125,000 died in a cyclone, mainly from its accompanying flood.

Unfortunately, it's not only people who are raised on Bangladesh's flood plains; 38 percent of the nation's food is raised there as well. So, floods have far-reaching effects.

Here are other places you wouldn't have wanted to be in the history of the world's water:

➤ **1228, Holland**—A total of 100,000 people reputedly drowned by sea flood in Friesland.

➤ **1642, China**—Rebels destroyed the Kaifeng seawall, and 300,000 drowned. (Okay, this was a seminatural disaster.)

➤ **1896, Sanriku, Japan**—An earthquake and tidal wave killed 27,000.

➤ **1889, Johnstown, Pennsylvania**—More than 2,200 died in a flash flood.

➤ **1953, Northwest Europe**—A storm followed by floods devastated North Sea coastal areas. The Netherlands was hardest hit, with 1,794 dead.

➤ **1954, Iran**—A storm over Iran produced flooding rains, resulting in approximately 10,000 casualties.

➤ **1959, Frejus, France**—A flood caused by the collapse of Malpasset Dam left 412 dead.

➤ **1963, Italy**—A landslide ran into the Vaiont Dam; the resulting flood killed about 2,000.

➤ **1966, Aberfan, Wales**—An avalanche of coal, waste, mud, and rocks killed 144 people, including 116 children in school.

➤ **1969, Southern California**—January floods and mudslides from heavy rains caused widespread property damage and left at least 100 dead. Another downpour (February 23–26) caused further floods and mudslides and killed at least 18.

➤ **1970, East Pakistan**—About 200,000 were killed by a cyclone-driven tidal wave from the Bay of Bengal. More than 100,000 went missing.

➤ **1971, Vietnam**—Heavy rains caused severe flooding in North Vietnam, killing 100,000.

➤ **1972, Man, West Virginia**—More than 118 died when a slag-pile dam collapsed under pressure of torrential rains and flooded a 17-mile valley.

➤ **1972, Rapid City, South Dakota**—A flash flood caused 237 deaths and $160 million in damage.

➤ **1972, Eastern seaboard**—Tropical storm Agnes caused widespread flash floods in a 10-day rampage. The death toll hit 129; 115,000 were left homeless. Damage was estimated at $3.5 billion.

➤ **1976, Loveland, Colorado**—A flash flood along Route 34 in Big Thompson Canyon left 139 dead.

➤ **1988, Bangladesh**—The country's heaviest monsoon in 70 years inundated three-fourths of Bangladesh, killing more than 1,300 and leaving 30 million homeless. Damage was estimated at more than $1 billion.

➤ **1993, Illinois, Iowa, Kansas, Kentucky, Minnesota, Missouri, Nebraska, North Dakota, South Dakota, Wisconsin**—Two months of heavy rain caused the Mississippi River and its tributaries to flood in 10 states, resulting in almost 50 deaths and about $12 billion in damage to property and agriculture. Almost 70,000 were left homeless.

➤ **1996–1997, U.S. West Coast**—Torrential rains and snowmelt produced severe floods in parts of California, Oregon, Washington, Idaho, Nevada, and Montana, causing 36 deaths and about $2 billion to $3 billion in damage.

➤ **1996–1997, Ohio and Mississippi Valleys**—Flooding and tornadoes plagued Arkansas, Missouri, Mississippi, Tennessee, Illinois, Indiana, Kentucky, Ohio, and West Virginia. Sixty-seven were killed, and damage totaled approximately $1 billion.

➤ **1998, Papua New Guinea**—Spurred by an undersea earthquake, three tsunamis wiped out entire villages in the northwestern province of Sepik. One tidal wave was reported by a survivor to be 30 feet high. At least 2,000 people were found or presumed dead. Many who were injured by the tsunamis were later killed by deadly gangrene infections.

➤ **1998, Central and Northeast China**—This was the heaviest flooding of the Yangtze and other rivers since 1954. More than 3,000 were killed, and 14 million left homeless. Estimated damages exceeded $20 billion.

➤ **1999, Asia**—Flooding plagued Asia again after weeks of torrential downpours. More than 950 were killed, and millions were left homeless in South Korea, China, Japan, the Philippines, and Thailand.

➤ **1999, Vietnam**—Devastating floods caused $285 million in damage and killed more than 700 people.

➤ **1999, Venezuela**—At least 10,000 were killed in floods and mudslides caused by torrential rains. The government proclaimed it the country's worst natural disaster of the century.

➤ **2000, Mozambique**—At least a million people were displaced in the nation's worst floods ever. At least 200 were dead, with more deaths to come as water-dislodged mines from the 15-year civil war accidentally are detonated in their new, and unknown, resting places.

The Least You Need to Know

➤ Levees built by the Army Corps of Engineers ironically contributed to the 1927 Mississippi Flood.

➤ The flash flood in Rapid City, South Dakota, killed 236, injured 3,000, destroyed 1,335 homes and 5,000 cars, and totaled $160 million damage in 1972 dollars.

➤ When deciding where to build or buy a home, or even rent one, find out the area's flood risk.

➤ Know the difference between a flood watch, a flood warning, and a flash flood warning. Listening to the warnings and heeding them saves lives.

➤ You must take responsibility for saving your pets and finding shelter where they'll be welcome as well as safe.

➤ Bangladesh is the most flood-prone area in the world.

Chapter 21

Blizzards and How to Survive Them

In This Chapter

➤ The blizzard defined

➤ The worst blizzards in U.S. history

➤ Snowstorm safety

➤ Avalanche!

You may have heard that Eskimos have a hundred words for snow. They do, sort of. But Eskimo has several dialects, spoken from Siberia to Greenland, all classified as the Eskimo language. The West Greenland dialect offers at least 49 words for various kinds of snow. The one closest to blizzard is the word for "snowstorm," *pirsuq.* (In Eskimo languages, *q* sounds like *k.*)

No matter what you or Nanook call it, blizzards are fierce storms in which the water turns hard and cold, and extremely dangerous. To be classified as a blizzard, a snow-storm must have low temperatures (usually below 20°F), winds must be at least 35 miles per hour, and falling/blowing snow must frequently reduce visibility to less than a quarter of a mile. The whole thing must last, in any one location, at least three hours. A *severe* blizzard must offer the same stuff at 10°F or less, with winds 45 of miles per hour or more, and just about zero visibility a good deal of the time.

Most often, blizzards strike on the northwest side of intense storm systems. Extreme differences in pressure within the storm and to the west of it create the strong winds. When the jet stream has dipped far to the south, drier polar air clashes with the warmer, moister air—and snow, sleet, or freezing rain develops.

Types of Blizzards

Because of topography and prevailing weather patterns, different regions experience slightly different kinds of blizzards. Although English isn't as extravagant as Inuit about it, there are different names for these:

Earthy Language

The term **blizzard** comes partially from the German word *blitz*, which means "lightning."

To Ensure Preservation

Ice is tougher to deal with than a blanket of snow. Ice is very heavy and brings down the power lines it coats. It creates multicolored ice blocks from ordinary automobiles. It makes a venture outside, without mountain-climbing boots and ice picks, a prescription for multiple fractures. Stay inside.

➤ **Nor'easters**—In states such as New York and Massachusetts, blizzard precipitation often turns to rain, or a mixture of snow and rain. These are the famous and ferocious nor'easters, so named because of the continuously strong winds blowing in off the sea. Together, the storm and the ocean produce heavy snow, rain, and huge waves that cause extensive beach erosion, sweeping summer homes on the shore into the ocean. Wind gusts often beat those of hurricanes in intensity. The storm may even display an eye, like a hurricane, in the center of whirling low pressure.

Some notable nor'easters have wreaked havoc upon major metropolitan areas of the Northeast. The Halloween Storm of 1991 damaged or destroyed more than 1,000 homes from Maine to the Carolinas. A fast-moving storm will dump precipitation for 6 to 8 hours, while one that stalls will dump the white stuff for 12 to 24 hours, or more, as it did in big storms in 1888, 1969, 1978, and 1996.

➤ **Ice storms**—To create a winter storm in the Deep South, there must be very cold temperatures and enough moisture in the air to make rain, sleet, snow, or ice. Usually, moisture is not a problem, and, fortunately, the temperatures plummet only a couple of times a winter. There must also be a low-pressure area moving across the northern Gulf of Mexico.

On January 7 and 8, 1973, Atlanta and areas of north Georgia were hard hit by 1 to 4 inches of ice that closed schools and left 300,000 people without power for up to a week. More than 2.25 inches of liquid in the form of freezing rain, sleet, and snow fell on Atlanta between 7:00 P.M. and 9:00 P.M. on January 7, while temperatures remained at 32°F.

➤ **Blue northers**—Texas and the southern Plains experience winter storms when a strong cold front moves down the eastern slope of the Rockies. Over the panhandle, winds come out of the north, and temperatures drop. If the cold front parks, the moisture in the air off the Gulf, rising over the colder air, falls as snow, freezing rain, or (more usually) sleet. The typical blue-black sky that accompanies the storm accounts for its name.

White Fright: Blizzards We Have Known and Loathed

Unlike hurricanes, blizzards don't have names. They have been "recorded," though, since the 1870s, when an Iowa newspaper applied the word *blizzard*, previously referred to as a volley of musket fire, to a fierce snowstorm with relentless snow. The term was accepted for use quickly and was in general use by the 1880s. Good thing, because the end of that decade produced one humdinger of a storm.

On March 11, 1888, a nor'easter dumped 21 inches of snow on New York City. Drifts rose to 20 feet, piled by winds of 70 miles per hour. New Yorkers were stranded in elevated trains, carriages, and office buildings.

Post-War Trauma

In 1947, a scant two years after the worst war in history, the climate decided to do what Hitler's armies had not gotten even close to doing—paralyzing the East Coast of the United States. And during Christmas week, no less.

The monstrous storm dumped as much as 26 inches of snow on New York City, 4 more inches than the Blizzard of 1888 had produced. Cars were left stranded where they stopped. Subways couldn't run. And people with new, inexpensive Kodak cameras took lots and lots of pictures.

Blizzard Andrew

In 1978, an East Coast blizzard woke up the population to winter storm dangers, much as Hurricane Andrew would reawaken Florida to hurricane danger in 1992.

On January 20, 1978, there was a low pressure area along the East Coast. Forecasters' models all said the same thing: There was going to be a big storm. But no one believed them. New York and New England had not experienced a truly fierce winter storm for at least a generation, so the residents had become a bit lax about it all.

233

Research Findings

In 1816, June and July acted like winter. Connecticut had a blizzard. Danville, Vermont, had snow and sleet. Crops failed in the unexpected cold all over New England. Even Savannah, Georgia, saw a high temperature of only 46°F on the Fourth of July. It was dubbed "The Year Without a Summer." The cause? Possibly the eruption of the Tambora volcano in Java, a year earlier. The eruption had expelled tons of sun-obscuring ash into the atmosphere.

Too bad. New York was hit with 17 inches of snow, which piled up in 3-foot drifts. Transportation was paralyzed. Schools and businesses closed. The snow fell for so long that people wondered, even as they dashed out for essential food supplies, when it would end. People were stranded on roads all over the area.

In New England, it was even worse. For two days, the storm raged. It left more than 2 feet of snow, and at least 54 people died. More than 2,000 homes were destroyed; 10,000 people spent time in storm shelters, even if they had a home to go back to. On Route 128, 3,500 cars and trucks were stranded when a whiteout overwhelmed drivers. Drifts piled up to 15 feet. Damage amounted to $1 billion, and it began to be called The Storm of the Century.

The "Greed" Decade Big Storm

Winter storm watches and warnings were issued for Washington and Philadelphia for February 11 and 12, 1982. The snow began to get heavy in late afternoon on the 11th all over the New York City metropolitan area. By nightfall, the storm had developed into a genuine blizzard. Emergency services had their hands full as drivers tested their skills on hazardous roads.

By midnight on the 12th, there was well over a foot of snow in most places. Airports were closed. By morning, depending on where you lived, you might have had up to 24 inches of snow.

Putting 1888, 1978, and 1982 in the Back Seat

This one was dubbed Superstorm '93. It was called a hundred-year storm. It affected 26 states with high winds, heavy rain and snow, and even a storm surge.

On March 12, 1993, a storm in the Gulf of Mexico was pounding western Florida with high winds, tornadoes, and a 12-foot storm surge. By the 13th, it had dumped heavy snow—as much as 20 inches—on the Southeast. Over the next couple of days, it traveled on to Pennsylvania, New Jersey (leaving an average of 20 inches in its wake), and New York City, where it left at last 15 inches.

The storm left behind a billion dollars in damage, and 240 people dead.

And You Thought '93 Was Bad!

You don't have to believe in the Little Ice Age theories to know that the blizzard of 1996 was a doozie. Scientists from the Northeast Regional Climate Center at Cornell University reported this:

Sound the Alarm

A really big snow storm can have as far-reaching effects as a really big hurricane. In 1993, hurricane-force winds from the blizzard were felt as far away as Havana, Cuba.

> Philadelphia and parts of New Jersey were hammered by the greatest one-storm snowfall totals ever. In Philadelphia, the storm left 30.7 inches of snow, breaking the old one-storm snowfall total by 9.4 inches—the previous record was the February 11–12, 1983, storm that blanketed the City of Brotherly Love with 21.3 inches of snow. This week's blizzard exceeded the 12 inches of snow left during 1993's so-called Storm of the Century.

> The all-time record snowfall for New Jersey—34 inches in coastal Cape May, in February 1899—was beaten by 1 inch at Whitehouse Station in northeastern Hunterdon County, New Jersey, which received 35 inches of snow through January 9.

> The snowfall record in Newark, New Jersey—22.6 inches set on February 3–4, 1961—did not measure up to the 1996 blizzard's 27.8 inches. The 1993 "Storm of Century" left but 12.7 inches in Newark, a faint match for this week's onslaught.

> Central Park in New York City recorded 20.2 inches of snow in this storm, making it the third highest snowfall ever there. On parts of nearby Staten Island, New York, more than 27 inches of snow fell. La Guardia International Airport, New York, recorded 24 inches of snow, which exceeds the normal for the entire season of 22.6 inches.

On January 7 and 8, 1996, 28 inches of snow fell in New York City. The storm reached from Maine to Washington, D.C., and west to Pittsburgh. But its worst rampage was to the north; in Connecticut and central Massachusetts, it raged for a day and a half and delivered 40 to 50 inches of snow, piling up at times to 40- and 50-foot drifts. Whole houses and trains were buried. Two hundred ships sank or were severely damaged from Maryland to Massachusetts. Four hundred people lost their lives on land and sea.

The storm was pretty much universal. Dulles International Airport in suburban Virginia outside Washington, D.C., set a new 24-hour snow record, 19.8 inches of the total of 24.6 inches they got.

Virginia, in general, got slammed. Shenandoah caught 37 inches, and Sperryville had 31. Nor was neighboring West Virginia spared. Pocahontas County was pounded with 40 to 48 inches of snow. Webster County recorded between 24 and 46 inches of snow, and Randolph County had between 20 and 40. Petersburg and Brandywine both were blanketed with 30 inches of snow.

Comparisons of Snowfall, 1993 and 1996 Blizzards

City	1996	1993	
Philadelphia, Pennsylvania	30.7	12.0	
Newark, New Jersey	27.8	12.7	
Washington Dulles Airport	24.6	14.1	
Providence, Rhode Island	24.0	10.2	
Elkins, West Virginia	23.4	18.8	
Baltimore, Maryland	22.1	11.9	
Wilkes-Barre/Scranton	21.0	21.4	
Charleston, West Virginia	20.5	18.9	
New York City, New York	20.2	10.6	
Boston, Massachusetts	18.2	12.8	
Hartford, Connecticut	18.2	14.8	
Washington National Airport	17.1	6.6	
Bridgeport, Connecticut	15.0	10.8	
Portland, Maine	10.2	18.6	
Pittsburgh, Pennsylvania	9.6	24.6	
Williamsport, Pennsylvania	8.6	15.9	

When the Weather Outside Is Frightful

If it's winter and you're not in Florida, you might get a blizzard. So stay tuned to weather reports, and prepare; winter storm effects—including power outages and closed shops and businesses—can last several days. Be sure you have plenty of food in the house, especially things that you can eat without heating and that do not require refrigeration.

If you heat with oil, be sure that your tank is fairly full all winter. If the furnace has an electric starter, you'll be just as cold as everyone else without power. So, if at all possible, add a fireplace or woodstove to at least one room of your home, and be sure that you have fuel for it.

Research Findings

The East Coast doesn't have an exclusive on blizzards. Chicago gets them, too, and badly. In 1967, the city was treated to two days of nonstop blizzard, leaving 24 inches of snow—24 million tons, by estimate. O'Hare International Airport was closed for three straight days. About 60 deaths were attributed to the storm.

Check the batteries in your flashlight and portable radio before the storm. Get a supply of candles. A fondue set with fuel might also be a good idea; you can at least heat soup and water for hot beverages.

If you must go out, remember this: Winds can intensify the effects of cold temperatures. Take this advice:

➤ Wear several layers of loose-fitting, warm clothing.

➤ Wear a hat or a hooded jacket; you lose enormous amounts of body heat through your head.

➤ Cover your face with a scarf; this will protect your face and help warm the air you breathe into your lungs.

➤ Wear thermal socks or several layers of socks; warm, preferably waterproof boots; and gloves or mittens. Mittens do a better job of keeping your hands warm; wear them if you don't need the dexterity that gloves allow.

You should also keep some equipment in your car to cope with winter emergencies, including these items:

➤ Extra layers of loose-fitting clothing, blankets, or sleeping bags

➤ Nonperishable food items and jugs of water

➤ A flashlight with extra, brand-new batteries

➤ Matches

➤ An ice scraper and a small or collapsible snow shovel

➤ Jumper cables

➤ Chains

To Ensure Preservation

Driving in blizzards of any kind is hazardous, especially for those who get little practice driving in them. At the very least, winterize your car before the snow flies: Check your oil and replace your car's antifreeze; ensure that the heater, brakes, and windshield wipers are working well; install snow tires if you're in a heavy-snow area; and keep your gas tank full so that you won't have to walk through a storm because you ran out. If you are stranded, stay in the car. Use your heater sparingly, with plenty of ventilation. Keep awake, and move your legs and arms frequently.

Extreme Snowfall: Avalanches

Any place with snow and mountains is avalanche country. An avalanche is the swift descent of a mass of loosened snow, ice, rocks, and debris down a steep slope. Usually, as the "snowslide" picks up material, it picks up speed and vice versa, and, despite its origin as snowflakes on a hillside, ends up a solid, deadly, ice-hard wall that crushes and buries everything in its path, from skiers to their lodges.

Types of Avalanches

There are three kinds of avalanches, and all require these three ingredients:

1. Snow
2. Sufficient slope
3. Instability within the snowpack

Here are brief descriptions of the three types and what it takes to trigger them:

➤ **Powder avalanche**—These avalanches move at up to 100 miles per hour and have a tumbling, dusty appearance. They are usually triggered by vibrations, such as a loud noise. If you are caught in one, wind will hit you first, pushed ahead of the deadly tumbling snow, which will catch you in its mass and probably tumble and bury you very quickly.

➤ **Slab avalanche**—These usually occur on a 30° to 45° slope when a rise in temperature causes recent heavy snow, laid loosely over older snow, to melt until both slip away as one large mass. In addition to the thousands of tons of snow that destroys everything in the path of the avalanche, ice lumps as big as houses may come with it. Triggers may be a storm, as can a temperature change or the weight of a person on top of the mass. These are the most dangerous to skiers.

➤ **Wet avalanche**—These don't look bad because they move only at about 5 miles per hour. But they still have enormous power.

How Disastrous Can an Avalanche Be?

Ask FEMA. In February 2000, Alaskan state officials requested FEMA assistance because of avalanches and severe weather in the Kenai Peninsula and Prince William Sound. Alaska's governor had already declared a state of disaster, for multiple reasons. Seward Highway, the major link between Anchorage and the Kenai Peninsula, was closed about 20 miles south of Anchorage by an avalanche. Other roadways were closed by avalanches or heavy drifting snow, isolating the communities of Whittier, Portage, and Valdez, as well as the entire Kenai Peninsula.

Scattered power outages plagued the region as avalanches and heavy winds downed power lines. Commercial cellular phone outages had hit numerous communities, along with some land line communication failure as the avalanches affected transmission equipment, including radio towers. At least two fatalities and several injuries resulted.

Around the World

In 1999, two avalanches, minutes apart, hit the town of Le Tour in the French Alps. Eleven chalets were buried. Residents of Le Tour, near the ski town of Chamonix (also host to a Winter Olympics in 1924, and not far from Albertville, site of the 1992 games), helped police and sensor-equipped crews search for survivors.

Avalanches and heavy snows had also hit Austria hard: Supplies and emergency equipment had to be flown in to towns completely cut off by impassable roads.

In at least one Austrian avalanche in February 1999, seven people died; 55 were buried but later rescued. According to a Reuters report, rescuer workers said that most of those saved were badly injured. A blizzard in progress kept the injured from being evacuated or more help being flown in.

Even people in non-resort countries such as Russia experience death by avalanche. In late December 1996, rescue workers freed dozens of people trapped in a Caucasus mountain tunnel by an avalanche. Heavy snows along the highway that links Russia's North Ossetia region with the breakaway Georgia province South Ossetia have triggered avalanches and rock slides, including the one that cut off the 2.5-mile Roksky tunnel.

The same week, in Turkey, an avalanche thought to have been caused by vibrations from a snow-flattening machine killed at least six at a ski resort near Erzurum. About 300 people had been killed by avalanches in the area during the three years before that.

Minimal Safety Measures for Avalanche Country

Very often, say experts, people trigger the avalanches that kill them.

Says Rocky Mountain Hiking, a winter sports service in the Rocky Mountains, "About half of all buried victims (of avalanches) will die if they are not rescued within 30 minutes. Many are killed during or within minutes of the avalanche from suffocation, the severe trauma of hitting boulders or trees during the slide, or having been crushed by massive blocks of snow."

The service recommends two things: venturing out only where fast, organized rescue services are in operation, and learning about avalanches and how to avoid them.

If you must enter an avalanche area, here's what you'll need:

➤ Help in finding the safest routes and places to be

➤ An avalanche transceiver, on your person at all times, to alert rescue workers in an emergency

➤ A shovel that's strong, light, and reliable

➤ A first-aid kit

How to Assess a Route—The Short Version

Terrain is the only factor that a non-expert can hope to assess, even minimally.

Where to Go

➤ Ridges are usually a safe route, as long as you don't step on cornices or the lee side of the ridge.

➤ Windward slopes, if winds have scoured them leaving shallow or patchy snow; beware of gullies or depressions, however.

➤ Traveling at the bottoms of broad valleys is usually safe, except in periods of high avalanche hazard. An avalanche can run down into the valleys, especially if there is an established slide path from previous avalanches.

Where Not to Go

➤ Lee slopes, unless you are confident that the slope is stable. In the Rockies, the east and north slopes are usually lee slopes.

➤ Cornices, which can collapse and trigger the slope below to avalanche; beware of them while traveling across ridges.

➤ Gulleys, which are natural funnels for avalanches.

This is a very simplified and condensed explanation for finding a good route and for rescue. Only with good training, practice, and experience is it safe to travel in avalanche terrain.

The Least You Need to Know

➤ To be classified as a blizzard, a snowstorm must have accompanying temperatures of below 20°F, have winds that blow at least 35 miles per hour, and produce falling/blowing snow that frequently reduces visibility to less than a quarter of a mile. The whole thing must last at least three hours.

➤ In North America, the worst snowstorms of the last century or so occurred in 1888, 1947, 1978, 1982, 1993, and 1996.

➤ Stock up on food and supplies before winter arrives.

➤ An avalanche can happen anywhere there is snow, sufficient slope, and instability within the snowpack.

➤ Learn how to assess the safest routes when in avalanche territory.

Chapter 22

Lackawatta Problems: Drought

In This Chapter

➤ How the Dust Bowl got started

➤ Recent droughts

➤ The other side of the world

➤ Planting rain, old ways and new

To most Americans—except those who survived and still recall the Dust Bowl—drought is just something the politicians talk about that may, at worst, cause a little inconvenience. Perhaps lawn-watering is restricted to once a week. Flow-restriction devices are provided to homeowners by the government for use in their shower nozzles. Refilling swimming pools is prohibited. That sort of thing.

But that's not real drought, not skin-thickening, tongue-coating, throat-parching, death-dealing drought as it is known still in many parts of the globe.

Between a Rock and a Hard Place

When Americans think of drought, it is usually the Dust Bowl of the 1930s that comes to mind. The Dust Bowl was born officially on Palm Sunday, April 14, 1935. On that day, in northwestern Kansas, a cloud much worse than the one that transported Dorothy to the Land of Oz was born.

A Black Cloud

It had been a clear day, with no wind, for a change, and residents of the drought-stricken plains thought it might be a good day for a little rest; they had been working feverishly, seven days a week, to keep crops and cattle in spite of the drought. Some visited friends; some caught up on household chores, such as taking the rugs outside for a beating, airing the stuffed furniture already silted from the migration of fine particles through double-hung windows.

But in mid-afternoon, their universe changed. A huge wind, rolling across the plains, had picked up, apparently, what remained of the topsoil in Kansas, Nebraska, Texas. It rolled across the plains, carrying an inky load of silty earth that choked car engines, blacked out radio transmissions, and transformed barbed-wire fence into running sparklers pinging electricity as the wind-driven highly charged particles struck them and changed magnetic fields.

Cows choked to death where they stood. Crops were buried. And the Dust Bowl was born in the biggest of the Black Blizzards that had started five years earlier; it would be 10 more years until they stopped completely.

To Ensure Preservation

Why didn't Americans starve in large numbers in the drought? On April 8, 1935, a week before the Day of the Black Blizzard—which delivered silt even to New York City and Washington, D.C.—President Franklin D. Roosevelt approved the Emergency Relief Appropriation Act, which provided $525 million for drought relief, and authorized creation of the Works Progress Administration (WPA), which would employ 8.5 million people.

More Than a Lack of Water

In addition to affecting agriculture, the drought of the 1930s affected wildlife and caused water-shortage hardships for even nonagricultural households. The agricultural disasters contributed to the bank closures, business losses, unemployment, you name it. Without water, people die and their institutions suffer.

Displaced farm workers headed west, and in turn displaced people already living there and looking for jobs. Between the two groups, relief and health agencies were often overwhelmed.

What Caused the Drought?

Although there was a shortage of rainfall, it became clear that the drought was intensified by human error. In the prosperous days before the drought, land was not as well managed as it should have been. Many farmers had forgotten lessons learned as long ago as Biblical times—lessons about letting some fields lie fallow every seven years so that they could replenish nutrients through sprouting indigenous plants, rotating crops, tilling around hillsides rather than up and down, and so on.

Research Findings

In the drought years of the 1890s, enterprising men hit the trail as rainmakers. Desperate Nebraskans sometimes hired them. Some even had success. In 1894, near Ravenna, Nebraska, five of seven rainmaking experiments actually produced rain. In the Texas Panhandle, rainmakers set off gunpowder and made little more than noise. Needless to say, they had trouble collecting their fees.

New technologies—gas-powered machinery and so on—allowed more crops to be planted on the same land than before. New fertilizers allowed planting and raising more plants per acre, but that also consumed more water per acre and helped deplete the other soil nutrients that much faster.

Research Findings

At a meeting in Pueblo, Colorado, in 1935, experts estimated that 850,000,000 tons of topsoil had blown off the Southern Plains during that year, and that if the drought continued, the total area affected would increase from 4.35 million acres to 5.35 million acres by the spring of 1936. C.H. Wilson, of the Resettlement Administration, proposed buying up 2.25 million acres and retiring it from cultivation.

Greed also had something to do with it. Before the Dust Bowl era, the world discovered wheat and was paying good money for it. Farmers had an outstanding crop yield in 1926, and they overplanted year after year, thinking only of short-term money and not of long-term healthy land. They planted marginal land, land that would wear out quickly. Once again, there was a bumper crop, in 1931. Unfortunately, that abundance forced down the price; even before the dust began to blow, farmers went broke by getting less for their grain than it had cost them to produce it. Some of those abandoned their fields, beginning a vicious cycle that would eventually affect the whole nation.

All these factors created the major drought in American history.

The Government Steps In

It's impossible to tell how much the drought really cost, but some estimates of government assistance rise as high as $1 billion in 1930s dollars. As any number of historical accounts will tell you, even at that, many people were passed over and passed

by, becoming hobos, living in shanty-towns beneath overpasses—doing anything they could do to survive.

Still, the United States had a strong central government to coordinate relief efforts across the region. Indeed, the measures instituted by the federal government during the 1930s—the New Deal—helped soften American reliance on self-help in favor of reliance on a much less passive government.

Whether or not one agrees with the political effect of the U.S. government's response to the drought, one thing is certain: Fewer people died during our great drought than might have been expected in any other part of the world.

The New Deal programs meant to cope with the Dust Bowl problems included these:

➤ Providing emergency supplies, cash, and live-stock feed, and transport to maintain the basic functioning of farms and ranches

➤ Establishing healthcare facilities and supplies to meet emergency medical needs

➤ Establishing government-based markets for farm goods, as well as higher tariffs and loan funds for farm market maintenance and business re-habilitation

➤ Providing the supplies, technology, and technical advice necessary to research, implement, and promote appropriate land-management strategies

By 1938, the WPA workers had planted trees as wind-breaks across the plains, replowed lands into proper furrows, and instituted other conservation practices. Soil-blowing had decreased 65 percent. In the fall of 1939, significant rain finally came. Between that and the start of World War II, the country began to emerge from the Depression, and the fields began to sprout golden wheat again.

Same Stuff, Different Year

Something was learned from the 1930s experience. When rainfall in the East was minimal in 1999, politicians were quick to take action. The following two examples also provide a glimpse at how drought can affect more than just water supply.

Maryland: Crabby from Lack of Water

The drought of 1999 threatened the crabs in the Chesapeake Bay. Maryland draws some water from the Susquehanna River, which flows into the bay; plans were afoot to draw even more, if need be, although the river was already down by two-thirds. That might well have affected the temperature of the bay, a critical aspect of successfully harvesting healthy crabs.

But it didn't happen. Just when Baltimore city was down to about a 35-day water supply, the rains came—too much rain, in the form of back-to-back hurricanes, but rain just the same.

Whew! Anyone who had driven by Maryland's extensive series of reservoirs the previous summer would have seen shoreline big enough to build homes on where there should have been water, and grasslands growing around fairly large puddles in some outlying fingers of the reservoirs. It was scary. But the drought emergency, with mandatory water restrictions, was ended on September 4, when the reservoirs had reached 40 percent of capacity.

Sound the Alarm

There are lingering effects of every drought. After the 1999 drought, ABC news reported, "The State Agricultural Department figures show the drought we had over the summer cost farmers in Maryland $72 million dollars in lost crops ... and $30 million dollars because of depressed prices."

West Virginia, Mountain Mama

If John Denver had been alive, he no doubt would have done a concert to raise funds to help the state glorified in his early opus.

In August 1999, under the headline "Family farms drying up," West Virginia Agriculture Secretary Gus Douglass said that 15 inches of rain would be needed to make up for the state's dry weather, but that the damage to crops was already irreversible. Douglass cited a farmer in Lewis County who had to sell every one of the cows he had spent a lifetime with, selectively breeding for the best possible herd: His pasture was dry and water was scarce, too scarce to properly raise the cows.

Rainfall on the East Coast had been between 50 and 80 percent below normal, and there had been little snow the previous winter. Up to 30 percent of rural water supplies in the region were gone.

In West Virginia, all 55 counties were declared official drought disaster areas by the federal government. Market prices, for beef especially, had been down before the drought; few farmers could afford the debt service of more loans for rebuilding herds or replanting fields, even at low interest rates. West Virginia farmers ended up at least $100 million in the hole.

Trouble in Paradise

The United Kingdom's Hadly Centre is predicting a future temperature rise this century. What does that mean? A warmer climate would bring increased evaporation, but it might also bring more severe storms, increasing runoff rather than water availability. If the water runs off, you can't use it. And that's not to mention the damage from winds and water.

What's that got to do with drought? In warmer conditions, climates become more variable, and more variability invariably means more severe droughts. The combination of severe rains and major runoff with no rains is, one might say, nature's balancing act. Both phases can be deadly.

Agricultural production is a $500 million industry in Hawaii, with 80 percent coming from crops, and almost half of that from irrigated land. Major crops, sugar cane and pineapple, would be affected only plus or minus about 10 percent in such conditions.

Sound the Alarm

Weather and Europeans have been bad for Hawaiian wildlife. An estimated 91 percent of flowering plant species, 81 percent of birds, and 99 percent of terrestrial snails and arthropods are found only in Hawaii. At the same time, Hawaii is the world's capital for species extinction and endangerment. Of the known U.S. extinctions, 70 percent have occurred in Hawaii. Since 1778, the year of first European contact, 263 species are known to have become extinct, including 50 percent of the bird fauna and perhaps 50 percent of plants and 90 percent of native land snails.

But the forests are another story. Native Hawaiian forests are already being reduced and, in some cases, eliminated by competition by non-native trees and plants. Climactic stress could render the already stressed native plants even more susceptible to funguses and insects. And drought conditions would affect the tropical cloud forest, one of the wettest ecosystems on Earth. Forest fires caused by dry conditions could further damage the forests.

Drought of Africa

The American Dust Bowl and more recent droughts took very few lives. The same cannot be said about a drought region called the Sahel in North Africa, roughly the same size as the United States. There, in just the final third of the twentieth century, at least 1.2 million people lost their lives through the effects of drought.

The Sahel forms the southern edge of the Sahara Desert, running 4,500 kilometers from Senegal through Maritania, Mali, Burkina Faso, Niger, and Chad. It is slightly more arid than the Sudan to its southern edge, and has supported agriculture of sorts, livestock herding, fishing, and some Allied occupations. Most food production in the Sahel depends on three months of rainfall in the summer, except along major rivers and lakes.

Since 1900, three major droughts have occurred: 1910–1916, 1941–1945, and a long period of below average rainfall beginning in the late-1960s and continuing, with some interruptions, into the 1980s.

But persistent drought is only one of a set of overwhelming problems affecting the Sahel, which has some of the poorest nations in the world. There are tribal disputes, international disputes, problems of linking up with the world's increasingly sophisticated monetary systems, and so on.

Still, lack of rain can be coped with as long as farmers can diversify and have sufficient assets and a little help from their friends. In the future, that might be enough. Since the early 1970s, there has been an increased international ability to warn of drought-induced food shortages and provide relief. Grain reserves have been established, although in remote areas, funds are frequently inadequate to maintain them properly. And, when needed, it doesn't always "trickle down" to the poor.

When Withering on the Vine Is Real

The very modern twentieth century offered some very medieval sorts of disaster, producing death on a scale that only sci-fi writers could imagine. But it was not the sinister Borg creatures from a galaxy far, far away that did the damage; it was the Earth's own atmosphere.

To Ensure Preservation

In the Sahel, the Niger and Senegal Rivers are still the main "roads." It helps to be near them in time of trouble.

Sound the Alarm

Droughts have an enormous capacity for changing the character of civilizations. Timbuktu is the home of the Tuareg, a nomadic, fair-skinned people known as the "blue men of the desert" because of the swaths of indigo cloth they wrap around themselves. Unfortunately, their nomadic life was disrupted by the droughts of the Sahel in the 1970s and 1980s: Many became urban residents or farmers.

Here are some of the worst of the worst of twentieth-century droughts:

➤ **The Chinese New Famine**—In 1935–1936, more than 5 million people died of starvation as a result of drought.

➤ **The Chinese Famine of 1928–1930**—Also known as "The Old Famine," this drought left more than 3 million dead.

➤ **Two other nameless Chinese droughts**—In 1907, more than 24 million died. In 1941–1942, more than 3 million died.

➤ **Indian drought**—India has suffered two major droughts (although there are lesser ones all the time). In 1900, as many as 3.25 million died; in 1965–1967, more than 1.5 million died.

➤ **Russian drought**—Russia, too, has had droughts. In the Ukraine and Volga areas, anywhere from one-quarter million to 5 million died in 1921–22.

➤ **The Sahel of Africa drought**—Drought is a repetitive—and often continuous—problem. Major drought periods include 1910–1916, 1941–1945, and 1970–1985. During the last extended period, in two waves, the drought claimed 1.2 million lives.

Of Biblical Proportions

Recent droughts are not the only ones worth worrying about. Connie Woodhouse and Jonathan Overpeck, of the National Oceanic and Atmospheric Administration, have made some interesting discoveries about historical droughts. By reviewing paleoclimatic literature, as well as data from historical documents and tree rings, archaeological remains, and sediments, they have been able to determine what droughts were like before mankind decided to track them.

They found evidence of two major droughts between the thirteenth and sixteenth centuries that were incredibly long, very severe, and widespread. The worst of the megadroughts occurred in the western United States in the latter half of the sixteenth century.

Their studies showed that conditions that lead to such droughts could recur, leading to a natural disaster of a dimension unprecedented in the twentieth century. Current land use practices and global warming could ensure that the megadrought we next experience will be more devastating than the Dust Bowl era's dry weather patterns. Even without the greenhouse effect, all the other factors could make future droughts very bad indeed, Woodhouse and Overpeck conclude.

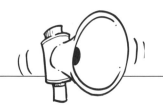

Sound the Alarm

Amazingly, Woodhouse and Overpeck found that droughts of the twentieth century have been only moderately severe and relatively short. In fact, we can expect droughts the size of the Dust Bowl once or twice each century.

Research Findings

After an Israeli scientist linked higher Middle Eastern rainfall levels to El Niño action, he speculated that the Pharaoh's Biblical drought could have been caused by several years without El Niño's impact.

As the twenty-first century began, a drought in Ethiopia was proving that their findings might be more accurate than we'd like.

What Science Can Do

For thousands of years, humans have tried to coax the weather into performing the way we would like it to, producing rain on demand.

They invented cloud seeding. Dr. Vincent J. Schaefer conducted the first field experiments following his basic discoveries in 1946 at the General Electric Laboratory in Schenectady, New York. Since 1946, various inorganic and organic materials have been known to alter the physical processes that lead to the formation and growth of water droplets and ice crystals in clouds.

Recently, extensive scientific experiments have led to the development of techniques that can provide predictable results when applied under proper supervision. Cloud and storm-related events that are often the target for cloud-seeding programs include rainfall, snow, fog, lightning, hail, and devastating winds from severe storms. In short, it's not only about making precipitation, but about making the right kind in the right place at the right time.

Cloud droplets form around microscopic particles—dust, smoke, salt crystals, soil, and other materials that are always present in the atmosphere. Without these nuclei, there would be no clouds.

To determine precipitation, three things must be taken into account: the vertical and horizontal dimensions of the clouds, the lifetime of the clouds, and the sizes and concentrations of cloud droplets and ice particles. Under proper conditions, one or more of these three factors can be favorably modified by seeding the cloud with appropriate nuclei.

Scientists can prompt rain by two processes, called "warm rain" and "cold rain." Depending on which is the method likely to create rain under current conditions, man can assist by furnishing the proper nuclei at the proper time in the proper place.

Usually, this is done by airplane. But on high mountain tops, snow can be created by using guns to spray the nuclei into the atmosphere; ski resorts in western states even today employ these modern rainmakers.

The Least You Need to Know

➤ In addition to low rainfall, bad land-management practices and greed played a role in causing the drought of the 1930s.

➤ In the past 100 years, at least the equivalent of the current population of the United States has died in Asian droughts.

➤ Africa is beset by drought at the edge of the Sahara.

➤ Droughts may become more severe in the next 10 years.

➤ The modern rainmaker knows that it's not only about making precipitation, but about making the right kind in the right place at the right time.

Part 6

Bugs, Bugs, and More

There are the creepy-crawly kind of bugs. And then there are the bugs you get that send you to bed coughing and sneezing with fever.

Either way, plenty of varieties have had us jumpin' and twitchin' since the beginning of time. And the much-maligned bedbug is among the least of them.

Bugs and bugs. Insects and bacteria. Fearsome fleas and flesh-eating microbes. Yikes! Read on.

Chapter 23

Creepy, Crawly Epidemics: Vermin

In This Chapter

➤ Plagues of locusts are Biblical—and still real

➤ Rat facts

➤ The buzz about killer bees

➤ 'Skeeters and the bad blood they can bring

➤ Ticks and cockroaches and lice, oh my!

If you live in a New York City high-rise, it's almost guaranteed that, no matter how fastidious you are, you share your home with the ubiquitous German cockroach. If you live in the Southwest, you are in an area particularly beset by the depredations of the South American killer bee. If you live anywhere from the Gulf Coast to Maine, from Long Island to San Francisco, you've seen a few mosquitoes in your time. If you stroll in the woods, you'll encounter ticks. And almost certainly, sooner or later your dogs—or your uninvited rat guests—will have fleas.

Is there no place safe from infestations of things that creep, crawl, and carry disease? Nope. Well, maybe Antarctica—unless someone brings lice to the research station.

Locusts

And then there are the locusts. Clouds of them have eaten every blade of food in just about every nation at one time or another, from ancient Egypt (the Book of Exodus mentions that a huge swarm covered the Earth "and there remained not any green thing") to twentieth-century America. The United States has seen plagues of locusts,

To Ensure Preservation

It's all in the way you look at it. To some, grasshoppers and locusts are vermin; to others, they are delicacies. Both types of insects were harvested by Utah settlers to avoid famine in the 1800s, when those very critters made grain crops fail. The Ute Indians made fruitcakes from grasshopper flour and currants. In Africa, still, grasshoppers are high-protein snacks. In Algeria, dried grasshoppers are munched on like dates.

or grasshoppers, throughout its history. In 1797, grasshoppers ruined crops in New England; in 1818 they destroyed crops in the Red River Valley of Minnesota.

Joseph Smith was the founder of Mormonism, but Brigham Young (1801–1877) took it to Utah in 1846–1847. No sooner had the people gotten settled and their farms planted than a plague of locusts descended upon them, in 1848. But they were saved: Flocks of gulls moved in and devoured the hordes of grasshoppers eating the crops. The wingless variety of grasshopper in question was later nicknamed the Mormon cricket.

One swarm of winged grasshoppers, in the locust decade of the 1870s, was reportedly 100 miles wide and 300 miles long, so huge that it obscured the sun. Even smaller swarms left the prairies barren, with holes in the ground where wheat had grown. They stripped trees of both leaves and bark, and they halted railroad travel.

Laura Ingalls Wilder wrote of the Locust Plague Tragedy of 1873–1878 in her book *On the Banks of Plum Creek:*

> A cloud was over the sun. It was not like a cloud they had ever seen before. It was a cloud of something like snowflakes, but they were larger than snowflakes, and thin and glittering. Light shone through each flickering particle …. The cloud was hailing grasshoppers. The cloud was grasshoppers. Their bodies hid the sun and made darkness. Their thin, large wings gleamed and glittered. The rasping whirring of their wings filled the whole air and they hit the ground and the house with the noise of a hailstorm.

With the advent of the plague of locusts, the dreams of her family for good crops, a large house, horses, and some luxuries all died. Many families gave up or sent the men to work in lumber camps to survive.

Some sought public or private help. The scale of destruction was so great, though, that local charitable resources were strapped; the state and federal governments stepped in, finally, with the U.S. Army distributing food and clothing to those in need.

The invention of *DDT* did a great deal to stop the plagues. Of course, that presented problems of its own: It became concentrated in the flesh of birds and fishes that ate the insects that had become, in a very short time, resistant to DDT. The birds and fish simply lived with it in their systems, passing it up the food chain and damaging or killing off populations of creatures higher up.

Earthy Language

DDT is the abbreviation for dichlorodiphenyltrichloroethane, a synthetic insecticide that kills by disrupting the nervous system. It was invented in 1874 but its insecticidal qualities were not realized until 1939 by Swiss chemist Paul Hermann Mueller. During and after World War II, DDT was used to control lice, fleas, mosquitos, the Colorado potato beetle, the gypsy moth, and other vegetable/grain eating insects.

Bee Wary

To people allergic to their stings, bees can be deadly. Still, the average honeybee has been around for a long time, and no one would have considered these insects a plague—until, of course, the African killer bees arrived.

Surprisingly, killer bees are only slightly more poisonous than the bees we are all used to in Europe and North America. But they are ferocious and relentless, the Terminator of bees. Where a European bee colony would send three or four bees to scout and sting an intruder, the African bees send 300 or 400.

Killer bees stop at nothing. Even if you jump into a lake and go underwater to get away from them, chances are that—unless you can hold your breath for several hours, or even a whole day—they will be hanging around up top to sting you when you emerge. So then you'll be wet *and* endangered.

Zounds! How did this all come about? And where can you go to avoid them?

Bee Story

It began in 1957, when 26 colonies of African killer bees, *Apis millifera scutellata,* escaped from an apiary in Brazil and mated with the calm little European honeybee.

By 1990, the bees had reached the southern tip of Texas. By 1994, they had wreaked havoc in the southwest, and parts of California were aswarm with them.

In Tucson, Arizona, on March 14, 2000, killer bees stung several workers on a roof at least seven times each; two were stung 50 times each, mainly on the head and neck.

"One minute I was tearing off the roof, and the next it seemed like everywhere I looked there were bees," said 50-year-old Michael Barrett, who was stung about 20 times, mostly on his face, head, and arms. Another man was so frightened by the attack that he jumped 20 feet from the roof to a lower ledge, and then jumped from the ledge to the ground to escape the bees.

Firefighters found the bees' nest next to the grocery store, where the roofers had thrown some debris. Unknowingly, one worker had been removing the debris from the nesting area. The Tucson Fire Department killed the bees with a foamy soap-and-water mixture and uncovered four large palettes of honeycomb.

The deaths of four people in the state, as well as the deaths of several pets, are blamed on the bees.

A report in the *Los Angeles Times* on November 11, 1999, said, "Africanized bees are considered the greatest threat to people in open areas—such as in fields or equestrian trials—where there is no immediate place for a person to take shelter, and a particular threat to the elderly or infirm who cannot run away or may fall and become easy prey."

So don't bother them and they won't bother you, right? Wrong. Killer bees respond aggressively to such everyday occurrences as vibrations from lawn mowers, traffic, and even people on foot.

Bee List

The Salt Lake City newspaper, the *Salt Lake Tribune*, ran an article in late 1999 about what to do when swarms appear. Here are some hints:

1. Run—fast.
2. Remove stingers by scraping; pulling releases more toxin.
3. See a doctor if you're stung more than 15 times.
4. Especially if you're allergic to bee stings, carry a bee sting kit when you're outside.
5. Inspect your home and yard for large holes and open spaces where bees can nest. Seal them.
6. If you find a hive, call the state extension service or fire or police officials. *Do not remove it yourself.*

German Cockroaches, or the Teutonic Plague

Orkin, the exterminating company, says there are myths about cockroaches and then there are facts. A myth is that cockroaches are disgusting, but not unhealthy, to have in your home. The fact is, they are very unhealthy. They can contaminate food and cause gastroenteritis, food poisoning, and diarrhea. They have been implicated in the transmission of a variety of pathogenic (disease-causing) organisms, including at least one parasitic protozoan, and they cause allergic reactions in many people.

They can come into your home a number of ways: via paper products or paper packaging such as grocery bags, cardboard boxes, and drink cartons; and via secondhand appliances, such as refrigerators, televisions, VCRs, microwaves, and so on. Rarely, they have been observed to migrate from building to building on warm evenings.

Keeping food properly stored won't starve them out, either. Cockroaches can eat starch-based paints, wallpaper paste, envelope glue, and bars of soap. And that's a fact.

To get rid of them, exterminate.

Rats!

In the 1960s, a television public service advertisement showed a ghetto child saying, "Here, kitty, kitty," without knowing she was actually calling to a huge, hairy rat.

Rats continue to be a problem in urban areas. They are a problem on farms, where any number of cats are kept just to deal with them. They are a problem on ships still, where Rat Guards, inverted cones big enough to prevent a rat from climbing over them, are installed on ropes tying even huge U.S. Navy vessels to the docks.

Rats were such a problem in Germany in times past that the story of the Pied Piper of Hamelin arose, codified by poet Robert Browning in 1888 in the poem, "The Pied Piper of Hamelin." Read over a few lines:

> Rats!
> They fought the dogs and killed the cats,
> And bit the babies in the cradles,
> And ate the cheeses out of the vats,
> And licked the soup from the cooks' own ladles,
> Split open the kegs of salted sprats,
> Made nests inside men's Sunday hats,
> And even spoiled the women's chats,
> By drowning their speaking
> With shrieking and squeaking
> In fifty different sharps and flats.

The tale refers to a time 500 years earlier—the time of the Bubonic Plague, spread by fleas that lived on rats.

Research Findings

The Bubonic Plague traveled on a merchant ship from Tana in the Crimea to Messina in Sicily in 1347. The ship's rats were in-fected with the disease, which took many forms. The plague attacked the lymphatic gland system and caused swelling. Pneumonic Plague attacked the lungs and was more devastating.

The Bubonic Plague (about which there is more in Chapter 24, "Ancient Plagues on All Their Houses") was caused by the bacillus *Yersina pestis*, primarily an internal parasite of wild rodents—rats, mice, and squirrels. It was spread by fleas looking to humans for a meal once their animal host had died. The plague could even enter the bloodstream through contact with the fleas' excrement.

Here are some rat facts that explain why rats are such a scourge:

➤ Rats will eat anything, including dead—and dying—members of their own species.

➤ Rats drag food to a safe hiding place to consume it.

➤ Rats don't need to see things to get around; they rely on smell, touch, and hearing. Guard hairs and whiskers help them move quickly just about anywhere.

➤ Rats chew wiring and cause fires.

➤ Rats eat and urinate in human and animal food they get into.

➤ Rats can get into your house through a hole as small as a quarter. They memo-rize routes, using the same ones habitually, although they can figure out new ones, too.

Mosquitoes

Generations have learned in school that digging the Panama Canal was dangerous, mainly because of the malaria and yellow fever carried by the indigenous and ubiqui-tous mosquitoes living on that isthmus. Since then, of course, mosquitoes—especially in the United States—have been considered more a nuisance than a plague.

Not so. Since 1972, reports the U.S. Centers for Disease Control, there have been signs that mosquito-borne illnesses are not just a tropical problem. One sign was the case of a man who went camping in northeast Michigan and came down with malaria.

So slather on some bug juice and read on. Here are other things you can get from "unauthorized blood donations"—that is, mosquito bites.

Malaria

Ebola caught the headlines, but *malaria* catches about 400 million people each year in its fevered, anemia-causing, repeatedly debilitating grip.

About 1,200 Americans catch malaria each year, mostly while traveling abroad. But in 1993, two New York City dwellers caught it, probably from mosquitoes that had fed on infected foreigners. New York is at least 1,000 miles north of "malaria country." However, the anopheles mosquito, which transmits it, lives all over the United States all summer. Until after the Civil War, malaria was endemic in parts of the Mississippi Valley and the Chesapeake Bay region.

Sound the Alarm

Malaria is most severe in Africa, where it kills two million people each year, either directly or with some help from acute respiratory infections. Most of the dead are children.

West Nile Fever

It's a bird. It's a plane. Well, it's a virus of birds that might have traveled by plane in the form of infected passengers. In any case, West Nile Fever, a new form of an old disease, hatched in birds and spread by mosquitoes, has arrived in the New World—New York, to be precise. It arrived in late summer of 1999, making several people ill and killing some.

West Nile Fever used to be limited to Egypt, Israel, India, France, Africa, and the northern Mediterranean area. Until those 1999 New York cases, the disease had never before been identified in the United States or any other Western Hemisphere nation, according to the Centers for Disease Control.

In early fall of 1996, Romania had 299 West Nile Fever patients; 15 died. Then the disease began spreading through that region, hitting Czechland in 1997.

Here's the kicker: Prior immunity to a different variant of dengue apparently *increases* the risk of developing grades II through IV.

Earthy Language

The word **malaria** comes from the Italian *mala aria*, or bad air. The disease was once attributed to the unwholesome air found in and near swamps. In fact, it is not the swamp air, but the mosquitoes breeding in the swamps that cause malaria by transmitting, through their bites, protozoa—one-celled organisms—that feed off red blood cells. The disease is characterized by severe chills and fever.

Sound the Alarm

There are four grades of West Nile Fever. Grade I includes headache, weakness, fever, skin rashes, and sometimes nausea and vomiting, but it is rarely fatal. Grade II adds spontaneous bleeding of skin, gums, and intestinal tract to that list, and is often fatal. Grade III, also often fatal, incorporates agitation and circulatory failure, including heart failure. Grade IV adds profound shock to the symptom list and is, of course, often fatal.

Yellow Fever

The *A. aegypti* mosquito transmits yellow fever when it sucks blood from an infected person and then infects a healthy person when it takes another blood meal. Until recently, these viral diseases were not found in the United States. Now, though, the *A. aegypti* mosquito is found in the southeastern United States and has the potential to spread the disease.

Research Findings

The District of Columbia in its early days was like a marshy wilderness, where pigs roamed the streets, and mosquitoes made people sick from malaria.

Yellow fever is characterized by fever, vomiting, and jaundice, or the turning yellow of skin and mucus membranes. In 1990, yellow fever cases worldwide reached the highest levels since 1948, according to the World Health Organization.

Dengue Fever

Dengue fever and dengue hemorrhagic fever (DHF) are caused by any of four different viruses. Naturally, they are pest-borne, transmitted by females of two species of mosquito of the genus *Aedes*.

The most effective preventive measure is the use of mosquito repellent. As yet, no successful vaccine for dengue fever has been developed.

Lice: Not Nice

Infestations of head lice beset schoolchildren and their mothers alike. But those aren't the kind of louse that's a plague—well, not a *real* plague.

The real louse is the one that spreads typhus, recognized as the only *rickettsial* disease that causes extensive human epidemics. The typhus organism lives in the lice as a parasite, infecting man and animals only when one of the lice bites.

Since World War II, typhus outbreaks have occurred primarily in Africa and mainly in Burundi, Ethiopia, and Rwanda. In 1996, Burundi reported 3,500 cases; that number jumped to 20,000 for the period from January to March 1997.

The Dirty Tricks of Ticks

Ticks carry a variety of disases in the United States.

Lyme Disease

More than 14,000 cases were reported to the Centers for Disease Control and Prevention (CDC) in 1994, primarily in the Northeast, the mid-Atlantic coastal states, and the north-central United States. Lyme disease is often thought at first to be a bad cold, but it is followed by debilitation and fatigue for indeterminate periods. A cure has not been found; time often diminishes the symptoms. Prevention includes staying away from tick-infested areas.

Rocky Mountain Spotted Fever

Most infections are acquired in the Southeast and the west south-central United States. More than 400 cases of Rocky Mountain spotted fever (RMSF) were reported in 1994. In recent years, prompt treatment has reduced mortality from 25 percent to 5 percent.

About a week after being bitten by a carrier tick, the victim will experience high fever, severe headache, prostration, and muscular pain. Fever will be as high as 104°F., and can linger for days. About the fourth day of the fever, a rash appears on the extremities and moves to the trunk. Blood tests confirm the disease, but even with a negative test—which

Research Findings

The word **dengue** comes from Swahili word dinga or dyenga, which means cramplike attack. Indeed, the disease causes pain and swelling in the joints and back, as well as an uncomfortable rash, severe enough to cause contortions of the limbs.

Earthy Language

Rickettsial diseases are those caused by rickettsia, named after American pathologist Howard T. Ricketts (1871–1910). They are microorganisms that are bigger than viruses but smaller than bacteria. They live inside the cells of ticks and other insects that pass these microbes to humans. The microorganisms cause a variety of uncommon illnesses characterized by fever, headache, malaise, and rash.

happens—sufferers of the symptoms are usually treated with the antibiotic tetra-cycline. Avoid tick-infested areas all over the United States, not just in the Rocky Mountains. Check for and remove immediately any ticks you find when coming in from outdoors.

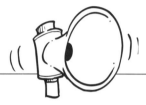

Sound the Alarm

Louse-borne typhus happens when people live in crowded, louse-infested conditions. A case begins with the sudden onset of high fever, chills, headaches, and generalized pain and exhaustion, which alternates with agitation. On about the fifth or sixth day, a dark spot appears, usually on the trunk, which spreads to most of the body except the face, palms, and soles of feet. Fatality is between 1 and 20 percent. Milder symptoms can recur years after the primary attack.

Babesiosis

This malaria-like illness is caused by a protozoan parasite that invades erythrocytes. Babesiosis most often occurs after a tick bite, although the disease also has been transmitted through blood transfusion. More than 450 cases have been reported since babesiosis first appeared in 1968, most occurring in the Northeast during the summer months. It is only occasionally fatal.

The parasite attacks the red blood cells. Symptoms, if any, begin with tiredness, loss of appetite, and a general ill feeling. As the infection progresses, these symptoms are followed by fever, drenching sweats, muscle aches, and headache. The symptoms can last from several days to several months. It is treated with a variety of antiparasitic agents.

Ehrlichiosis

This is the latest tick-borne disease in the United States, first described in 1987. It has been reported in many areas, but most cases have occurred in the Southeast and the south-central United States. Ehrlichia bacteria parasitize white blood cells, causing illness that may range from mild to severe and even fatal. Most patients, however, recover completely without treatment.

Ehrlichiosis is transmitted by the same ticks that carry Lyme disease and babesiosis; sometimes, all three are transmitted at once. The symptoms of ehrlichiosis are severe headache, nausea, chills, high fever, malaise, fatigue, muscle aches, and drenching sweats. The fatality rate is five percent. Usually, there is no rash. It is treated most often by tetracycline; avoidance of tick-infested areas is key to preventing it.

Tick-Borne Relapsing Fever

This disease, transmitted by the soft tick Ornithodoros, is found mainly in remote mountainous settings. Ornithodoros ticks feed at night for only 5–20 minutes, and their bites usually go unnoticed. Infants and the elderly may become severely ill and require hospitalization, but deaths are rare.

Colorado Tick Fever

Also known as "mountain fever," this is transmitted by the Rocky Mountain wood tick, *D. andersoni*, and occasionally by blood transfusions. Between 200 and 300 cases are reported annually in the United States, but the actual incidence of the disease is likely to be much higher. This is an acute viral infection, causing abrupt onset of fever, excessive sweating, severe muscle aches, joint stiffness, headache, sensitivity to light, general weakness, and sometimes a faint rash. Although it can lead to various forms of encephalitis, it is usually self-limiting with or without treatment.

To Ensure Preservation

And to avoid a double whammy, make sure that your mountain cabin is free of rats. Why? Epidemics of relapsing fever have been traced to vacation cabins infested with rodents.

The Least You Need to Know

➤ The locusts didn't die off with the Pharaohs; they still plague regions of the globe today.

➤ Killer bees are only slightly more poisonous than ordinary honey bees—but they attack in droves.

➤ Cockroaches are able to survive on starch-based paints, wallpaper paste, envelope glue, and bars of soap.

➤ Rats eat anything, can squeeze through holes the size of a quarter, start fires by chewing through wiring, and urinate in your food.

➤ Mosquitoes' tropic travels take terrible tolls; they can cause malaria, West Nile Fever, yellow fever, and dengue fever.

➤ Lice, fleas, and ticks are not just a nuisance; they're a plague on all our houses.

Chapter 24

Ancient Plagues on All Their Houses

In This Chapter

➤ Where the Bubonic Plague was born

➤ Who got it and why

➤ Leprosy, most ancient of plagues

➤ Disease or sin?

Today, most people are terrified of catching AIDS. Few fear Bubonic Plague. And yet, as diseases go, AIDS is probably preferable. Chances are, with the Bubonic Plague, you would be dead in three days or less; with AIDS, you could live for years, maybe even until someone finds a cure. We also know how AIDS is transmitted; with care, we can prevent its spread. In the mid-1300s, they didn't have a clue that Bubonic Plague was transmitted by rats and their fleas; you can't stop something if you don't know how it starts.

The Black Death

The Bubonic Plague, also known as the Black Plague and the Black Death, for all its virulence, was not totally new. A smaller version, the Plague of Justinian, had visited Europe in 558. In Egypt, that onslaught continued until 590.

As far as the Middle Ages plague, you might blame it all on Marco Polo. The micro-organism that causes Bubonic Plague (and its cousins, Pneumonic Plague, co-existent with Bubonic in the fourteenth century; the Septicemic Plague; and the ever-popular

Enteric variety) is not endemic to Europe, but to Asia. Without the increasing trade, the infected rats couldn't have made it to Europe so quickly and so well. The rats rode the Silk Road caravans and the spice trade sea routes. The sea also is how the plague got to Greenland, not to mention England and Ireland.

To Ensure Preservation

If you're going to quarantine, know what you're quarantining against. Often, when a merchant ship full of dying and dead men came into port, the port authorities would order it quarantined, thinking that the men were transmitting disease. This proved to be of little use. The quarantine was meant to keep sick sailors and traders from entering the town, but the disease–bearing rats and fleas would scurry down the ropes tying the ship to the dock.

Research Findings

Some estimates indicate that as much as half of the population of Europe died from Bubonic Plague. Even Viking settlements in Greenland were ravaged, and equally high death rates were felt in the Middle East, North Africa, South Asia, and East Asia.

Some experts believe that Bubonic Plague might have begun in earnest in the winter of 1338–1339 in Central Asia near Lake Issy-Koul. It then spread east to China, south to India, and then to Crimea. By October 1347, it had made it to Sicily, easily spreading outward from there to the mainland of Italy, to North Africa, and to Spain by ship. By August 1348, it had arrived in France, killing young Princess Joan. By January 1349, this plague was so fierce in England that King Edward proclaimed it unsafe to walk the streets of London. Many evacuated, but it didn't do much to save them; England was especially hard hit by the plague because of its many seaports and huge coastline, hospitable to ships and their rats.

Fleaing to Europe

Plague bacteria normally resides, because of climate, in Central Asia, Yunan China, Arabia, East Africa, and limited areas of Iran and Libya. The weather in northern Europe is hostile to the plague-bearing fleas to such an extent that regular outbreaks would not be possible even in the summers, let alone the winters of fourteenth-century Europe. But there were extenuating circumstances.

A Hans Holbein engraving of the Plague era.

People had recently figured out how to build fires indoors (via chimneys) without burning down the house. Consequently, houses were warmer than they had ever been, for both people and rats. Because there were a lot of ships, the rat population was continually replenished. Even if they died quickly (rats, too, died of Bubonic Plague), lots more arriving afterward perpetuated the infection. And it was a rapidly progressing disease.

Plague Facts

Rats may have died of Bubonic Plague, too, but not before passing the microbes out of their bloodstreams into the digestive tracts of fleas. The fleas, in turn, bit people, either after jumping directly off the rat (sanitation was not too good back then), or by hitching a ride on an intermediary, a dog, a car, or even a farm animal. (But not a horse: Horses do not harbor fleas. Apparently, their blood is inhospitable. So knights did not get it from their chargers.)

If a housecat had contact with the burrow of a dead rat, even if the rat had been eaten by other rats—not uncommon—the plague could still be passed along. Plague bacteria can live in dark, moist rat burrows even after the rats are of blessed memory.

Bubonic Plague's incubation period averages about six days. The first symptom is a blackish pustule over the site of the flea bite, with swollen lymph nodes nearby. Then comes hemorrhaging under the skin, producing purple blotches (buboes). These will swell into painful, burning lumps on the neck and at the groin and armpits. The lumps turn black, split open, and ooze pus and blood. The nervous system is affected next, causing insomnia, delirium, and stupor. About 50 to 60 percent of victims die within a week, after passing great amounts of foul-smelling fluids from every bodily cavity. Some experts say Bubonic Plague was 90 percent deadly.

Types of Plague

Pneumonic Plague victims had no buboes, but they suffered severe chest pains, sweated heavily, and coughed up blood. This type of plague is airborne, contracted

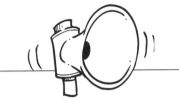

by inhaling the infected water droplets exhaled (or coughed) by a victim. The pneumonic form spread much more quickly and just as invisibly. Virtually 100 percent of its victims died.

The Septicemic Plague, which infected the bloodstream, could be transmitted by direct contact with a carrier through a cut or open sore. Enteric Plague—another variant that affected the gastrointestinal tract—could also be transmitted by contact. Both Septicemic and Enteric Plague killed within a day, and they probably account for the stories of healthy people going to bed for the night and never waking up. Both forms were almost always fatal.

To Ensure Preservation

Medieval remedies were as unappealing as they were ineffective. They included bathing in human urine, placing dead animals in the house, being bled by leeches, drinking molten gold and powdered emeralds (for the wealthy), eating figs before dawn, chopping up a snake daily, sleeping on the left side of the bed, and refusing to eat desserts.

Charnel Houses of Europe

People died so swiftly and in such high numbers that burial pits were dug, filled to overflowing, and abandoned; bodies (sometimes still living) were shut up in houses that then were burned to the ground; and corpses were left where they died in the streets.

There had to be someplace to take the bodies before they were buried or burned. Whole houses in cities such as Rouen, France, received those bodies; they were known as *charnel houses*.

One quarter of the population would die of the plague. A quarter of the European population at the time was about 25 million people, more than the combined population of Virginia, West Virginia, North Carolina, South Carolina, Maryland, and Delaware. Most of those deaths occurred in a three-year period, 1347 to 1350, a shorter period than World War I, which killed only a third as many people.

Research Findings

A visit to Rouen put it all together for me. My companion had the guidebook; I was happily walking and observing. When we got to the head of a street packed with four-story half-timbered medieval houses, I stopped in my tracks and began to cry. I had no idea why. My companion referenced the street in the guidebook; it was the very street where the charnel houses for the Black Plague stood. Psychics would say I was picking up the incredible sadness that had lodged in the wattle walls. I might agree.

Plague Days

Aside from the incredible number of deaths, what did the life of the mid-1300s look like?

First, there were open sewers, which overflowed when it rained hard. Cities were sealed off when the disease struck. Good idea? No. Uninfected residents were more likely to become infected as fleas jumped off the dwindling supply of live rats and live humans to find healthy new hosts. Needless to say, the populace was terrorized. Because government workers also became ill, governments ground to a halt; the British Parliament, for one, and the courts were suspended for the duration. People adopted a fatalistic, not to say pessimistic, view of life. And they starved. Farms were often abandoned as farmers and their help died, leading to food shortages—which led to malnutrition, which led to greater susceptibility ... well, you can see where this leads.

Earthy Language

The term **charnel house** comes from the middle English, middle French, and medieval Latin word—common to all—*carnale*. That, in turn, came from late Latin for "of the flesh." As used in medieval times, it meant a building or chamber in which bodies or bones were deposited.

It leads to a compendium of what some experts say it was like in various spots around Europe and the Mediterranean:

➤ Cairo, at the height of the plague, lost between 10,000 and 15,000 a day.

➤ In China, more than 13 million are believed to have died.

➤ India was basically depopulated.

➤ Mesopotamia, Syria, and Armenia were covered with dead bodies, too many even for mass graves because there was hardly anyone left to bury them.

➤ In Aleppo, 500 died each day.

➤ In Gaza, 22,000 people and most livestock and pets died within six weeks.

➤ Cyprus was virtually depopulated.

Following are some fairly well-accepted plague fatality figures for various cities:

City	Fatalities
Florence	60,000
Venice	100,000
Marseilles	16,000 (in a single month)
Sienna	70,000
Paris	50,000
St. Denys	14,000
Avignon	60,000
Strasbourg	16,000
Lubeck	9,000
Basle	14,000
Erfurt	At least 16,000
Weimar	5,000
Limburg	2,500
London	At least 100,000 (probably more)
Norwich	51,100
German Franciscan Friars	124,434

If these numbers, in the days before accurate census-taking, are even approximately correct, it isn't hard to believe that a great many country towns and villages became ghost towns. In some parts of France, only two of every twenty residents survived; the houses of their dead neighbors fell to ruins as survivors watched.

Strange Measures

Sealing off contagion has often been a popular idea, but depending on how it's done and where the contagion comes from, it doesn't always work. Archbishop Visconti of Milan ordered the first three houses of plague victims there walled up, entombing both the dead and the living. Plague continued to spread anyway, as it did in Leicestershire, England, where the village of Nosely was completely torn down at the behest of the local noble to prevent plague's spread to the manor house.

While strange measures to prevent the spread of plague didn't work, strange measures to cope with all the sudden death seemed to be a bit more effective, if gruesome. Pope Clement, in Avignon, consecrated the Rhone River so that bodies could be tossed into it without funerals; churchyards could not hold the dead. In Vienna, with 1,200 deaths a day, the dead were arranged by the thousands in layers and were buried communally in six large pits outside the city. This had been necessary in Paris and Cairo before that. In London, too, the dead were buried row upon row in pits.

In Europe, despite the large number of Franciscan Friars who died, Germany was hit least hard. Ireland was also substantially spared. Scotland would have been lightly hit, too, except that it chose that time to invade England and got a lot more than it bargained for. Most severely visited by the plague was Italy; in Florence, it was prohibited to publish the numbers of dead or to toll bells at their funerals so that the living wouldn't die of despair.

There developed a shortage of priests; many died, and too few were young and willing to take their place. But monks were aplenty; laymen who had lost their wives often joined monastic orders for both the respectability it conferred and for the wealth. Monasteries received huge stores of riches from nobles trying to buy spiritual insurance against the plague. (It didn't work.)

Then there was the Jewish question. Foreshadowing the Holocaust of the twentieth century, Jews were persecuted and murdered by the thousands during the plague. The entire Jewish population of Basle, Switzerland, was burned alive in a building constructed for that purpose. In Strasbourg, 2,000 Jews were taken to a burial pit. If they converted, they were allowed to live—at least until the plague got them. If not, they were tied to stakes, burned, and buried in the pit.

Research Findings

In March 2000, Pope John Paul II visited Israel, the Jewish homeland. There he made it clear that historic persecutions of Jews by Christians are deplored by the Church. Pope Clement VI, in 1348, went further. In the face of the terrors being perpetrated against Jews because of the plague fright and ignorance, Clement welcomed them to the Papal Court, despite persistent rumors that Jews had carried Bubonic Plague.

A Pox upon Our Households

The Black Plague has not disappeared. Outbreaks continue, even in highly developed nations, such as the United States, and despite medical and public health measures beyond anything dreamed of in 1350.

Plagues After the Plague

Area of Outbreak	Dates	Comments
Europe, Asia, elsewhere	1663–1668	Pandemic along the lines of the fourteenth-century outbreak, but smaller
Austria	1711	Localized outbreak
The Balkans	1770–1772	
Surat, India	1994	1,400 cases of Pneumonic Plague in New Delhi, 900 in Bombay; 855 deaths

In the early twentieth century, Bubonic Plague popped up sporadically in Britain, with the earliest cases in port cities—Cardiff, Liverpool, Bristol, London. Just as before, the rats came off ships from plague-endemic regions and infected the locals. Suffolk, England, experienced bouts of Pneumonic Plague between 1910 and 1918. Fortunately, few lives were lost.

Today, plague appears in the western United States from time to time. Amazingly, 350 cases of plague were reported in the United States between 1970 and 1997, with 80 percent in New Mexico, Arizona, and Colorado. Nine percent came from California, with the rest reported in nine other western states.

In 1997, four cases were reported, two in California, one in Arizona, and one in Colorado. One case was fatal. Septicemic Plague was diagnosed postmortem; if you can't tell that a person is sick, you can't treat and save him. In that respect, nothing has changed, at least with that variety of plague.

Plague also occurs in animals; in 1997, plague-infected prairie dog fleas were identified in Kansas, the first such report of plague in an animal there since 1950. In fact, plague is endemic in western U.S. rodent populations, including ground squirrels and prairie dogs as well as rats.

Sound the Alarm

An outbreak of rat-borne plague occurred in Madagascar's port, Mahajanga, from 1995 through 1997. The outbreak revealed the first multidrug-resistant strain of plague in the world.

Wearing Bells: Lepers from the Holy Land to Hawaii

Leprosy retains an enormous power to send chills down the spine, possibly because one effect of the disease is disfigurement. And yet, leprosy never achieved the huge mortality numbers of the Black Death. A sort of whitish, lingering death, it insinuated itself into the global consciousness as a most terrifying kind of plague. Its association with sin and moral decay, from the earliest times, hasn't helped its reputation any. Christians and Jews, banking on Biblical references, equated leprosy with sin. So did the Chinese and many Hindus. On the other hand, a few priests in Europe thought that the disease was a gift from God because he chose lepers to bear such a heavy burden.

In eleventh-century Britain, leprosy was the plague to be reckoned with: The first hospice was founded near the cathedral at Canterbury by the Archbishop, Lanfranc, sometime between 1070 and 1089.

The daughter of William the Conqueror, Matilda, founded a hospice near the gates of London in 1101 and dedicated it to the patron saint of outcasts, St. Giles. Matilda allowed the condemned prisoners on their way to Tyburn to be hanged to take a "cup of charity" from the lepers as they passed the hospice.

A Lonely Legacy

Some commentators think that the separation leprosy caused its victims was as horrific as the disease itself. David W. Lloyd, in a sermon at Seekers Church in suburban Washington, D.C., in 1998, explained it thus:

> … It may be that such separation from human contact has been the most painful part of the disease. … To see [a] character wearing something like cheesecloth over his head to protect others from the sight, and to see lepers beaten by those who feared the lepers were approaching too closely as they begged for alms, gives you a sense of the loss of community, of humanness, that befell lepers ….

Father Damien

Native Hawaiians, like Native Americans on the mainland, were very susceptible to European diseases. When leprosy appeared on the islands, officials rounded up the lepers and dumped them on the island of Molokai to live as best they could.

Enter Father Damien de Veuster (1840–1889), who lived for 16 years among people who had leprosy on the island of Molokai. Until Damien arrived, sailors heaved supplies and cattle overboard to be hauled to shore by anyone who was able to do so.

275

Of the 2,000 exiled there, about 800 still lived. They had a chapel, dedicated to St. Philomena, but little else. At first Father Damien didn't have a house and slept beneath a tree.

He had to beat down his own revulsion to help them. He wrote:

> The flesh decays and yields an infectious odor. The breath of the lepers poisons the air .... I sometimes experience a feeling of repugnance. I am quite puzzled how to administer extreme unction when the hands and feet are but one sore. It is the sign of approaching death.

Eleven years into his work, Damien discovered that he, too, had leprosy. Brother Joseph Dutton, a U.S. Civil War veteran, came to help. A group of Catholic nuns opened a school for the children of leprosy victims. Robert Louis Stevenson, who would later succumb to tuberculosis (caused by a bacillus related to that which causes leprosy), wrote about Father Damien's work to help stir the world to help.

Sound the Alarm

Leprosy cannot be cultured in a petrie dish, but only in the flesh of humans and armadillos—of which there are a lot in Louisiana. But before you get down on the armadillo, consider this: The discovery that the germ occurs naturally in that animal helped take some of the stigma out of leprosy. If an armadillo could harbor it, clearly it wasn't some sin or fault of man's that got him afflicted. Still, you may not want to go playing around with armadillos.

Leprosy is still endemic in Hawaii and six mainland states, including Louisiana. Slaves brought from Africa might have carried the disease with them, or French Canadians might have brought it when they were expelled from New Brunswick in the eighteenth century. By 1817, leprosy had receded of its own accord in Europe.

The Symptoms

What does leprosy do? What are the symptoms? Early ones are scattered bumps and patches on the skin with red, raised borders and pale, hairless, and somewhat numb interiors; enlarged nerves; and areas of the body, especially hands and feet, lacking nerve sensation.

If untreated, disfiguring patches and bumps appear all over the body; the skin of the face, eyebrows, and ears swells; eyebrows are lost; and nose cartilage is destroyed, producing deformity. Leprosy may also destroy the testicles; the decreased testosterone leads to breast development. Eventually, the larynx is constricted and the voice is lost; eyesight may be lost as well. Bones of fingers and toes may be lost to injury and infection.

A Poverty-Belt Affliction

The following table shows the approximate number of leprosy cases in 1998, according to the World Health Organization.

Country	Number of Cases
India	634,901
Brazil	43,933
Indonesia	18,367
Myanmar	14,357
Madagascar	8,957
Nepal	6,570
Ethiopia	4,457
Mozambique	3,764
D.R. Congo	3,781
Niger	2,549
Guinea	3,684
Cambodia	2,438

India, Indonesia, and Myanmar account for 70 percent of the world's leprosy cases, according to the World Health Organization. In the beginning of 1998, the worldwide total of leprosy sufferers was about 800,000.

Africa is the second most affected area, but the situation there is fraught with terrible possibilities. The AIDS epidemic, the resurgence of major tropical diseases (malaria), and discovery of new ones (the Ebola virus), plus poor health delivery systems and armed conflicts all over the continent, make elimination of leprosy there seem far-fetched indeed.

In South America, Brazil is badly affected; it alone accounts for more than 80 percent of that continent's cases.

Western Europe is virtually leprosy-free; Central and Eastern Europe continue to report sporadic outbreaks, but many go unreported because of the political climate there.

The Least You Need to Know

➤ The Black Plague is endemic to Asia and made its way to Europe via trade routes.

➤ At least a quarter of medieval Europe's population died from the Black Plague.

➤ The Black Plague is still around. New strains are antibiotic-resistant and can still kill in 24 hours or less.

➤ Leprosy was considered a sin as well as a disease in ancient times. The stigma and isolation was as horrible as the disease itself.

➤ Leprosy is still around, even in the United States.

 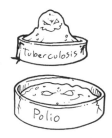

Chapter 25

Modern Maladies

> **In This Chapter**
>
> ➤ Modern epidemics: TB, flu, polio
>
> ➤ Modern plagues: AIDS and Ebola
>
> ➤ Mad cows and flesh-eating bacteria

Just because the modern world has antibiotics doesn't mean that it doesn't have illness. Indeed, many people think we have illnesses that are all the worse *because* we have antibiotics; none can doubt that antibiotic-resistant strains of just about every sort of disease are cropping up, as hard to cure now as they were before the first drug company made its first million bucks.

Tuberculosis

One third of the world's population—almost two billion people—have or carry tuberculosis, or TB. Because everyone travels internationally these days, and because the average person cannot tell a TB cough from an allergy without medical assessment, that number is likely to rise unless prevention efforts are increased.

Worse yet, TB is spread person to person, through the air. Estimates say that 10 million to 15 million Americans harbor the TB bacterium; each could develop TB, and 10 percent of them actually will. In 1999, more than 17,000 cases of active TB were reported in the United States.

Sound the Alarm

Although 1998 marked the seventh consecutive yearly decrease in TB cases in the United States, don't breathe easy yet. There had been a resurgence of TB in the mid-1980s (following a decline beginning after the turn of the century), and there are disturbing trends. In some areas of the United States, drug-resistant strains of the disease are cropping up, and an increasing proportion of new cases is found among U.S. residents who were born in foreign countries. In 1998, 19 states reported either no change or an increase in TB cases.

History of a Killer Cough

TB used to be called consumption; it consumed all a person's energy to breathe as lung tissue became diseased and useless, and it wore them out with a persistent cough that produced white phlegm and sometimes blood. TB is also characterized by night sweats and fatigue. It is a wasting sort of disease.

TB was once the leading cause of death in the United States. In 1900, 195 per 100,000 people died of it. In 1925, that number was 85 per 100,000. Then, there was no reliable treatment for TB. Bleedings and purgings were used; resting, eating well, and spending time outside in the sun were recommended. But very few people recovered. Those who did were likely to experience another bout if they overworked; after TB, an active life was out of the question.

It has been estimated that, at the turn of the century, 450 Americans died of TB every day, most between ages 15 and 44. The disease was so common and so terrible that it was often equated with death itself.

In the 1940s, drugs to treat it were discovered. (Note, the word is not "cured." TB sufferers harbor the bacillus in their bodies, and an active case can still flare up years after the initial, even successful, treatment.) By 1960, 6 deaths per 100,000 cases resulted, and that seemed to be dropping, until a spike appeared beginning in 1985. That year, complacency set in and TB prevention efforts and funds were redirected. Between 1985 and 1992, there was a 20 percent increase in new cases.

What's the Problem Now?

The problem is getting people to do what needs to be done to finish off this insidious killer. If those who have an active case of the disease fail to complete their therapy for the full six months, they can develop and spread drug-resistant germs. In 1998, 1.1 percent of active cases already showed multiple drug resistance—worse yet, that resistance was to the two most important TB-fighting drugs.

In 1993, Congress increased resources for the public health infrastructure, partly to bring TB back under control. Public health officials instituted directly observed therapy (DOT) to be sure that patients took what was prescribed, hoping to halt increase of drug-resistant organisms.

That's fine for here. But TB is global and still endemic in places where people live in crowded conditions with substandard food, water, and air to breathe. Now, more than ever before, people travel and migrate.

Although easier diagnostic tools and better drugs will help, a vaccine would be of great benefit. As it stands in 2000, TB continues to kill more people worldwide than any other infectious disease.

To Ensure Preservation

Public health organizations will need to do a better job of marketing TB prophylaxis (protective treatment) to certain U.S. populations to avert disaster. TB is endemic in Asia, Africa, and Latin America; cases among U.S. residents from those areas increased from 22 percent of the national total (4,925 cases) in 1986 to 42 percent (7,591) in 1998.

The Flu of 1918

Hah! Flu, you say? Some medical experts seriously doubt that it was flu—or, at least, not the flu as we know it.

Think about it: At its worst, the Black Plague killed at most 2 million a year, while the "flu" killed 25 million in a single year worldwide. In that year, nearly 20 million cases were reported in the United States; almost 1 million people died.

The Beginning

The disease is supposed to have begun in the United States, on the morning of March 11, 1918, to be exact, at Camp Funston, Kansas. A cook named Albert Mitchell came down with low-grade fever, mild sore throat, slight headache, and muscle aches—flu. He was sent to bed.

By noon, 107 other soldiers were sent to bed. Within 48 hours, 522 people were sick, many with severe pneumonia. And this was happening on bases all over the nation. Sailors at East Coast docks were sick; prisoners at Alcatraz were sick. Within the first week, there were cases in every state. Within a month, France had it. Two weeks later, China and Japan had it. In May, it was knocking 'em dead in South America and Africa.

How many died? In the United States, 158 of every 1,000 residents of Philadelphia, 148 of 1,000 in Baltimore, and 109 of a thousand in Washington, D.C., died. The disease did all its dirty work in two to three weeks in each city it attacked, and then was not heard from again.

Still, 850,000 Americans dying in so short a time frame is nothing to sneeze at. And although the disease began in the United States, the country was spared, compared to the rest of the world. In Nome, Alaska—a territory, not a state, at the time—60 percent of the native population died. In Samoa, a U.S. protectorate, as much as 90 percent of the population was infected. Of those who survived, many died of starvation, lacking the energy to feed themselves.

On transatlantic voyages, as much as 7 percent of the passenger list was absent on arrival, having died and been buried at sea. And we're not talking famine ships here; we're talking luxury ocean liners with physicians on board.

From Pigs to People

In March 1997 (this bug has an affinity for March!), researchers at the Armed Forces Institute of Pathology in Washington, D.C., reported that they had isolated genetic material from the virus, kept under glass all that time in formaldehyde in part of the lung of a soldier who had died and been autopsied.

It took two years, but after examining the genetic code, they concluded that it was a virus passed from birds to pigs to humans. Why? The virus is stable in birds—no problem there. When it enters a pig, the pig's immune system kicks in. To survive that, the virus mutates. When it enters people, it's a tricky devil; having mutated to cope with the unknown once, and able to do it again, it overwhelms man's immune system.

But then again, the researchers had only 7 percent of the genetic code under scrutiny, so could the virus have been something else? A Maryland physician raised the question about whether it might have been a form of hantavirus pulmonary syndrome (HPS). That would make sense in view of its American origins; hantaviruses are a pan-American germ, not native to Europe, the Far East, or anywhere else.

Hantaviruses are pretty darn deadly. By March 31, 1998, 179 cases of HPS had been reported in 29 states, with a fatality ratio of a whopping 44.7 percent. That's getting up there with Black Plague. In fact, like the Black Plague, hantaviruses are rodent-borne, and lots of rodents can carry it. HPS has attacked people in the United States, Canada, Argentina, Brazil, Chile, Paraguay, and Uruguay. Already, several New World hantaviruses are involved in those cases. But all are rodent-spread.

Flu? Think about it again. Most of the 1918 deaths were not from "flu," but from the pneumonia it caused. And then there's HPS. Pneumonia by any other name ....

Polio

If you were a child in the 1950s, you might recall polio (poliomyelitis, infantile paralysis) as vividly as you recall air raid drills for potential nuclear attack. Both changed lives. Both struck fear into huge populations around the world.

Of course, polio is another virus. This one, spread mainly through contaminated food and water, binds to the intestinal epithelium, where it has just what it needs to multiply. Its secondary effect is on the brain and spinal cord, producing permanent paralysis of varying degrees of severity.

The Spread of Polio

The first polio epidemic recorded in detail was in Sweden in 1887, and epidemics continued throughout the early twentieth century, primarily in Europe and North America.

Polio was first recognized in the United States in 1916, when 27,363 cases were reported, causing 7,000 deaths. In 1949, 42,173 cases were reported, with 2,720 deaths. In 1951, 3,300 died from among 57,628 cases reported.

President Franklin Roosevelt had polio as a young man and was unable to walk unaided. News photographers of the time had a tacit agreement not to call attention to his handicap, and he was usually shown either sitting or, if standing, already in place, with the heavy braces that supported him concealed by his clothing. Film clips hardly ever showed him taking steps or being pushed in a wheelchair.

Parents were justifiably terrified of polio in the 1950s. Public swimming pools were closed, probably a good measure in view of the means by which the disease was spread. Children were taught not to drink from public fountains. And everyone knew someone who had polio.

The iron lung, properly called the Drinker respirator, saved many and led to the development of more compact portable respiratory devices used today in cases of paralysis from other causes, such as spinal cord injury.

Of course, iron lungs prevented any muscle exertion or exercise; patients' muscles became foreshortened and immobile. Thus, the iron lung crippled many patients while keeping them alive. Today, patients would be connected to a ventilator so that therapists could keep their muscles working until they could be weaned from respiratory support. Still, that experience helped to create a better understanding of how to support weak limbs.

Intense pain was characteristic of the disease, especially in the beginning when the virus was killing nerves. This aspect of the disease led to the development of transcutaneous electroneural stimulation (TENS) devices that are in widespread use now for sports injury therapy and postsurgical pain relief. Back then, the most that caregivers could do was to apply moist heat packs for the muscle pain.

283

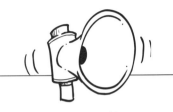

Polio vaccines were introduced in the mid-1950s. Today, there is very little new polio. But many of the 250,000 survivors of the 1940s/1950s attacks are experiencing another visitation from the disease. Not that they are experiencing another active bout of the disease; rather, the normal pains and creaky joints of aging are intensified. Why? Post-polio syndrome is the polio victim's manifestation of the aging process; with fewer nerves than they had before the virus destroyed some, victims become weaker with age at a faster rate than others.

A Disaster That Shouldn't Have Been?

Some organizations, notably Australia's Campaign Against Fraudulent Medical Research, suggest that polio need not have been the scourge and terror that it was.

In fact, it may not have been a "natural" disaster, but one caused by the prevalence of mass vaccinations against smallpox, diphtheria, and other childhood diseases by the late 1940s. The organization makes the point that the polio virus is normally benign; most cases are so mild that they usually are diagnosed as a cold or flu, rarely progressing to the paralytic form. If they do progress, it is because of other stressors, such as poor diet, poor hygiene, poor living conditions, or injection of a poisonous vaccine.

AIDS

At least 16.3 million men and women have died of AIDS (acquired immunodeficiency syndrome) since it was first recognized. By the end of 1999, the United Nations and the World Health Organization expected that 32.4 million adults and 1.2 million children would be living with Human Immunodeficiency Virus (HIV) by the start of the year 2000. HIV is the precursor to AIDS. At the beginning of the year 2000, the disease remained fatal.

About half of those who acquire HIV become infected before they turn 25 and typically die of the life-threatening illnesses called AIDS before their 35th birthday. Ninety-five percent of the global total of people with HIV live in developing countries, where poverty, poor healthcare delivery systems, and limited prevention resources fuel the spread of the virus.

But HIV is a challenge even in developed nations, maybe more so as complacency sets in due to recent successes in controlling the disease for longer periods and as hopes for a cure become, people think, more realistic.

The Spread of AIDS

Contrary to expectations when AIDS was first identified, the epidemic has taken different forms in different parts of the world. In some areas, HIV rapidly became common among men and women throughout the population. In others it became entrenched in certain subpopulations whose sexual or drug-injecting behavior carries an especially high risk of contracting or passing on the virus—particularly sex workers and their customers, men who have sex with men, and drug injectors (the virus is spread through blood and bodily secretions).

Sharing drug-injecting equipment without sterilizing it between users is an extraordinarily efficient way of spreading HIV. Because of the way drug solutions are prepared in Eastern Europe and Central Asia, there is also a danger that the solutions themselves are contaminated with HIV. This means that even if clean needles are used, there is still a danger of transmitting the virus.

India, too, has a very unusual AIDS problem. In the southern and western parts of that country, HIV has a significant grip on the urban population, with more than 1 pregnant woman in 50 testing positive for HIV. In the northeast, HIV infection has shot through networks of men who inject drugs and has spread to their wives. Yet other states of India detected their very first HIV infections just in the last year or two. Estimates indicate that about four million Indians are HIV-positive. But that number is lower than would have been expected from earlier disease progress.

Africa, especially south of the Sahara, is the area of the world worst affected by HIV and AIDS. Complicating that, access to care is lowest, and social and economic safety services that might help people cope are rudimentary.

At the start of the twenty-first century, some 23.3 million Africans south of the Sahara are estimated by UNAIDS/WHO to have HIV infection or AIDS. That is almost 70 percent of the world's total in a region that is home to just 10 percent of the world's population.

To Ensure Preservation

HIV is thought to have spread throughout central Africa by truck drivers sleeping with infected prostitutes along highway stops. Trade continues to have a strong connection with the spread of deadly diseases.

A New Theory

And then there's another point of view—controversial, but worth noting. That view, the Drug-AIDS Hypothesis, was presented in 1997 by Peter Duesberg and David

Rasnick. It more or less rejects sexual experiences as the main method of transmission. It also rejects transmission via contaminated needles. What it proposes is that recreational drugs and the highly toxic drugs used to treat the disease/syndrome themselves cause AIDS.

Research Findings

The hypothesis about HIV-AIDS is that HIV causes a list of 30 previously known diseases in various combinations, including pneumonia, tuberculosis, candidiasis, diarrhea, and classical nonimmunodeficiency diseases such as Kaposi's sarcoma, dementia, weight loss, and lymphoma. Any of these may be diagnosed as a disease in itself, but if there is HIV in the body, they are diagnosed as AIDS. This means that there is more TB around, for instance, than statistics would suggest.

Duesberg and Rasnick propose that HIV is a long-established virus in the United States because the number of carriers has remained stable since its discovery. But AIDS is a recent development. Therefore, HIV is not the cause.

They propose that we ban AZT and all other anti-HIV drugs because they are known carcinogens, terminate illicit recreational drug use, and treat AIDS patients for their specific disease when it appears, whether Kaposi's sarcoma, TB, or anything else. You might want to check out the entire hypothesis on their Web site: www.virusmyth.com/aids/index.htm.

Ebola

This one hasn't spread much—yet. The Ebola virus, named after the Ebola River, most often appears near the river in Zaire.

Ebola is a lot like the Black Plague of old. It causes a severe hemorrhagic fever, usually within 7 to 14 days after exposure. It often kills its victim in less than 10 days; it is spread by bodily fluids, making it difficult for those taking care of the victims. Indeed, the lack of sanitary conditions, including clean needles, syringes, and water, and methods to sanitize an area after it comes into contact with the fluids of a victim, are prime ways in which the disease is spread. Airborne transmission is thought unlikely in humans, although the disease is spread that way in monkeys.

The specifics of the fever are horrific: fever, headache, flu-like symptoms to start. Then the blood congeals and the victim's capillaries, blocked by dead cells, collapse. That happens to bigger blood vessels, and soon the organs begin to fail. Indeed, the organs disintegrate, and tissue bleeds uncontrollably.

Visual symptoms include bruised skin that blisters and falls away, and uncontrollable bleeding from every orifice. Then there is delirium, and the patient literally vomits internal organs and tissues. Little wonder it creates a crisis when it appears.

The Ebola virus is to be feared. Scientists have classified it as a Level 4 pathogen, while HIV is Level 3. And, like all the epidemics of old—and not, by the way, HIV particularly—it is following trade routes in its spread.

Two Real Pips

Really horrific diseases make the news, whether they have reached epidemic proportions or not. Two of these, from the end of the twentieth century, are Mad Cow Disease and flesh-eating strep.

And boy, are they nasty. They deserve inclusion as natural disasters because of the true horror they wreak, albeit on a relatively (thankfully!) small population.

Research Findings

Ebola is not limited to the third world and to places where monkeys abound in the wild. There may be a pet monkey or two in Reston, Virginia, but they were not the cause of an outbreak there. Nor was the Reston version deadly—it just made people sick. So did a similar virus found in cynomolgus monkeys imported to Italy from the Philippines. No humans were infected by that one, either.

Mad Cow Disease

The full name of this disease is bovine spongiform encephalopathy (BSE), and it was—or used to be—a rare, chronic degenerative disease of the central nervous system of cattle. First diagnosed in 1986 in Great Britain, it has not been found anywhere in the United States—yet.

Upon investigation, scientists decided that the "Mad Cow Disease" in Britain was caused by feeding calves meat and bone meal processed from sheep infected with scrapie—a similar disease of that species—and byproducts from BSE-infected cattle that hadn't shown signs of the disease.

"Mad cows" display nervousness or aggression, abnormal posture, lack of coordination and difficulty in rising, decreased milk production, or loss of body weight despite continued appetite. Affected cattle die. The cause is not known, and there is no cure.

What has that got to do with humans? BSE is caused by uncharacterized agents similar to those that cause Creutzfeldt-Jakob disease (CJD) and Gerstmann-Straussler

Sound the Alarm

Some scientists suggest that Alzheimer syndrome is related to Mad Cow Disease and may come from prions, otherwise known as proteinaceous infectious particles, which some researchers believe underlie both inherited and communicable diseases. These proteins convert normal proteins into dangerous proteins that cause neurodegenerative diseases. They could be the proteins in the tissues of cows with the disease.

syndrome, rare degenerative diseases of the nervous system. People who have eaten BSE-infected cows also have died.

Creutzfeldt-Jakob Disease (CJD) is a neurodegenerative condition of humans, classified as a "slow virus" because of the extremely long incubation period (10–40 years). Brains from affected humans are histopathologically classified as having spongiform encephalopathy (SE). Kuru is a human SE disease seen in certain New Guinea natives that practice cannibalism of brains.

Flesh-Eating Strep

It's too horrible to contemplate: a bacteria that not only infects you, but that also kills your flesh as it moves deeper into your body from the wound through which it was introduced—often at the alarming rate of an inch an hour. In some cases, the only cure is to amputate above the infection. If the bacteria has already entered the trunk of the body, well ....

The real name of the disease is necrotizing fasciitis, and it is caused by streptococcus A. Usually, strep A—the same stuff that causes strep throat—is killed by antibiotics. But the one that causes "flesh eating" also destroys soft tissue at the subcutaneous level and often is coupled with toxic shock syndrome; each can be deadly alone, but together they are even more so.

The bacteria can enter the skin through a paper cut, a staple puncture or a pin prick, or through weakened skin, such as over a bruise. Or, this can happen after major surgery, and sometimes it happens with no identifiable point of entry.

The symptoms are varied but often include these:

➤ Pain in the general area of the trauma, disproportionate to the injury, and often feeling like a muscle pull

➤ Flu-like symptoms

➤ Intense thirst as dehydration starts

➤ All these symptoms combined

You will feel worse than you've ever felt, probably, and not know why. Advanced symptoms include swelling with a purplish rash, proceeding to blisters filled with blackish fluid. Then the flesh becomes necrotic—that is, dead—appearing bluish, white, or dark, and mottled. After that, in the critical stage, blood pressure drops and the body goes into toxic shock. If the body becomes too weak to fight the infection, unconsciousness will occur.

Treatment ranges from aggressive antibiotic intravenous therapy to no-holds-barred intensive care: throw-everything-at-it-including-radical surgery.

For those lucky enough to survive, most often at least some removal of skin is required. Often this requires skin grafting. Amputation also is sometimes needed to remove the affected limb. Legs, hands, fingers, toes, and arms all have been sacrificed to save the life of NF patients.

If you don't want your arm amputated from a paper cut, what can you do? Here are some preventive measures:

➤ Buy antibacterial soap and use it often.

➤ Avoid people showing sore throat symptoms; 15 to 30 percent of the population carries strep A at any given moment without showing symptoms. It could be you.

➤ Cover your mouth when you cough or sneeze, and throw away tissues.

➤ Clean and care for even the smallest traumatizing wound using antibiotic ointment, and frequently change sterile coverings.

The Least You Need to Know

➤ TB or not TB: The ancient scourge is still among us and still bears watching.

➤ The "flu" of 1918 was pandemic—global—and more deadly than the two world wars put together.

➤ Polio caused lots of suffering but led to medical breakthroughs.

➤ Some researchers take issue with the common wisdom about AIDS.

➤ If you want a rotten way to die, try Ebola, Mad Cow Disease, or flesh-eating strep.

Let Them Eat Cake: Famine

Famine was simply part of the human condition before means of preserving food were found. Fat times came when the harvest was in; lean times of varying degrees came in between, depending on what could be dried and what could be foraged.

Things got better after it was found that salt could preserve food, or that it was possible to heat food really well, store it in airtight jars, and eat it long after it should have gone bad.

But, of course, it's necessary to have the food in the first place, or the salting, drying, and canning are all for naught. Even after the invention of food science, there have been famines.

Out of Sight, Out of Mind

Here's a look at the Famine of 1315:

In England, meat and eggs ran out, fowl were scarce, animals died of disease, and even the pigs who lived could not be fed because of the high price of fodder. When the king went to St. Albans to celebrate the feast of St. Laurence, the local nobles had a tough time finding enough bread to feed even the king's household.

It was a typical famine of the period, and of the type that happens in Africa even now—a famine of the time between planting and harvest, when the old harvest's stores run out and the new harvest isn't yet ripe. But in 1315, that was made worse because of summer rains so heavy that grain couldn't ripen. Some was able to be harvested and made into flour—and bread—by the end of September, but by Christmas, that short, low-nutrient supply had run down. Even those who had lots of the late grain flour wasted away from the lack of nutrition provided by the substandard wheat. Even the rich, it was said, were constantly hungry. The poor? Contemporary reports said they were "lying stiff and dead in the wards and streets."

The Great Hunger and the Irish Diaspora

Arguably the most famous of famines was the Irish Potato Famine. The first mention of it was made in the Irish press on September 9, 1845. The last mention of it was probably yesterday, in some news report somewhere in America.

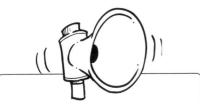

Sound the Alarm

Even today, with food technology, weather forecasting, and international aid agencies on a scale unimaginable even 100 years ago, someone dies of hunger every 3.6 seconds; 75 percent are children.

There are reasons, of course, that the Irish Potato Famine is top-of-mind for many Americans. Those of us who can trace our ancestry to Ireland either have a great-great-grandparent who arrived in the United States because of it, or we have a more recent ancestor who came here from a country still impoverished—between the single-source antiquated diet and the lengthy foreign occupation, right up until the Celtic Tiger of galloping development took hold in the late 1980s.

The Great Hunger, as it was called in typical Irish lyricism, was caused by a crop disease, potato blight. It was made worse (some say) by the actions of a hostile foreign government, that of Great Britain, which had not even begun to think of an Irish Free State, never mind imagining the birth, in the 1920s, of the Irish Republic. On the other hand, it was ameliorated by the actions of (some say) subjects of that government who went out of their way to prevent at least some of the starvation in the Irish countryside. The verdict still is mixed. But one thing is certain: In just a few years, Ireland lost two thirds of its population from a combination of famine and the emigration that resulted from it.

Historians blame the famine on more than simply a biological disaster in the form of a plant blight. The Penal Laws, enacted in 1695 by the British government, were intended to destroy Catholicism in Ireland; under those laws, native Irish were considered "insignificant slaves, fit for nothing but to hew wood and draw water," wrote Cecil Woodham-Smith in *The Great Hunger; Ireland 1845–1849.*

Catholics—that is, Irish—were barred from the armed forces, law, commerce, and civic activities such as judgeships and mayoralties. If an Irish landowner's eldest son became Protestant, he inherited all his father's land, no matter how many brothers he had. If not, then all the brothers got equal shares. Catholics could not vote, hold Crown offices, purchase land (so Irish could own only what their ancestors had owned before the Penal Laws), or attend school, or even send their children abroad to be educated.

A few hundred years of that, and one can see that the Irish were ill-equipped to cope with a disaster affecting what little they had.

Some historians also blame the Irish culture; they were not, these historians hold, willing to fish although the seas ran with life. However, the Irish had little more than wooden and canvas curraghs, which would not hold up to serious fishing in Atlantic gales. And British boats fishing the Irish waters sent their catch to England for the higher prices.

Fat Potatoes

The Irish peasants were dependent on the potato, although it was not indigenous to the island. Found probably near Lake Titicaca in South America, it was introduced in Europe as a curiosity in the sixteenth century. Sir Walter Raleigh introduced it to Ireland, where it was eagerly adopted. With some milk and some greens, it made the basis of a fairly healthful diet.

The potato does the same nutritional job in many parts of the world today. In fact, the potato is the fourth most important food crop on the planet, after wheat, rice, and corn. It accounts for about half of the global output of all roots and tubers. Amazingly, it makes up 22 percent of planted acreage in India and China, and 28 percent in the Russian Federation and Poland. In developing countries, increases in potato acreage have been higher than for any other food crop. More than a

Earthy Language

You can see "famine walls" all over the Irish countryside to this day. They don't often contain anything or enclose anything of note. Rather, they were construction projects initiated by the more enlightened and generous British landowners as an excuse for paying starving Irish tenant farmers some wages so that they could feed their families.

To Ensure Preservation

Potatoes provide very good nutrition and can keep diseases such as scurvy and pellagra at bay. They are easy to grow with minimum labor and training; most of the labor is in the digging at harvest time. They'll keep in pits in the ground, for up to a year under the right conditions. Potato plants also produce more calories per acre than any other crop that can be grown in the climates of northern Europe. All you need to cultivate potatoes is a spade.

billion people worldwide eat potatoes as a large part of their diet; fully half of that total is eaten in developing countries, although Europe is still the potato-eating capital of the world.

Research Findings

The 1845 disaster was not the only one that Ireland had ever had. In 1740 and 1741, the island nation suffered a great famine, perhaps with more loss of life than in 1845. Another famine happened in 1800–1801, killing about 60,000, and another one like it occurred in 1816–1819. Another one came on its heels in 1821–1822, but the British instituted some welfare assistance that lowered mortality. During the Europe-wide famine of 1830–1831, Ireland was knocked about again, and Britain helped out. In 1839 and 1842, some potato crop distress was reported in the south and west of Ireland, a hint of things to come.

Sound the Alarm

Don't try to raise potatoes from seed. The flowers produce seed-balls, which are poisonous. Instead, plant chunks of potato containing "eyes," the buds of aborted leaves that are apparent as knotty whorls when you cook the tubers. These buds are genetically identical, of course, to the plants they came from. But they also can harbor any infection that might have attacked the parent plant, even though they might appear just fine.

Slim Pickin's

This deep dependence on the white tuber today parallels what was happening in Ireland in the 1840s.

Contemporary accounts of what was happening appeared in newspapers all over the nation in the late 1840s. Donegal, in the far west of Ireland, had already suffered through two pre-famine seasons of relatively bad crops.

In 1845, the fungus *Phytophthora infestans* arrived accidentally from North America. That year was unusually warm and wet, and the fungus thrived. The potatoes didn't.

Potatoes cannot be stored longer than 12 months, so all of one harvest is eaten before the next; because of that short "shelf life," there was never any surplus to fall back on beyond the first year after harvest. Enough potatoes were still edible from the previous harvest that first winter that most of the populace made it through; in the spring, however, problems began. And the following winter, when there were absolutely no edible stored potatoes, the blight, dormant inside the seed tubers, began again, unrecognized until the plants were well along ... not that there was an antifungal agent to use back then even if they had known what was lurking below the surface. Although the growing seasons were good and Irish farmers were producing lots of other crops, those were for export to England, and the Irish could not afford to buy them.

In *The Ballyshannon Herald*, a report about the situation in Donegal in 1845 said this:

> ... the parishioners of this parish of West Tullaghabegley, in the barony of Kilmacrennan, and county of Donegal, are in the most needy, hungry, and naked condition of any people that ever came within the precincts of my knowledge, although I have traveled a part of nine counties in Ireland, also a part of England and Scotland, together with a part of British America; I have likewise perambulated 2,253 miles through some of the United States, and never witnessed the tenth part of such hunger, hardship, and nakedness.

> They have no means of harrowing their land but with meadow rakes. Their farms are so small that from four to ten farms can be harrowed in a day with one rake.

> Their beds are straw, green and dried rushes, or mountain bent; their bedclothes are either coarse sheets, or no sheets, and ragged filthy blankets; and, worse than all I have mentioned, there is a general prospect of starvation.

Mass Graves

Recent famines in Africa have provided photos of mass graves, with corpses piled up like felled trees. It was not much different in Ireland during the famine. There were so many bodies that not enough coffins existed to bury them in. Mass burials had to be conducted, and a way had to be found to reuse the few coffins there were. The Irish developed coffins with hinged bottoms, to let the body drop out into the hole, while the coffin would be carried away and used again.

At times, even that was too slow a treatment and too cumbersome to deal with the huge numbers of bodies. Near hospitals and workhouses—as in the Black Plague—people were buried in pits and mass graves.

Ballyshannon, situated at the most southerly point in Donegal, was relatively unaffected by potato blight in 1845. Everything was different in 1846, however, as *The Ballyshannon Herald* reported:

> The weather continues extremely fine and the crops are stacking in good condition, with the exception of potatoes, which no one thinks of digging except to search through whole fields to make out a basketful which those who have no other employment do. The Indian meal which a few merchants have brought

here from Sligo, has been the means of keeping hundreds from starvation—but why don't the merchants get in cargoes of it as is done in Sligo and elsewhere?

And what about the health of the other crops? Why didn't that save the Irish? Simple. Those crops were grown for export, often by veritable indentured servants in their own land, and were meant for export to the British, who could afford to pay for them; the Irish could not. In part, the famine wasn't just due to lack of food, but to lack of the means to get hold of what there was. This is not terribly different from the famines in developing countries today, with many reports of food being hijacked by government officials and black-marketed for profit rather than distributed to the populace.

However, there were *workhouses,* although they preexisted the famine and had always housed a percentage of the Irish peasants who lacked land, skills, and hope. The Ballyshannon workhouse was built for the shelter of 500; by 1848, that figure was at 769, despite occasional illnesses that wiped out some of the residents from time to time.

Hundreds more were on "outdoor relief," which meant that people got some food to subsist on and some blankets to wrap up in, and then had to find shelter as best they could in a damp and cold climate, where there is sunlight in winter on an almost Arctic schedule.

Before the potato blight, the workhouse diet was wholesome, if not fancy, including oatmeal porridge, potatoes, and buttermilk. After the blight, potatoes were not to be had, and imported corn was substituted. It was considered unpalatable but was better than nothing, although it had much lower nutritional values than potatoes. It would not keep scurvy and pellagra away; it would merely keep many alive until things got better.

The Society of Friends contributed to relief pound for pound with what the town of Ballyshannon could raise to establish a soup kitchen. One of the major landlords reduced his rents in Donegal by 25 percent. A medical officer, Dr. Kelly, had the children of the local workhouse removed and cared for in a separate building, which reduced both the outbreaks of dysentery and their mortality a great deal.

The workhouse continued to experience fevers that killed those who had been barely saved from starving. In July 1847, a temporary fever ward was erected with 50 beds, although there had been 100 fever cases the previous month.

No wonder. The overpopulated workhouse had an overflowing cesspool. One inspector complained to the Poor Law Commissioners, who oversaw workhouses and outdoor relief, of "the sewers leading from it without a sufficient discharging power: the smell arising from this cause is most offensive, and distinctly to be perceived through the house itself." The problem persisted, and in November 1847 the Master reported that the sewage was backing into the water tank. So water was in short supply as well.

Fire in the Belly—and on the Roof

Despite a few benevolent landlords and the attention to workhouses and outside relief, there were still evictions, and they were horrible. The Ballyshannon Union offered this account:

> The usual procedure after an eviction was to burn the thatched roof to prevent the tenant from entering the house again after the bailiff and his assistants had left the scene. A man named Diver, who lived in this townland, was among those who were evicted out of their homes. The landlord himself was present on this occasion, and he offered the sum of one pound to anybody who would set fire to the house.

> Diver, who was standing out on the street with a number of neighbours, stepped forward and said he would earn the money. He thereupon stepped into the kitchen where some turf was still smouldering on the hearth, brought them out on a shovel and placed them among the thatch of the roof. In a few moments it was ablaze, fanned by a strong southwesterly breeze, and in a short time his home was gone .... When the landlord tendered Diver the money which he had thus so strangely earned, he coolly put it in his pocket, turned on his heel, nodded to the neighbours, and disappeared from the scene.

Research Findings

Potatoes are grown in all 50 states and about 125 countries. The average American eats about 140.6 pounds of potatoes per year.

When the Irish Potato Famine began, the population of Ireland was about 9 million. When it was over, the population was about 3 million. And there it has basically stayed to the present day. Where did all those Irish go? Many of them into the grave, and many more to America.

Sudan and Soldiers Means Starvation

The Sudan is home to 28.5 million people. The country has virtually no roads, no telephones, no electricity, and very often no food. Skeletons walk the dusty expanses, often dying before they reach a place where there might be a little food.

In all, over the last few years of the twentieth century, death by starvation stared 2.6 million Sudanese in the face every day of their lives. At any given moment, estimates were that 350,000 were near death, irretrievable. The few international relief agency feeding stations were often shut down because of the continuing war.

A Complex Emergency

Humanitarian aid experts have called the Sudanese situation a "complex emergency." This means it is not a simple natural disaster, the result of a plant blight. Nor is it the result alone of wars and other human events. It is a combination of man and nature working in concert to deliver the utmost devastating experience of hunger they can muster.

Research Findings

In events like those in the Sudan, it's hard to decide how much death is from which cause. At least 1.5 million people were slaughtered by bullets or lack of food in the first 15 years of the war.

The civil war between the Islamic government in Khartoum and the rebel Sudan People's Liberation Army (SPLA) has been raging for almost 20 years. At times, the government tries to starve the rebels into submission. At other times, the rebels take food from civilians to feed themselves. Aid agencies have felt that they must accede to the government's hand-binding strictures, lest they be barred from operating at all in a humanitarian fashion.

All this is in addition to the ordinary "hunger gap," the time between April and September of every year when the food from the previous harvest runs out and it's too early for the next. Every year is problematical. Add war to that. Then add drought, as in 1994 and 1998. Result? Wholesale death.

And all this is despite the work of the USAID Famine Early Warning System, which predicted the 1998 situation. Initial estimates were that the nation would need to obtain 30,000 tons of food a month. That was raised quickly to 35,000 tons. Finally, the program said that 15,000 pounds a month might do it.

Earthy Language

USAID stands for United States Agency for International Development, and carries out projects globally—when invited—to improve conditions through industrial, commercial, and humanitarian assistance.

And then there was "donor fatigue." The developed nations of the world have been active—even when reluctantly so—in the Sudan for most of a generation and are simply overwhelmed by the continuing problems, by the task of finding enough people willing to put their lives on the line to deliver aid to a country that has rebel factions within its rebel factions, killing and marauding apparently willy-nilly.

Then, too, the Khartoum government has occasionally barred all relief flights, the only effective way to deliver food to a vast country without roads. The United Nation's Operation Lifeline, which struggled with the restrictions for most of two decades, feared that the government would shut it down. Even a U.S. State Department official was quoted on the subject: "As an institution, [Operation Lifeline] has been consumed with trying to survive."

"The only way to put an end to this," said Catherine Bertini, executive director of the World Food Program, "is to stop the war."

That's about as likely as the British voluntarily getting out of Ireland in 1845, apparently. In 1998, Sudan's government reportedly had been buying off rebel leaders and turning them loose on the people—although how it could be worse is hard to imagine. The Popular Defense Force militia had also sprung up, formed of bands of Arab horsemen who raided villages, stole cattle, shot young men, and kidnapped women and children.

Deadly Toll

What's the tally? In 1998, the number of famine victims per day was estimated at 69 per 10,000; two deaths per day per 10,000 is considered an emergency by aid workers. Worse, for children under 5 years, the rate was 133 deaths per 10,000 per day.

If the people lived, it was to wait another day for death in camps like those at Ajiep, Southern Sudan, where CNN described conditions as "purgatory ... for more than 7,000 malnourished people, naked or clothed in rags, who await food, or certain death."

The Rasta Men Who Left Are Lucky

For *Nikolai Vavilov*, Ethiopia was the cradle of wheat culture in the world. For millions of Rastafarians spread out over the globe, it is the center of a religious world. It is homeland for Coptic Christians, the third and little-known branch stemming from early Christianity (the better-known two being Roman Catholicism and Eastern Orthodox).

Yet, despite its glory days, Ethiopia has been humbled repeatedly by famine. The new millennium was no exception. At this writing, failed rains, lost harvest, and war between Ethiopia and Eritrea

Earthy Language

Nikolai Vavilov (1887–1943) was a Russian botanist and geneticist. Tracing the origins of various crops by locating areas with the greatest number and diversity of their species, he reported that Ethiopia and Afghanistan were the birthplaces of agriculture and hence of civilization. He reportedly died in a Soviet concentration camp after losing favor to a scientist whose theories he opposed but who had greater Kremlin patronage.

caused a huge famine threat. Estimates ran that six million people would need 250,000 tons of food over the middle months of the year.

To add to the misery, the World Bank had refused to fund any new projects in either nation because it objects to the money spent fighting each other rather than providing for their people.

The Millennium Famine was not the first recent one for Ethiopia. A drought-caused famine of 1969–1973 killed 300,000; thousands more fled.

In 1977–1978, the Ogaden War and a 1978 drought in eastern Ethiopia created an exodus, with more than 700,000 refuges showing up in neighboring Somalia.

Another famine in 1984 and 1985 killed almost a million and displaced 100,000 to Somalia, 10,000 to Djibouti, and more than 300,000 to Sudan.

In 1988, a drought-caused famine placed 6,000,000 Ethiopians at risk. In the 1994 famine, only 5,000 to 10,000 died because of a huge relief effort that was effective in the main.

The Least You Need to Know

➤ The Famine of 1315 was a famine of the time between planting and harvest, when the old harvest's stores had run out and the new harvest wasn't ripe.

➤ The potato is a high-nutrient vegetable that, even today, feeds at least one-quarter of the world.

➤ The Great Hunger of Ireland was the result of a crop disease—potato blight—caused by the fungus *Phytophthora infestans.*

➤ Easy-to-cultivate plants can cause overdependence on one variety, equaling famine pretty easily if one little thing goes wrong.

➤ The Sudan experiences a normal "hunger gap," the time between April and September of every year when the food from the previous harvest runs out and it's too early for the next batch. This, plus war and drought, adds up to almost insurmountable obstacles for aid agencies.

➤ At this writing, failed rains, lost harvest, and war with Eritrea is causing a huge famine threat in Ethiopia.

Part 7

Where and How to Live

Everyone has a pet fear. For some, it's earthquakes. For others, it's weather: lightning, tornadoes, hurricanes. For many, it's disease. How can you get away?

Forget about it. No matter where you go on Earth, you're likely to be in the way of one of them. The best you can do is pick the least risky, according to your own assessment of what constitutes real danger. Then move there and, well, forget about it.

Chapter 27

For Thrill Junkies and Safety Freaks

In This Chapter

➤ Nations with natural disasters in abundance

➤ True disaster areas and occasional disaster locations

➤ Places with virtually no natural disasters

Some people are attracted to places that offer danger, while others would rather be as far from harm's way as they can manage.

Guess what? No matter where you live on the globe, you'll get some excitement. The opening line from a United Nations online dispatch from August 1997—filed under the headline "UNDAC Team Dispatched to the Seychelles Following Heavy Rains"—said it best:

> Floods demonstrate that no country in the world can be considered disaster free. From 13 to 17 August, continuous heavy rains in the Seychelles caused extensive damage to homes and infrastructure, forests and agricultural land, estimated at U.S. $5.5 million. Never before had the Seychelles been afflicted by such a disaster. Three islands were affected: Praslin, La Digue, and especially Mah, where 80 to 100 locations were severely damaged. The floods affected in particular the tourist industry.

Oops. No doubt the tourists had chosen the Seychelles partially because of its reputation as a warm and peaceful place with the world's two major international tongues, French and English, as its official languages, despite the republic being strung out north of Madagascar in the Indian Ocean.

The disaster was projected to cost about $6.8 million in U.S. dollars.

Sound the Alarm

No matter where you go, or when, there it is: disaster. While the UN took care of the Seychelles, the following situations were also demanding attention from aid groups: Montserrat, with an exploding volcano; Myanmar, with serious floods; China, with a typhoon and resulting landslides; the Philippines, with torrential monsoon rains and floods and slides; India, Pakistan, and Thailand, with both monsoon rains and the lingering effects of drought; Romania, with heavy rains and hailstorms that damaged crops; and Burundi, with famine.

The USGS Says ...

The United States Geological Survey keeps tabs on natural disasters in this country—except for diseases—and in others as well. Here are some tidbits from its storehouse for 1999, which you may want to use in determining places that seem safe, or unsafe, to you:

➤ **Kansas, Oklahoma, Tennessee, and Texas**—Huge property losses from tornadoes in May.

➤ **Bahamas**—Huge property losses from Hurricane Floyd in September.

➤ **Japan**—Huge losses from Typhoon Bart in September.

➤ **Taiwan**—Lots of damage from an earthquake.

➤ **Sydney, Australia**—Huge hailstone damage from a storm in April.

➤ **Turkey**—Property damage from an August earthquake; at least 17,000 people died.

➤ **Orissa, India**—Extensive property damage from a second October cyclone; at least 20,000 fatalities occurred immediately, before disease and famine set in.

➤ **Venezuela**—At least 30,000 fatalities from flooding and landslides; maybe as high as 50,000 deaths from hunger and disease altogether.

➤ **Colombïa**—A death toll of 1,185 from a January earthquake.

These are the nations that appear repeatedly, for many sorts of disasters, on a list of 100 worst disasters of all time, maintained by disastercenter.com:

➤ Bangladesh
➤ Republic of China
➤ India
➤ Former Soviet Union
➤ Ethiopia
➤ Uganda
➤ Sudan
➤ Japan
➤ Mozambique
➤ Niger
➤ Italy
➤ Peru
➤ Pakistan
➤ Guatemala
➤ India
➤ Martinique
➤ Iran (Islam Republic)
➤ Turkey
➤ Cape Verde Islands
➤ Somalia
➤ Indonesia
➤ Hong Kong
➤ Nigeria
➤ Morocco
➤ Canada

Those appearing only once, along with the type of disaster that got them on the list, include these:

➤ **Canada**—Epidemic, 1918
➤ **Peru**—Earthquake, 1970
➤ **Hong Kong**—Typhoon, 1937
➤ **Morocco**—Earthquake, 1960
➤ **Martinique**—Volcano, 1902
➤ **Guatemala**—Earthquake, 1976
➤ **Italy**—Earthquake, 1908
➤ **Japan**—Earthquake, 1923
➤ **Indonesia**—Earthquake, 1917

So, from this unscientific survey of those left with multiple disasters in the top 100, where might you not want to live?

➤ Bangladesh
➤ Republic of China
➤ India
➤ Former Soviet Union
➤ Ethiopia
➤ Uganda
➤ Sudan
➤ Mozambique
➤ Niger
➤ Pakistan
➤ Guatemala
➤ India
➤ Iran (Islam Republic)
➤ Turkey
➤ Cape Verde Islands
➤ Somalia
➤ Nigeria

What do these dangerous places have in common? Many are on active earthquake faults. Many are in the typhoon areas of the Indian or Pacific Ocean. Many are in drought zones. Virtually all have infrastructures fraught with problems, making disaster preparedness and recovery difficult.

The Best Revenge Is Living Well

If you want to get back at Mother Nature for all the damage she has done to humanity, there are some pretty safe places to live. The United States would be one of them. Despite the fact that we have earthquakes, volcanoes, floods, droughts, blizzards, avalanches, hurricanes, tidal waves, tornadoes—just about any kind of weather, not to mention virtually all the germs (if you count the modern version of plague, the hantaviruses, which are endemic), fewer fatalities occur in the United States than in similar disasters elsewhere.

But here are some really safe bets:

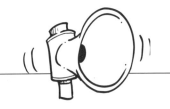

Sound the Alarm

Two thirds of all property loss from natural disasters in the United States can be chalked up to hurricanes, says the USGS.

Tonga: Island Paradise with a King, Coconuts, and Everything

Right on through the first sunrise on the first day of the new millennium (Tonga is 13 hours ahead of Greenwich Mean Time, and the sun really does rise there first), Tonga was a virtually pristine paradise, except for the odd cyclone.

In March 2000, it had a pretty bad one, one that did $2.28 million in damage. But Tongan officials said the nation would not need food aid or replanting help; it had sufficient food supply because of the success of the rehabilitation program after a 1998 cyclone. Radio Tonga reported that bananas, breadfruit, and cassava were the main crops affected by the cyclone, with root crop damage in Tongatapu estimated at 400,000 Pa'anga ($240,009 U.S. dollars). Tonga's Electric Power Board had restored about 90 percent of the lost power very quickly.

In short, the king in that kingdom has a handle on getting things back to normal after a natural disaster. That, coupled with the ease of living and natural beauty, suggest it as a place for those weary of the war against the elements, or the elements' war against us.

Where is Tonga exactly? On a South Pacific map, it is just west of the international dateline where it meets the Tropic of Cancer. From the Island of Niuafo'ou in the north, Tonga stretches nearly 1,000 kilometers to the Minerva Reef in the south. Tonga consists of 171 islands, spreading over 700,000 square kilometers of the South Pacific. The total land area is 290 square miles (750 square kilometers), located between latitude 15 to 23 south and longitude 173 to 177 west. Only 45 of the islands are inhabited, with about two thirds of the population on the island of Tongatapu.

Tonga: Dramatic bluffs overhang Pacific beaches. Nice and calm, except for a cyclone now and again. (Kingdom of Tonga photo)

Here's another pleasant surprise: Tonga's climate is slightly cooler than that of most tropical areas. Mean annual temperature in Nuku'alofa is 23.7°C, with a mean humidity of 76 percent. English is widely spoken. The tiny nation is, believe it or not, the host for a huge number of Internet domain names, despite its continued dependence on agriculture, handicrafts manufacturing, and tourism. Tipping—*mirabile dictu*—is not expected, although it wouldn't be considered insulting, either.

Casual attire is the norm most of the time, although there are laws against appearing in public places without shirts. Mainly, water is chlorinated and safe to drink.

When do we leave?

If You Can't Stand the Heat, Get Out of the Kuching

Another tropical island seems tailor-made for man and beast: Kuching.

Kuching is the capital city of Sarawak, Malaysia's largest state, which is situated on the island of Borneo. The World Health Organization chose it as an exemplary model of a healthy city, so you can be pretty sure that plagues won't get you there. But what else about it puts it in the Best Revenge Is Living Well category?

Earthy Language

In the Malay language, Kuching means "cat." Like many cats, the city is built for comfort, not for speed. In fact, the city has its own breed of cats and a Cat Museum, which houses feline exhibits from all over the world. It's a safe haven, then, for cats and cat lovers.

The climate is not quite as perfect as Tonga's; the average daily temperature is 32°C, and humidity is high. Annual rainfall is about 160 inches, so you'll find no drought here. Food is plentiful, and restaurants serve world cuisines as well as indigenous foods.

Kuching is a very tolerant place, as long as you extend tolerance back and avoid criticizing the government, religious beliefs, or ethnic/racial characteristics. Dress is more formal than on Tonga, and you will need to remove shoes when you enter homes. Don't enter mosques or longhouses where mourning is going on, unless you're invited.

Outside Kuching, you'll still find peace. There are very few dangerous animals in the jungles. There are no earthquakes, volcanoes, or cyclones. And, amazingly enough, there is little crime, no terrorism, and no internal strife—and no epidemics.

Spain

Spain doesn't appear on any significant natural disaster lists. This country has lots of high mountains, but it lacks the frequent and deadly avalanches of the center of Europe.

Research Findings

After Switzerland, Spain is the highest country in Europe. Its highest peaks are: Pico de Teide (Tenerife), Mulhacen (Sierra Nevada), Alcazaba (Sierra Nevada), Les Poset or Lardana (Pyrenees), Monte Perdido (Pyrenees), Cilindro (Pyrenees), Perdiguero (Pyrenees), Maladeta (Pyrenees), and Pico de Camachinos or Vignemale (Pyrenees).

Because of its position as a peninsula between the Mediterranean and the Atlantic, it offers scenery and climate conditions for all tastes. The beaches to the south are flat and sandy; the ones to the northwest are rugged and fjord-like because of the Pyrenees that flank the coast.

Spain's climate is temperate, although it does experience some of the European big winds. But it is not prone to earthquakes, volcanoes, hurricanes, or blizzards. Still, its rugged features allow for a great diversity of climates.

North of the Cantabrian mountains is "rainy Spain," the Basque country with its maritime climate, marked by mild winters and cool summers, plus frequent rainfall, especially in winter. Northern European vegetation thrives there, which accounts for about a third of the country. Spain is dry to the south of the mountains; there is often a burning sun, a blue sky, and fierce, local thunderstorms. To the south of the Cantabrian range lies "dry Spain," which has an extremely varied climate, always characterized by scarce rainfall and a pitiless burning sun in an intensely blue sky, occasionally crossed by short-lived, fierce local thunderstorms.

Although the landmass was called by many names in antiquity, the one the Romans gave it, Hispania, stuck. Hispania is, in turn, a word from the Phoenician language, derived from "shepham" or "coast or island of rabbits." Spain also boasts a couple of island chains: the Balearics and the Canaries.

A Very Large, Very Safe Island: Ireland

Ireland has no volcanoes, no earthquakes, no hurricanes, no blizzards (very little snow, despite its northern location, due to the Gulf Stream that skids by its west coast), no droughts, no floods, no famine since the nineteenth century, and no ugly endemic germs. No tidal waves have struck. No tornadoes have hit. No meteors have set towns on fire. And there are no snakes.

To Ensure Preservation

If you're going to be safe, you may as well be tanned and healthy. Fortunately, many of Spain's beaches are world-famous among those who wish to live a healthful—and wealthful— lifestyle. They include Costa Brava, Costa del Sol, Costa Dorada, Costa de Azahar, Costa Blanca, Mar Menor, Costa de la Luz, Rias Bajas and Rias Altas, Costa Cantabrica, Costa Canaria, and Costa Balear.

Research Findings

The Balearic archipelago contains many of the romantic islands of travel posters: Mallorca, Ibiza, Menorca, Formentera, and Cabrera. The Canary Islands are comprised of Tenerife, the best-known, and Gran Canaria, Ferteventura, Gomera, Lanzarote, Palma, and Hierro.

Research Findings

St. Patrick, Ireland's patron saint, did not rid the land of snakes; it never had any. Nor was he Italian, as some claim. He was a Roman slave from Britain.

What's not to like? The weather.

Rain is seemingly constant, although it's not a hard rain. Sometimes it's barely rain, what locals call a "soft day." The west gets the most rain, with as many as 270 days containing some rain.

But the temperatures are amazingly constant. The coldest months see an average low temperature of 39°F; the warmest months have an average high of 53°F. Because Ireland is so near the Arctic Circle, summer days provide up to eight hours of sunlight at summer's height.

The Republic of Ireland also has the longest river in Ireland and Great Britain, the Shannon, which flows for 160 miles. There are spectacular cliffs on the west coast, where the Shannon empties into the Atlantic. There are sandy beaches—if somewhat chilly—on the east coast. There are mountains, really overgrown hills, and an extinct volcano, Mt. Erigal. There's a unique outcrop of stony ground on the west of Ireland called The Burren; at the far north, there are upended columns of stone called The Giant's Causeway.

In short, the island is visually interesting without offering the sort of natural "fright theater" that other varied landscapes usually provide.

The Least You Need to Know

➤ No country is completely safe from natural disaster—but some recover better.

➤ The world's 100 most deadly natural disasters have occurred in a handful of countries.

➤ Among the safest places on Earth are some remote islands and some close-in European nations.

➤ Spain has mainland, islands, mountains, beaches, wetness, dryness, and virtually no natural disasters—unless you're a bull.

➤ Ireland has a wet, rainy, chilly climate, but little to alarm one in nature—not even a snake.

Chapter 28

Being Prepared in an Active Disaster Zone

In This Chapter

➤ What documents you should gather, in case

➤ What kinds of insurance are available

➤ Sources of help after the event

When disaster happens, it is almost always unexpected, even when there's warning. Naturally, anything that upsets daily life usually is. Even pleasant events—births, weddings, winning the lottery—are stressful.

Disasters are even more upsetting when you do not have access to the documents that will help you deal with agencies—public and private—that could help you recover.

Life will also get back to normal for you sooner if you've taken steps in advance for both financial and personal recovery. Granted, there might be a time when you end up living in a tent provided by the National Guard for a while. Who can forget the distressed faces of victims of Florida Hurricane Andrew when they were interviewed after the rampages of that nasty boy?

Still, it might help to have a pocketful of mental roses to keep you going through the transition from normal to totally messed up to recovery. This chapter gives you some pointers.

Paper Trails

In the United States, we don't need a lot of documents to live—just our birth certificate, driver's license, maybe a passport if we intend to travel abroad. But at least we have never heard the phrase "May I see your papers?" that struck fear in the hearts of Soviet citizens in times past, and in parts of Europe during the Middle Ages.

Research Findings

When medieval lords were warring and the feudal lifestyle was breaking down, it was hard for people to travel from one place to another without a guarantee of safe passage. Most successful in granting these guarantees were the Counts of Champagne in France, who protected trade between Flanders and Italy, helping commerce-based towns to spring up along the route.

Still, having some documents readily available will make life easier. Here's what you should have:

➤ Birth certificates for each family member

➤ Passports of all family members who have them

➤ Driver's licenses

➤ Automobile registrations and insurance documentation

➤ Health insurance membership cards

➤ Inoculation records for each family member

➤ Continuing prescriptions for each family member

➤ Extra copies of eyeglasses and contact lens prescriptions

➤ Any medical care instructions that would be needed if the patient was not treated in the usual place

➤ Insurance policies for houses, cars, and livestock

➤ Copies of mortgages or leases

➤ Records for pet and livestock healthcare, and licenses if required in the area

➤ Documents pertaining to any businesses owned, including articles of incorporation, business insurance, and leases

➤ Bills of sale for any recently transferred objects

➤ Tax returns for the past three years

➤ Contracts

➤ Living wills for any family members who have them

➤ Trusts and deeds

➤ Powers of attorney for any family members who have them

➤ Last wills and testaments for any family members who have them

Who said Americans don't have a lot of documents?

Most people have their documents in several places, with some of the important ones often lodged in a safe deposit box. That's not a bad idea—as long as you put copies of those documents that you need daily or weekly in the box with the originals of those that you access only occasionally.

But here's something to consider: In a disaster, you may not be able to reach a safe-deposit box, or the building it is in may be damaged or even destroyed. What then?

Your best bet is to have copies of all documents in a single, portable strongbox in a location that will allow you to pick it up easily if you need to evacuate. This box also should have a chance of withstanding damage to your house.

Insurance

Most homeowners have insurance on their dwelling that also covers their possessions. Many tenants have no insurance on their possessions, and yet, they would be lost in a severe disaster. Renter's insurance is relatively inexpensive and usually has the added benefit of offering protection from liability if a visitor trips on your entryway rug or if your dog bites someone. In many states, even your horse, lodged in a boarding barn somewhere, would be covered for any damage he did to another person; a pleasure horse, under such policies, is considered a household pet housed elsewhere.

When it comes to disaster, you might want to beef up your car insurance. Your car might be lost in a disaster; if it is old and you have only liability and not collision coverage, you might want to rethink that unless you have cash on hand to replace it outright after a disaster.

Homeowner's policies might be written with some exclusions, the most important of which concerns floods. In areas where flooding is common and severe—where river flood plains and shoreline areas are subject to storm surges and beach erosion—flooding coverage is usually excluded from private policies. But you can obtain this insurance through a program underwritten by the federal government.

Federal Flood Insurance

The Standard Flood Insurance Policies offered by the National Flood Insurance Program cover direct physical losses caused by flooding. They also cover losses caused by flood-related erosion via waves or currents outside normal activity of those forces, or damage caused by a severe storm, flash flood, or tidal surge that results in flood damage. Damage caused by mudslides is also covered. In short, if it isn't normal and it flows, it's probably covered.

Of course, all this must meet the program definition of a flood: a general and temporary condition of partial or complete inundation of normally dry land by the following:

➤ The overflow of inland or tidal waters.

➤ The unusual and rapid accumulation or runoff of surface waters from any source.

➤ Mudslides (that is, mudflows) that are proximately caused by flooding, as defined previously. These are akin to a river of liquid and flowing mud on the surfaces of normally dry land areas, including your premises, as when earth is carried by a current of water and deposited along the path of the current.

➤ The collapse or subsidence of land along the shore of a lake or another body of water as a result of erosion or undermining caused by waves or currents of water exceeding the cyclical levels.

The flood must affect two or more adjacent properties or two or more acres of land, and must have a distinct end point and beginning point to qualify as a "temporary condition." The waters also must be surface waters that cover land ordinarily dry. In addition, to qualify, the flood waters can be only surface water that covers land that is normally dry.

Of course, there are peculiarities in flood insurance coverage. For example, the program defines a basement as any area of a building with a floor that is below ground level on all sides. These policies do not cover any improvements to that area, such as finished walls, floors, and ceilings, or any personal items, including furniture. But they do cover structural elements and basic household gear usually kept and used in basements, such as the following:

➤ Sump pumps

➤ Well water tanks and pumps, as well as cisterns and the water in them

➤ Oil tanks and the oil in them, and natural gas tanks and the gas in them

➤ Pumps and/or tanks used in conjunction with solar energy

➤ Furnaces, hot water heaters, air conditioners, and heat pumps

➤ Electrical junction and circuit breaker boxes, and required utility connections

➤ Foundation elements

➤ Stairways, staircases, elevators, and dumbwaiters

Cleanup also is covered.

In addition, the program covers a few items under "contents coverage": clothes washers, clothes dryers, and food freezers and the food in them. There are also limits on the dollar amount the program will pay, as shown in the following table.

Type of Building	Regular Program Coverage Limit
Single-family dwelling	$250,000
Two- to four-family dwelling	$250,000
Other residential	$250,000
Nonresidential	$500,000
Residential contents	$100,000
Nonresidential contents	$500,000

Naturally, the premiums will depend on how much coverage, up to the limit, you need. Here are some examples from average policies of each type in 1998.

Type of Building	Amount of Coverage	Program Premium (Yearly)
Single-family dwelling	$124,270	$411
Two- to four-family dwelling	$101,707	$419
Other residential	$85,883	$423
Nonresidential	$218,570	$1,041

Other Kinds of Insurance

The long and short of the government underwriting insurance for other sorts of disasters that beset Americans is this: There is none, at least as the new millennium got underway.

In early 2000, federal legislators tried again to create some sort of national insurance plan to protect homeowners against damage by earthquakes, hurricanes, tornadoes, and fires, in addition to what is already available for floods. (While flood insurance is federally underwritten, it is obtained through commercial insurance agents.)

Many people think that federal umbrella disaster insurance is a good idea; homeowners could purchase the insurance at an affordable cost while reducing the number of circumstances under which companies would cancel the policies because their exposure was too high.

But the insurance industry itself was split about the matter, making legislation hard. Proponents got support from a bevy of very bad tornadoes—60 of them—that shredded Oklahoma and Kansas and killed dozens the previous spring. But detractors still kept the legislation, House of Representatives Bill 21, "Homeowners' Insurance Availability Act of 1999," from getting very far.

In addition to the infighting in Congress and lobbying by various factions, there was the inevitable competition for any excess federal budget dollars, as well as lifestyle questions.

According to Bruce Hahn, president of the American Homeowners' Foundation based in Arlington, Virginia, "The argument is often raised about those of us with common sense subsidizing those fools who built homes on the San Andreas fault and to a lesser extent those who live in Tornado Alley. Insurers will and can insure anything for a profit, but they don't like to add high risk things they can't make a suitable markup on."

The common wisdom was that Washington would not succeed in passing an all-disasters underwriting program anytime soon. So what can you do?

Assess your home's vulnerabilities, and work to improve the structure's strength where possible. Join disaster-preparedness programs. Shop for as much insurance as you can get that will include most of what you might experience.

If all else fails, move to a safer area.

Knowledge Is Power

In a natural disaster or its aftermath, he who knows the ropes probably has less chance of being strung up or strung out by them. Here's the least you should be in touch with if disasters are expected or have struck:

➤ **NOAA Weather Radio**—The National Oceanic and Atmospheric Administration provides continuous broadcasts of the latest weather information from local National Weather Service offices. Weather messages are repeated every 4 to 6 minutes and are routinely updated every 1 to 3 hours, or more frequently in rapidly changing local weather or if a nearby hazardous environmental condition exists. Most stations operate 24 hours daily.

➤ **The Federal Emergency Management Agency Web site**—On this site, you can find information about how to find insurance and how to apply for federal assistance.

➤ **The University of Illinois Cooperative Extension Service (UIUC)**—This service hosts a disaster home page that contains news releases and information on current disasters, plus information on preparing for disasters, getting disaster assistance, and helping disaster victims.

➤ **Quake Safe**—Provided by Stanford University, this is a program and Web site that tells you what to do during an earthquake. It offers tips on how to prepare your home, office, and community for earthquakes; there's also a section on how to make a three-day survival kit.

➤ **Putting Down Roots in Earthquake Country, Southern California Earth-quake Center at the University of California**—This Web site provides tons of earthquake preparation information, including how to prepare your house. It also explores and explodes some earthquake myths.

When Is a Disaster Not a Disaster?

When it's a disaster on top of a disaster.

Few people think of heat and humidity as natural disasters, and yet, these are responsible for an awful lot of suffering and death. After a disaster, heat and humidity may cause additional problems, after tornadoes certainly, and after just about anything else except the cold, snowy disasters.

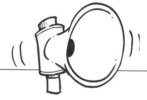

Sound the Alarm

Estimates are that more than 1,000 will die of heat-related causes in the United States' 15 largest cities in an average summer. There may be more; some deaths are attributed to other causes, and heat's implications are ignored. The elderly are most vulnerable because of stress on aging hearts; their bodies are also less capable of controlling internal temperatures. Anti-psychosis drugs and some other medications also can impair the body's ability to keep cool.

Heat and humidity aren't too awful if you're in good shape. But in a disaster and its aftermath, even if you've got the body of Arnold Schwarzenegger and the blood pressure of a turtle, you'll be stressed and more easily overheated. Overheating can cause life-threatening conditions such as heatstroke.

This happens because the humidity reduces the evaporation of sweat from the body, one of the major cooling mechanisms. Here's what could happen:

➤ Heat cramps, especially in the legs. A brief imbalance of body salts causes it. To prevent this, take it slow and easy.

➤ Heat syncope, or fainting, from a quick drop in blood pressure; take it easy.

➤ Heat exhaustion from loss of fluid and salt through perspiration. Dizziness and weakness might occur, and body temperature might rise, but not past 102°F. Take it easy, and drink lots of water. Only take salt tablets if approved by a doctor. Some elderly and other victims will need to be hospitalized.

➤ Heatstroke, which can upset the body's thermostat and cause the temperature to rise to 105°F or higher. Lethargy, confusion, and even unconsciousness may occur. Immediate medical aid is required.

To Ensure Preservation

In the brutally hot summer of 1999, Washington, D.C., got to test its new heat wave warning system. It also got to house people overnight in the air-conditioned metro rail stations, as did suburban Maryland. People really did use the rather odd shelters.

Ostrich Behavior

Disasters are often worse than they have to be because people don't heed the information they are getting. Before tornadoes, people might get only 30 minutes to take shelter. However, they could purchase a special radio that automatically turns on and sounds a warning as a twister nears; it costs about $25.

Some victims still ignore warnings, figuring that it won't happen to them, whatever the danger, from tornadoes to hurricanes to heat waves. Admittedly, often warnings are broader than they have to be, and some people are not affected, leading them to a "cry wolf" conclusion and reaction.

New equipment is being installed all the time, and prediction of earthquakes actually is improving. Although most weather experts say that site-specific warnings are five years away at this writing, it's better safe than sorry in the meantime, even if you're needlessly inconvenienced a little. (Specific earthquake prediction is probably farther off than that, but avalanche prediction is pretty darn good right now.)

Sound the Alarm

The heat wave of 1999 saw 466 die as temperatures rose as high as 106°F. Many of those were elderly who were too afraid or frail to evacuate; others simply didn't believe that the heat was dangerous.

Help from Other Sources

You can help yourself: You can listen to what others try to tell you. But sooner or later, you may still experience a natural disaster that requires some additional significant assistance. Where will it come from?

The Red Cross

The Red Cross operates virtually worldwide. In the United States, it has staff in more than 1,300 communities, poised to respond when disaster strikes.

Red Cross disaster workers are trained and come from all walks of life; they bring not only their skills, but also their life experiences to the site.

Materials needed to help, including supplies, vehicles, and communications equipment, are located all over the United States, its territories, and its possessions so that they can be present at a disaster site almost instantly.

Each year, disaster workers respond immediately to more than 60,000 disasters, which can be as localized as a house or apartment fire, or as all-encompassing as an earthquake or tornado. They also deal with man-made disasters, such as transportation accidents and explosions.

Between July 1993 and June 1998, the Red Cross responded to a total of 322,328 disaster incidents in the United States and its commonwealths and territories. At least 571,048 people were sheltered and fed, and 623,190 families were given financial assistance.

In 1905, Congress chartered the Red Cross to "carry on a system of national and international relief in time of peace and apply the same in mitigating the sufferings caused by pestilence, famine, fire, floods, and other great national calamities, and to devise and carry on measures for preventing the same." The Red Cross is not a government agency, but rather it carries on its work through volunteer support and donations.

When disaster strikes, the Red Cross provides shelter, food, and health and mental health services. The aim is to enable people to resume their normal daily activities as soon as possible; it also helps long-term, though, when community and personal resources are inadequate after a verified disaster.

The Red Cross also handles inquiries from outside the affected area concerning loved ones who might have been involved in a disaster.

Red Cross assistance is free; more than 85 percent of those who help through the Red Cross are volunteers.

The American Red Cross relies on contributions of time, skills, and money. To donate any of those, contact your local Red Cross chapter or write P.O. Box 37243, Washington, D.C. 20013. You also can call 1-800-435-7669; in Spanish, call 1-800-257-7575.

Research Findings

Clara Barton founded the Red Cross in 1881. After jobs in teaching and with the U.S. Patent Office, Barton resigned to work as a volunteer at the outbreak of the Civil War. She advertised for supplies and distributed bandages, socks, and other goods to help the wounded soldiers. After the war, President Lincoln gave her permission to begin a letter-writing campaign to search for missing soldiers. Because of her efforts, the United States signed the Geneva Agreement in 1882. Barton died on April 12, 1912, from complications of a cold.

U.S. Agency for International Development (USAID)

This is the U.S. federal government agency that implements America's foreign economic and humanitarian assistance programs. USAID's history goes back to the Marshall Plan for reconstruction of Europe after World War II and the Truman Administration's Point Four Program. In 1961, President John F. Kennedy signed the Foreign Assistance Act into law and created USAID by executive order.

The agency received guidance from the Secretary of State, providing humanitarian assistance in Africa, Asia, and the Near East; Latin America and the Caribbean; and Europe and Eurasia.

USAID has working relationships with more than 3,500 American companies and more than 300 United States-based private voluntary organizations.

Mennonite Central Committee

Among the most successful private groups in disaster relief is the Mennonite Central Committee, a relief service, community development, and peace agency of the North American Mennonite and Brethren in Christ churches. MCC has more than 1,400 workers stationed in 58 countries. All work under the guidelines of the Biblical call to care for the hungry and the thirsty, the stranger and the naked, and the sick and those in prison.

The Red Crescent

The Red Crescent has the same intentions and same way of working as the Red Cross, except that it works in Islamic nations. The Red Cross and Red Crescent are international partners.

The Least You Need to Know

➤ The one time that you may need your documents is when you are trying to re-build your life after a disaster.

➤ The only disaster for which the U.S. government underwrites insurance is flood.

➤ Heat and humidity can compromise efforts to recover from a great many sorts of disasters, from hurricanes to tornadoes.

➤ The Red Cross can be counted on to help after disasters, for free.

➤ USAID gives enormous aid to foreign countries coping with the aftermath of natural disasters.

➤ Among private groups, the Mennonite Central Committee takes it as a reli-gious duty to give aid in disaster situations, and it does so in 58 nations.

Glossary

aftershock   Coined in 1894, it describes a minor shock following the main shock of an earthquake. This term also has come to mean any aftereffect of a distressing or traumatic event.

alluvium   Clay, silt, sand, gravel, or similar material deposited by running water, usually in a fan shape.

amphitheater   From Greek and Latin, a circular, open, natural space with sides on which seating can be arranged. It has a flat place at the bottom so that performances or games may take place. This term also has come to mean a building that mimics the natural space and is used for the same purposes.

anthracite   A highly lustrous hard coal that burns very brightly and cleanly in comparison to softer bituminous coal.

antibiotic   A substance that tends to inhibit, destroy, or prevent the growth of biological organisms.

apiary   Quite an old word, dating from 1654, meaning a place where bees are kept.

bacillus   From the Latin for "small staff"; it refers to rod-shaped bacteria and also to some parasites of similar shape.

barrier island   A long, broad, sandy island that parallels the shore and has been built up by wave action, currents, and onshore winds. These islands protect the shore of the larger land mass from the ocean's effects. This term did not come into use until 1943—after barrier islands had been damaged by the Long Island Express hurricane of 1938.

Bermuda Triangle   The area of the north Atlantic Ocean defined by Bermuda, Florida, and Puerto Rico, where numerous airplanes and ships have disappeared, many with no explanation.

biodiversity   A very late term, dating from 1986, meaning numbers of different species of animals and plants inhabiting a particular environment.

bluff   A land mass having a broad, flat front, usually rising steeply from the ocean or land below.

bog   A Scottish and Irish Gaelic word dating from the fourteenth century referring to spongy, poorly drained ground with lots of accumulated plant material, and having a distinctive type of flora, such as sphagnum moss.

boll   The pod or capsule of a plant (as cotton).

caldera   A word that comes from the late Latin for "cauldron," it is a volcanic crater that is shaped much like a cauldron; it has a diameter many times that of the **vent** and is created when the central part of the volcano collapses or there are explosions of extraordinary violence.

carbonic acid   A weak dibasic acid (made of both oxygen and carbon) solution, H_2CO_3, that reacts with bases (other forms of oxygen or carbon) to form carbonates, such as limestone.

cave   A natural underground chamber or series of chambers that open to the surface.

Celts   One of the early Indo-European peoples who became prevalent over an area extending from the British Isles and Spain to Asia Minor; they were also found in what is now Germany.

chasm   Related to the Latin word for "yawn," it means a deep cleft in the surface of the earth.

cholera   Any of several diseases of humans and domestic animals usually marked by severe gastrointestinal symptoms, often with acute diarrhea, produced by a **bacillus.**

cold front   The advancing edge of a cold air mass. This term was coined when meteorology began to be respectable, and even sometimes accurate, around 1921.

Continental Divide   A movie with John Belushi. Or, the watershed of North America that separates the rivers flowing west from those flowing north, east, or even south.

Coriolis effect   Named after Gaspard G. Coriolis, a French civil engineer who died in 1843, it means the deflection of air currents as a result of the Earth's rotation. The deflection is to the right in the northern hemisphere and to the left in the southern hemisphere.

cultivar   An organism, generally a plant, that originates and persists under cultivation.

destabilization   To make unreliable, subject to change.

endemic   Belonging or native to a particular people or country, or characteristic of or prevalent in a particular region or environment.

epicenter   A "new" Latin word, coined from the old Latin for "center," plus the prefix "epi," it means the part of the Earth's surface directly above the locus of an earthquake.

fissure   As it applies to geology, a narrow opening or crack of considerable length and depth usually occurring from some breaking or parting in the Earth's surface.

fuller's earth   A substance used as an absorbent or filter medium or catalyst that is made primarily of clay but lacks plasticity.

fumarole   This term comes from Latin by way of Italian, where it originally meant a smoke chamber for aging wine. Now it means a hole in a volcanic area through which gases can escape.

fusiform   Tapering toward each end.

geophysics   Study of the physical processes of the Earth and objects and forces that affect the Earth.

hybrid   The offspring of two animals or plants of different races, breeds, varieties, species, or genera.

incendiary   Igniting combustible materials.

inundate   To cover with water, as in a flood.

jet stream   A meandering current of high-speed, high-altitude winds generally blowing westerly, usually in excess of 250 miles per hour.

leeward   Facing in the direction toward which the wind is blowing.

levee   A continuous embankment built for containing a waterway, or a ridge built to keep water from dispersing off lands irrigated by purposeful flooding.

mangrove   Any of a genus of tropical maritime trees or shrubs that send out many prop roots and form dense masses; they are important in building up coastal areas by trapping sediments carried by wind and waves.

massif   A block of the Earth's crust, bounded by faults, that has been uplifted without experiencing internal change, such as a volcano.

metamorphosis   A change of physical form, structure, or substance; usually a rather abrupt developmental change in the form or structure of an animal (such as a butterfly or a frog) occurring subsequent to birth or hatching. Or, this term may mean a similar drastic change in the character of a rock through the application of intense heat.

meteorite   Literally, a small meteor, but commonly denotes any meteor that comes through Earth's atmosphere without being completely vaporized and lands as an object.

meteorology   The science of weather, weather forecasting, and the Earth's atmosphere.

molybdenum   A metallic element, resembling chromium and tungsten in many ways, that is used especially in strengthening and hardening steel, and that is a trace element in plants and animals.

Mycenaean   Characteristic of the Bronze Age Mycenaean culture of the eastern Mediterranean area during the period from 1,400 B.C.E. to 1,100 B.C.E.

neurology   The scientific study of the nervous system, especially in respect to its structure, functions, and abnormalities; amazingly, the word dates back to 1681.

oceanography   A science that deals with the oceans, their extent and depth, the physics and chemistry of their waters, marine biology, and the exploitation of their resources.

orogenic   The process by which folding of the Earth's crust creates mountains.

oscillation   A swing from one extreme to the other, or a periodic complete change of directions by an energy or force.

outcrop   Part of a rock formation that appears above the ground surface while the rest of the formation remains below.

parameter   Any of a set of physical properties whose values determine the characteristics, behavior, or extent of something.

pennyroyal   An old word, dating from 1530, that describes a European member of the mint family with aromatic leaves, or an aromatic American mint used in folk medicine to drive away mosquitoes.

pestilence   Originally, this term referred to an infectious epidemic disease that was particularly devastating—for example, Bubonic Plague. Now it also means something that is destructive and pernicious.

physics   A scientific branch that deals with matter and energy and the interactions between them.

phytoplankton   Passively floating minute aquatic plant life.

precursor   A substance, cell, or cellular component from which another substance, cell, or cellular component is formed.

prophylaxis   Measures designed to preserve health (as of an individual or of society) and prevent the spread of disease.

pyroclastic   Formed as a result of volcanic or igneous action.

radiocarbon dating   Another fairly recent term, this means the determination of the age of archaeological, geological, or paleontological material by measuring the heavy radioactive isotope known as carbon 14 remaining in the material.

Sahel   The semidesert southern fringe of the Sahara that stretches from Mauritania to Chad.

seismic   Caused by or relating to the activity of an earthquake.

silt   Probably from the Danish *sylt*, for "salt marsh," this term means sedimentary material with very fine rock particles, usually 1/20 millimeter or less in diameter; also, soil made up of 80 percent silt and very little clay.

Spanish Main   This term has two meanings: the east coast of South America; and the Caribbean Sea and adjacent water bodies, especially when the region was infested with pirates.

stratosphere   The part of the Earth's atmosphere that extends from about 7 miles above the surface to 31 miles, and in which temperature increases gradually to about 32°F, where clouds rarely form.

subduction   The process by which the edge of one crustal plate descends below the edge of another.

subterranean   Under the surface of the Earth. It has also come to mean working in secret.

sump pump   A pump in a basement used to remove liquids, such as flood waters or intermittent streams.

superconductor   A material in which there is a complete disappearance of electrical resistance, especially at very low temperatures.

syzygy   A nearly straight-line configuration within a gravitational system of three celestial bodies (such as the sun, moon, and Earth during a solar or lunar eclipse).

temblors   From the Spanish; literally, "trembling."

troposphere   The lowest, densest part of the Earth's atmosphere, in which most weather changes occur and temperature generally decreases rapidly with altitude; it extends from the surface of the Earth to the bottom of the stratosphere.

typhoon   A tropical cyclone occurring in the region of the Philippines or the China Sea.

vent   In geology, an opening for the escape of a gas or liquid, or for the relief of pressure; it has also come to mean expressing one's emotions forcefully.

virulent   Rapid, severe, and malignant course of activity, or very poisonous or venomous, or very full of malice, or objectionably harsh. It can apply to objects (such as bacteria) or to emotions and conduct.

vortex   The vacuum or cavity formed by whirling liquids or air masses; it can also be used as a metaphor for other objects and activities that are reminiscent of a process: "a hellish vortex of requirements."

Disaster Resources

No matter what sort of disaster strikes, one thing is always needed: food.

If the disaster is of great magnitude or long duration, or if the disaster is a drought or famine, food is the one thing that no one will turn down. Below are some brief descriptions of food donation programs, followed by agencies that you might want to contact if you can provide food or (we hope not) if you need some after a disaster.

Food Programs

> ➤ **America's Second Harvest**—You can make a donation over the Internet through the group's Click to Give program, and the Chicago-based giant food bank takes care of the rest. This organization works with growers, processors, retailers, and the public. It works mainly in the United States, year-round rather than just after disasters, and helps feed 21 million people a year.
>
> Reach America's Second Harvest at 116 S. Michigan Ave., #4, Chicago, IL 60603. Phone: 312-263-2303

> ➤ **The Hunger Site**—This is a real clicking-and-giving program run by The Hunger Site. If you visit and click where indicated, you can make a serving of food happen. How? Sponsors pay for the food and its transportation through international relief organizations to wherever it is needed. The United Nation's World Food Program distributes for the group. The Hunger Site began on June 1, 1999—and it gave 32,389 pounds of food that month. That amount increased every month; by December 1999, it was up to 3,128,712 pounds, with declines in January and February to less than 3 million pounds.
>
> Reach The Hunger Site at 720 Olive Way, Suite 1800, Seattle, WA 98101.

➤ **The Heifer Project**—Based in Little Rock, Arkansas, this group uses the "teach a man to fish" principle. Instead of giving food, it gives heifers (cows that have not had calves), sheep, goats, pigs, chickens, and other food animals to those who need them. The group does accept contributions: a heifer costs $500. Actress Susan Sarandon has been involved with this project; she likes to give llamas, which provide wool for sale. But she has also given water buffalo, sheep, camels, and bees to the poor. Says The Heifer Project, "Susan is dedicated to helping people enjoy better nutrition and income from animals that provide milk, eggs, fiber, and other benefits."

Contact The Heifer Project International, P.O. Box 808, Little Rock, AR 72203-8058. Phone: 1-800-422-0474.

Other Folks Feeding Other Folks

Other U.S. relief organizations providing food after disasters include these:

➤ Action Against Hunger. 875 Sixth Avenue, Suite 1905, New York, NY 10001. Phone: 212-967-7800.

➤ Adventist Development and Relief Agency International. 12501 Old Columbia Pike, Silver Spring, MD 20904. Phone: 301-680-6380.

➤ American Red Cross, ARC International Response Fund. P.O. Box 37243, Washington, D.C. 20013. Phone: 1-800-435-7669 (English) or 1-800-257-7575 (Spanish).

➤ American Refugee Committee, World Headquarters. 2344 Nicollet Ave. South, Suite 350, Minneapolis, MN 55404. Phone: 1-800-875-7060.

➤ CARE. 151 Ellis Street NE, Atlanta, GA, 30303-2439. Phone: 404-681-2552.

➤ Catholic Relief Services. 209 W. Fayette St., Baltimore, MD 21201. Phone: 1-800-736-3467.

➤ Childreach. 155 Plan Way, Warwick, RI 02886. Phone: 401-738-5600.

➤ Doctors Without Borders (*Medecins Sans Frontieres USA*). 11 E. 26th St., 19th Floor, New York, NY 10010. Phone: 212-679-6800.

➤ Food for the Hungry. 7729 E. Greenway Road, Scottsdale, AZ 85260. Phone: 602-998-3100.

➤ International Medical Corps. 1223 W. Olympic Blvd., Suite 280, Los Angeles, CA 90064. Phone: 310-826-7800.

➤ International Rescue Committee. 122 E. 42nd St., New York, NY 10168. Phone: 212-551-3000.

➤ Lutheran World Relief. Church Street Station, P.O. Box 6186, New York, NY 10277. Phone: 1-800-597-5972.

➤ Map International. 2200 Glynco Parkway, P.O. Box 215000, Brunswick, GA 31521. Phone: 912-265-6010.

➤ Mennonite Central Committee. 21 South 12th St., P.O. Box 500, Akron, PA 17501-0500. Phone: 717-859-1151.

➤ Near East Foundation. 324 Madison Ave., Suite 1030, New York, NY 10173. Phone: 212-867-0064.

➤ Operation USA. 8320 Melrose Ave., Suite 200, Los Angeles, CA 90069. Phone: 1-800-678-7255.

➤ Save the Children. P.O. Box 900, Westport, CN 06881. Phone: 1-800-403-0505.

➤ World Relief. P.O. Box WRC, Wheaton, IL 60189. Phone: 1-800-535-5433.

The "Second Disaster": A Word About Donations

Do you know disaster response experts commonly refer to the influx of used clothing and other misguided donations as "the second disaster"? That's because truckloads of inappropriate donations can clog roads, use valuable volunteer time for sorting, and even cause disaster survivors psychological trauma.

After Hurricane Andrew, truckloads of used clothing blocked the highways for hours, then was put on the side and left for weeks because there was no storage space. Many truckloads finally had to be burned just to get rid of them! More recently, after Hurricane Floyd, one rural North Carolina town was so inundated with donated shoes that they filled two warehouses. Each person in the small town had enough shoes to last a lifetime—six times over.

If you want to help people after a disaster, don't just clean out your closet and send your old clothes! Instead, make a financial contribution to a trustworthy organization that is responding. Or, if you must send something else, check with your favorite disaster response organization to see what's really needed.

Index